the MORTGAGE KIT

Fifth Edition

Thomas C. Steinmetz

Dearborn™
Trade Publishing
A **Kaplan Professional** Company

This publication is designed to provide accurate and authoritative information in regard to the subject matter covered. It is sold with the understanding that the publisher is not engaged in rendering legal, accounting, or other professional service. If legal advice or other expert assistance is required, the services of a competent professional should be sought.

Acquisitions Editor: Mary B. Good
Senior Project Editor: Trey Thoelcke
Interior Design: Lucy Jenkins
Cover Design: KTK Design Associates
Typesetting: the dotted i

Printed in the United States of America

02 03 04 10 9 8 7 6 5 4 3 2 1

Library of Congress Cataloging-in-Publication Data

Steinmetz, Thomas C.
    The mortgage kit / Thomas C. Steinmetz.—5th ed.
      p.   cm.
    Includes index.
    ISBN 0-7931-5371-9 (pbk.)
    1. Mortgage loans—United States.   I. Title.
HG2040.5.U5 S72 2002
332.7′22—dc21

                    2002017419

Praise for the Previous Editions:

"Beacons amid confusion . . . advice, diagrams, and worksheets that help show you how to pick a mortgage."
—*U.S. News & World Report*

"An excellent handbook on purchasing a mortgage to finance a personal residence or investment property."
—*Booklist*

"For most of us, the single largest purchase we will make in our lifetime is our home. Doing it right the first time is made considerably easier with this trilogy of homebuying/selling books [*The Mortgage Kit, The Homebuyer's Kit, The Homeseller's Kit*]. . . . Steinmetz, well-versed in mortgage lending, offers practical strategies, illustrations, worksheets, forms, and ten appendixes of tables, lists, and statements for surviving the financing process."
—*Library Journal*

"There is no finer guidebook than this one that explains to homebuyers how to get the best home loan and to homeowners how to profitably refinance mortgages. The book is filled with easy-to-understand charts and graphs and an excellent appendix that includes loan-payment tables, application forms, and refinance worksheets. If you need a real estate loan, read this book first."
—Robert Bruss, syndicated real estate columnist who included the book in his annual end-of-the-year list of favorite real estate books

"A straightforward treatment of the basics any homebuyer should know before buying a home. The information is all here in one concisely written package."
—*Financial Planning*

"Sorting out and balancing all the factors in choosing a mortgage can be complicated. Fortunately, Thomas C. Steinmetz has made the job almost simple with *The Mortgage Kit*. . . . Steinmetz, a former strategic planner for the Federal National Mortgage Association (Fannie Mae), has developed ingenious charts and worksheets that walk you through the entire mortgage process, from shopping for one that best meets your needs to qualifying for it; he also has a chapter on refinancing."

—*New Choices for Retirement Living*

Dedication

This fifth edition of *The Mortgage Kit* is dedicated with love to my wife and best friend, Barbara, and to our children, Bill, Brian, and Jenny.

Contents

Appendixes, Worksheets, Forms, and Tables   157

Glossary   264

Index   270

About the Author

Thomas C. Steinmetz has worked in the real estate finance industry since 1974 when he started as a commercial loan officer.

He is currently Chairman of the Board of Mortgage Banking Systems, which he founded in 1987 to provide the real estate finance industry with computer services and software. To date, more than 600,000 families in all 50 states have signed mortgage documents prepared using Mortgage Banking Systems' document preparation services.

Prior to founding Mortgage Banking Systems, Steinmetz worked at PRC Loan Express, a computerized loan origination network, as Director of Marketing and Planning. He also has served as Senior Strategic Planner for the $1.4 trillion government-sponsored agency, Federal National Mortgage Association (Fannie Mae).

He has been a speaker at workshops of the Mortgage Bankers Association of America and has written articles for industry trade journals on the new uses of computers in mortgage lending. He also has appeared on local and national television and radio shows advising consumers about residential mortgages. Steinmetz received an MBA from Harvard Business School, concentrating in real estate and finance, and he received a BA from Dartmouth College in mathematics.

Introduction
Mortgage Basics

What is the largest purchase that you will make during your lifetime? It's your home, right? Wrong, it's your mortgage!

If you buy a $120,000 home financed with a $20,000 down payment and a $100,000 mortgage at 8 percent interest for 30 years, you will pay $165,849 in interest over the life of the loan. That's more than the purchase price of the home.

Most people do not consider obtaining a mortgage the same as choosing and buying a product. But a mortgage is a product like any other, and as with other products it pays to be a smart consumer. By shopping around and knowing what you are shopping for, you can save thousands of dollars, whether it is for your first home or your umpteenth. Saving 0.5 percent on the interest rate of a $100,000 mortgage lowers your payments by $450 a year and saves you $13,400 in interest over 30 years.

Making you a smart consumer is the whole point of this book. It tells you what you need to know when shopping for your mortgage.

What This Book Covers

The Mortgage Kit is strictly a consumer's guide and covers what consumers should know. It is not for people who work in the mortgage industry and need more in-depth knowledge of the topics discussed, although it may be a useful overview of the mortgage process for real estate agents and those just entering the business. It does not cover the history of mortgage lending or the arcane mathematics that underlie mortgages. Time is valuable, so to the extent possible, the fifth edition of *The Mortgage Kit* is short and to the point.

Chapter 1 explains the application process. Getting a mortgage is complicated, often taking one or more months. Knowing what information your lender needs can help you shorten that time and eliminate much of the frustration surrounding the process.

Chapter 2 tells you what a lender looks at before deciding whether or not to make a loan. It answers the questions "How large a loan can I get?" and "What can I do to help myself qualify for a mortgage?"

Chapter 3 is written for (the almost half of all) mortgage applicants whose employment history, income, savings, or property they are financing does not fit the national standards imposed by mortgage lenders. It describes in some detail how you can build your case to obtain a favorable consideration on your loan application.

Chapter 4 describes the various types of mortgages available today, including fixed and adjustable rates, level and graduated payments, FHA, VA, and conventional loans. Different types of mortgages satisfy different consumer needs—lower rates, easier qualifying, fast payoff, low down payment, and low initial monthly payments. This chapter helps you pick the right type of mortgage for your needs.

Chapter 5 reveals how to save money by shopping. You should expect to save at least $1,000 by shopping, but you must know what to look for and what to look out for. This chapter also helps simplify and organize your shopping efforts.

Chapter 6 covers several topics that do not fit neatly into any other chapter but need to be covered to make this guide complete. These include:

- Assumability
- Buydowns
- Late payment charges
- Mortgage insurance
- Internet lending
- New developments in mortgage lending

- Prepayment penalties
- Second mortgages

Chapter 7 is for anyone getting a mortgage on a small residential property bought as an investment rather than as a residence. It covers the additional qualification and documentation required for loans on investment properties (but not the advisability of making such an investment).

Chapter 8 is about refinancing. It helps you figure out whether you should refinance your existing mortgage, how much you would save and how much it would cost. It also offers some tips on how to reduce your refinancing costs.

The rest of this introduction is devoted to five topics that are basic to understanding mortgage:

1. What is real estate?
2. What is a mortgage?
3. Mortgage pricing
4. Loan-to-value ratio
5. Monthly payments

What Is Real Estate?

A *mortgage* is a method of financing real property, or real estate as it is commonly known. Real property, unlike other types of property, such as automobiles, jewelry, and clothing, is not portable. You can't pick it up and move it around. Ownership of land is defined by the location of that property. A lot survey defines the parcel of land that you buy in terms that relate to other fixed points of reference that are known and agreed on by all. This information is usually recorded in permanent records that are maintained by local governments. Following are some common ways to own real estate:

- *Fee simple property versus leasehold estates.* All states recognize fee simple ownership of real property. *Fee simple* means that the land and all improvements on the land (e.g., the house) transfer with the deed to the property. *Leasehold* means that the land is owned by a leaseholder who collects rent for the land. If you purchase a leasehold property, you obtain ownership of the improvements, but you incur an obligation to make leasehold payments, also known as ground rent, to the lease-holder. Residential leasehold properties are common in Hawaii and occur occasionally in Maryland.

- *Condominiums.* When you buy a condominium, you do not acquire land but a three-dimensional space defined as being within the exterior walls, ceiling, and floors of the condominium unit. The condominium unit itself may be an apartment unit in a high-rise or low-rise building, but it can also be a townhouse or even a freestanding, detached single-family home. The land on which the condominium is located is owned by the condominium owners association, which is governed and controlled by the condominium unit owners and is almost a minigovernment complete with bylaws and procedures, including the right to assess "taxes" in the form of association dues for maintenance and capital improvements to the common areas. The definition of the condominium unit is described in the condominium documents that created the condominium. Condominiums are common in most states.

- *Cooperative units or co-ops.* When you buy a co-op, you do not acquire title to any real property. You actually buy "shares" in a cooperative that owns the real estate and all the improvements thereon. The cooperative, in return for your purchase of shares, grants you the right to occupy a specified living unit, the structure of which can take any form as with condominiums. Cooperatives can be found in almost all states but are most common in large cities such as New York and Washington, D.C. Because cooperative ownership is substantially and legally different from other types of ownership, many lenders do not offer cooperative loans. The loan is not secured by real estate; it is secured by a lien against the shares of the cooperative.

Different types of ownership do not affect how you will qualify for a home loan, but they do affect the types of documents that you sign at settlement and may affect some of the costs associated with ownership. For example, leasehold payments for leasehold estates and condominium or homeowners association fees are included in your total housing cost for qualification purposes (see Chapter 3).

What Is a Mortgage?

Mortgage is a generic term used to describe several different combinations of legal documents that allow you to get financing to buy a home. The documents *(note, bond, mortgage, deed of trust, open-end-mortgage, security deed,* and *riders)* that you will use depend on the state in which the property is located and the type of loan you are getting. (See Appendix K for a list of what system each state uses.)

A *mortgage* is a financial claim against your real estate. You *give* a mortgage to a lending institution, along with a *bond* or a *note,* which is a personal promise to repay. In return, the lender gives you money—cash. You do not "get a mortgage"; you do the mortgaging—you are the *mortgagor.* The lender *takes* your mortgage, *holds* your mortgage and is the *mortgagee.*

Loans secured by properties located in deed of trust states are secured by a document called a *deed of trust.* When you sign a deed of trust, you actually transfer ownership of the property to a *trustee.* The trustee holds the deed to the property in trust until such time as the loan is paid off. If a dispute arises between lender and borrower, the trustee must resolve the dispute according to state law. If the borrower stops making loan payments, the trustee must hold a foreclosure sale to pay off the lender. The procedure for a foreclosure is clearly spelled out in the deed of trust and state law, and in most states, a court hearing is not required. In most mortgage states, however, the lender must go to court, argue the case before a judge and obtain judge's approval before a foreclosure sale can be held. Lenders prefer to have loans secured by deeds of trust because foreclosing on a deed of trust is cheaper and quicker than on a mortgage. As a borrower, you can consider *mortgages* and *deeds of trust* as generally interchangeable terms in this book.

The Price of a Mortgage

Question: Which is a better deal: (1) a 30-year fixed-rate mortgage at 8 percent interest plus three points or (2) one at 8.25 percent interest plus only one point?

Answer: It depends.

Comparing prices of different mortgages is complicated. In addition to the quoted interest rate, lenders charge a variety of additional up-front fees:

- Discount points
- Origination fee
- Appraisal and credit report fee
- Inspection fee (for new homes)
- Underwriting/review fee
- Document preparation fee

Discount points, often referred to simply as *points,* are usually the largest fee that lenders charge. Each point equals 1 percent of your loan amount. If you borrow $100,000 but have to pay three points, you really get only $97,000. However, you have to repay $100,000, and you have to pay interest on $100,000.

Points change the interest rate that you pay. The real rate is called the *effective interest rate.* For a 30-year loan at 8 percent plus the three points repaid over its full 30-year term, the effective interest rate is 8.32 percent.

The *annual percentage rate* (APR) is the effective interest rate for loans that are repaid over their full term. After you apply for a loan, truth-in-lending laws require lenders to tell you a loan's APR within three business days. While this is better than not knowing what rate you are paying, there are two problems with this procedure:

1. Finding out the APR after you apply does not help you with comparison shopping.
2. The APR calculation assumes that you will keep your loan for its full 30-year (or 15-year) term. However, most people sell or refinance their home within 6 to 12 years.

The effective interest rate depends on how long you keep your loan. If the $100,000 loan were repaid after 6 years rather than 30 years, its effective interest rate would be 8.66 percent, not the 8.32 percent APR.

You need a computer or financial function calculator to determine effective interest rates precisely, but the following formula is a fairly accurate way of estimating it for comparison shopping:

Effective interest rate = Quoted rate + (Number of points ÷ 6)

(If you *know* that you will be keeping your loan for more than 12 years, divide the points by 8 instead of 6. If you plan to stay for only 4 to 6 years, divide the points by 4. If you plan to stay for 1 to 3 years, divide the points by the number of years.)

Let's go back to the question posed at the beginning of this section: "Which is better, (1) a 30-year loan at 8 percent plus three points or (2) one at 8.25 percent plus one point?" Loan Number 2 is better.

Loan Number 1: Effective rate = 8.00% + (3 points ÷ 6) = 8.50%
Loan Number 2: Effective rate = 8.25% + (1 point ÷ 6) = 8.42%

That small percentage difference does not seem like much, but for a $100,000 loan paid off after 12 years, you would save $1,000. If you paid off the loan after only 6 years, you would save $1,500. Shopping and knowing how to shop saves money!

Sometimes lenders charge a one point (or half-point) *origination fee.* This has the same effect as discount points. You should add an origination fee to the discount points before you calculate your effective rate.

For purposes of comparison shopping, you usually do not have to add the other miscellaneous fees (credit report and appraisal, inspection, etc.) into your rate calculations. Although they increase your effective interest rate somewhat, they are less significant than points, and most lenders charge about the same amount of miscellaneous fees as their nearby competitors.

Down Payment and Loan-to-Value Ratio

Lenders prefer a borrower who makes a large down payment and a mortgage with a low *loan-to-value (LTV) ratio.* Your loan-to-value ratio is simply your mortgage amount divided by the value of your property (see Figure I.1). The *value* of your property is your purchase price or the appraised value, whichever is lower. Usually, they are the same.

Throughout this edition of *The Mortgage Kit,* there are many references to LTV ratio. The amount that you can borrow, your effective interest rate, and the availability of certain types of mortgages depend

FIGURE I.1   Loan-to-Value Ratio

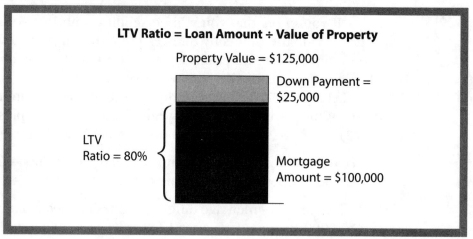

on your LTV ratio. Mortgage insurance (see Chapter 6), which costs hundreds of dollars a year, is required if your LTV ratio is more than 80 percent. Investor loans (see Chapter 7) are difficult to find with an LTV ratio higher than 85 percent. Qualification ratios (see Chapter 2) are stricter for high LTV ratios. Very large loans are available only with LTV ratios of 80 percent or lower, which means that your down payment must be at least 20 percent of the property value.

For all of these reasons, it is important to know approximately what your LTV ratio will be. Chapter 5 and the Mortgage Data Form in Appendix D will help you estimate your LTV ratio.

Calculating Your Monthly Payment

Your monthly mortgage payment includes not only principal repayments and interest on your loan, but also an additional amount known as *escrow* to cover real estate taxes, homeowner's insurance, and mortgage insurance (if required). Your lender then pays your tax and insurance bills for you when they come due. Sometimes lenders require that you pay enough to cover condominium/homeowners association dues as well. This whole package of payments is known as *PITI* (principal, interest, taxes, and insurance).

The sample PITI form in Figure I.2 shows how to calculate a total monthly mortgage payment for a 30-year loan of $100,000 at 8 percent interest. (A blank form and detailed instructions are in Appendix A.)

The principal repayment and interest make up the largest portion of your monthly payment. This is calculated by multiplying your loan amount by your loan's payment factor divided by 1,000. The payment factor depends on the interest rate and term of your loan. The payment factor for an 8-percent, 30-year loan is 7.3376. The instructions for the PITI Form in Appendix A include an abbreviated table of payment factors for 15-year and 30-year loans from 2.000 percent interest to 17.875 percent interest. Appendix I contains a complete table of payment factors for fully amortizing loans with terms of 1 year to 30 years, 35 years, and 40 years, and with interest rates from 2.000 percent to 19.875 percent.

FIGURE I.2   Sample PITI Form

Loan Amount:	$100,00
Interest Rate:	8.000%
Term of Loan:	30 years

Principal and Interest Payment	
$100,000 × 7.3376 ÷ 1,000 =	$733.76
Annual Real Estate Tax	
$1,380.00 ÷ 12 =	+115.00
Annual Homeowner's Insurance Premium	
$324.00 ÷ 12 =	+ 27.00
Mortgage Insurance (if required)	
$100,000 × 0.003 ÷ 12	+ 25.00
Premium rate = 0.3% × Loan Amount	
Condominium/Homeowners Association Dues	
$390.00 ÷ 12 =	+ 32.50
Annual Assessment	
Total Monthly Payment	$933.26

1

The Application Process

Getting a mortgage can be a long and sometimes frustrating ordeal. Applying for a mortgage is not quick nor simple. In fact, it is a lengthy, complicated process (see Figure 1.1) that often involves many different people and companies, such as:

- Borrower
- Real estate agent
- Mortgage broker
- Lender (loan officer, loan processor, underwriter, and/or loan committee)
- Credit bureau
- Appraiser
- Borrower's employer(s)
- Borrower's banks and creditors
- FHA, VA, or mortgage insurance company
- Inspector
- Surveyor
- Title insurance company
- Settlement attorney

Each of these people and companies can play a part in the processing, approval, and settlement of your loan.

FIGURE 1.1   The Application Process

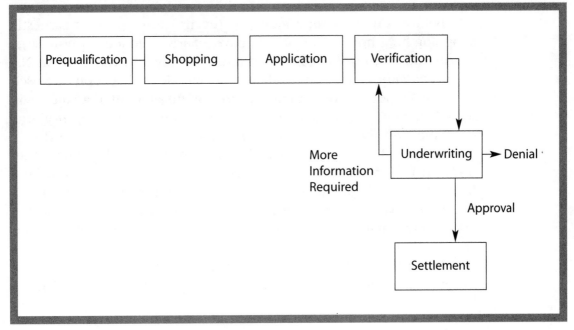

The whole process, from the time of the loan application to the settlement (also known as the *closing*), can take from 15 to 60 days. Under normal conditions, you should plan on 30 days. During the peak homebuying season or periods of heavy refinancing activity, count on 30 to 60 days. When applying, ask your lender what its processing time has been averaging.

Problems arise when one or more people involved in this process make a time-consuming mistake or get backlogged with work and fail to get their parts completed on time. The borrowers themselves also can delay the process by not supplying the necessary information on time.

Although the paperwork starts with submitting a loan application, two steps in the process precede the application: prequalification and shopping for a loan.

Prequalification

Before you apply for a mortgage (even before you start earnestly shopping for a home), you should have a fairly solid idea of how large a loan you will *qualify* for—how much money you can borrow. National guidelines based on family income and debt obligations are used by most lenders to determine the maximum amount that they will lend. The first step in getting a mortgage is known as *prequalifying,* determining how much a lender will lend to you. (See Figure 1.2.)

Chapter 2, "Qualifying for a Mortgage Loan," provides you with an in-depth understanding of how a lender decides whether to make a loan. The table in Figure 1.3 is not a substitute for reading Chapter 2, but it will give you a rough idea of how much you can borrow with a 10 percent down payment given the prevailing interest rate and your annual income.

For example, if your annual family income is $40,000 and prevailing mortgage interest rates are around 8 percent, you could get a

FIGURE 1.2   Step 1: Prequalification

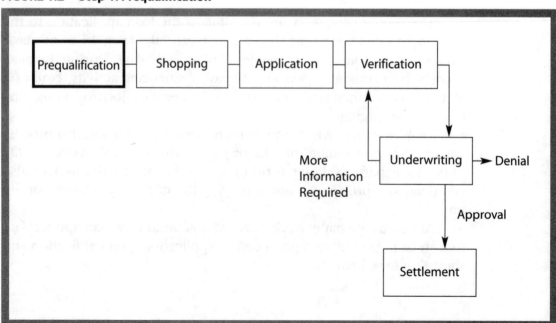

FIGURE 1.3   Conventional Loan Qualification Table

Maximum Mortgage Amount with a 10 Percent Down Payment							
Annual Income	**Mortgage Interest Rate**						
	4.0%	**5.0%**	**6.0%**	**7.0%**	**8.0%**	**9.0%**	**10.0%**
$ 20,000.00	$ 73,000.00	$ 67,000.00	$ 61,000.00	$ 56,000.00	$ 52,000.00	$ 48,000.00	$ 45,000.00
25,000.00	92,000.00	84,000.00	77,000.00	71,000.00	65,000.00	60,000.00	56,000.00
30,000.00	110,000.00	101,000.00	92,000.00	85,000.00	78,000.00	72,000.00	67,000.00
35,000.00	129,000.00	118,000.00	108,000.00	99,000.00	92,000.00	84,000.00	79,000.00
40,000.00	147,000.00	135,000.00	123,000.00	113,000.00	105,000.00	97,000.00	90,000.00
45,000.00	166,000.00	152,000.00	139,000.00	128,000.00	118,000.00	109,000.00	101,000.00
50,000.00	184,000.00	168,000.00	154,000.00	142,000.00	131,000.00	121,000.00	113,000.00
60,000.00	221,000.00	202,000.00	185,000.00	170,000.00	157,000.00	145,000.00	135,000.00
75,000.00	277,000.00	253,000.00	232,000.00	213,000.00	197,000.00	182,000.00	169,000.00
100,000.00	369,000.00	337,000.00	309,000.00	284,000.00	262,000.00	242,000.00	226,000.00

$105,000 conventional first mortgage from most lenders (assuming a 10 percent down payment, good credit, and manageable debts). Chapter 2 also describes other requirements and tells how you can qualify for a larger loan.

You can use several ways to prequalify yourself. In addition to using the table in Figure 1.3, you can use the Do-It-Yourself Prequalification Worksheet in Appendix C. You can also ask a loan officer of a local lender to prequalify you.

Shopping for a Loan

Shopping for a loan (see Figure 1.4) is an important step in the process. Saving 0.25 percent on the interest rate of a $100,000 loan saves $5,000 over the 30-year term of the loan. Saving a half discount point on a $100,000 loan saves $500. Lenders' prices vary widely, so comparison shopping is valuable to you. Chapter 5, "Shopping for a Mortgage," explains how.

Part of shopping is deciding what type of loan you want. Chapter 4, "Choosing the Right Type of Mortgage," describes the different types of mortgages most commonly available and their advantages and disadvantages.

FIGURE 1.4   Step 2: Shopping for a Loan

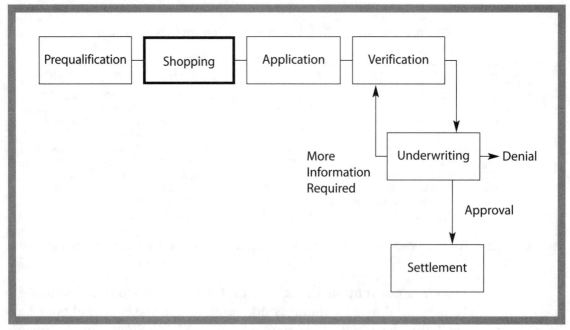

A professional, qualified loan officer also can describe the benefits of different loan products. Be aware, however, that most loan officers are commissioned salespeople, and they try to sell the loans that they have to offer and are most familiar with. Find out for yourself what kind of loan you need so you can shop more effectively.

Applying for a Loan

After you select a loan type and complete your shopping for a lender, you must submit an application (see Figure 1.5) and sign numerous forms that allow your lender to contact your employers and banks. Just as there are national guidelines for qualifying, there also are national standards for application forms and required information. Most lenders will request some or all of the following so you should gather the information ahead of time:

FIGURE 1.5   Step 3: Applying for a Loan

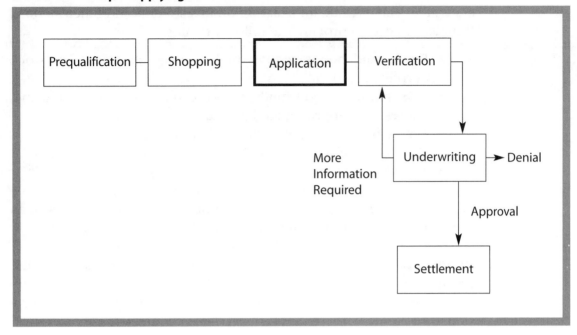

General Information

- Social Security numbers for each applicant
- Current address and prior addresses for the past two years
- Name and address of current mortgage lender (if any)

Employment Information

- Names and addresses of current employers and prior employers for the past two years
- W-2 forms or 1099s (sometimes required if you are paid by commission or if you work out of a trade union hiring hall)
- Past two years' tax returns and current profit-and-loss statement (if self-employed)

Assets

- Bank accounts (account numbers, bank name, address, and approximate balance)

If your income from salaries is sufficient to qualify you, some lenders will let you exclude information on investments and other income. If not, you need to provide the following information:

- Stocks and bonds (copies of brokerage statements or stock certificates)
- CDs, money market funds, IRAs (account number, bank name, address and approximate balance)
- Family trusts, pensions, and other annuities
- Cash value of whole life insurance policies
- Automobiles (copy of registration or title)
- Statement of personal property (furniture, etc.)
- Other real estate (mortgage lender's name and address, loan number, monthly payment amount)

Debts. You must provide information on your debts, including the creditor's name and address, loan number, monthly payment, and approximate balance required for each loan. You also will need to provide the following information:

- Charge accounts and credit cards (provide a copy of last monthly statements)
- Car loans
- Mortgage loans
- Personal loans
- Student loans
- Other installment loans

Miscellaneous. Other information that may have to be provided includes:

- Copy of signed sales contract (for home purchase) or copy of deed (for refinance)
- Condominium or co-op documents (if applicable and lender does not already have them)
- Alimony, child support, and separation maintenance payments due (copy of divorce decree or separation agreement)
- VA Certificate of Eligibility, DD-214, or Statement of Service (VA loans only)

- Copy of real estate tax bill for the past year
- Copies of utility bills (required by some lenders for FHA or VA loans)

The more complicated your financial situation, the more information you must supply. However, some lenders offer loans that require only minimal information from the borrower. If your down payment is 30 percent or more (LTV ratio of 70 percent or less), ask lenders if they offer these loans. It could cut your processing time and eliminate much of the hassle.

The application interview may take place in the lender's office, in the real estate agent's office, in your office or home, or sometimes over the telephone. A loan officer probably will help you fill out the loan application. (A sample application is provided in Appendix B.) Bring all the required documents to the interview to help speed the application process. In addition, when you apply for a mortgage, you must pay a nonrefundable application fee of from $300 to $400. This covers the cost of an appraisal and a credit report.

Locking In the Rate

In many areas of the country, lenders will allow you to lock in the price (i.e., the rate and points) of your mortgage when you apply. Many lenders require payment of a commitment or lock-in fee, especially for refinance loans. Others will set the rate and points for your loan after you have been approved or shortly before the day of settlement. During times of heavy refinancing volume, some lenders may require that you lock in a rate at the time of settlement *and* pay a nonrefundable commitment fee.

The major benefit of shopping for a loan is to lock in the best rate available for the product that you select. If lenders in your area will not let you lock in a rate and points when you submit an application, shopping for a low-priced loan becomes more difficult. You must look for a lender with a reputation for low rates.

If you do lock in the price of your loan, get a written statement from the lender that clearly spells out the rate, points, other fees, and conditions of the lock-in agreement. An oral promise is not enough to protect your interests.

The purpose of a price (rate) lock commitment is to protect you from a rate increase that might occur between the time that you apply for your mortgage and the time that you go to settlement/closing. What happens if rates *fall* during that period? If you have gotten a commitment at a higher rate, you are generally stuck with it. You can ask your lender for the lower rate, but do not expect to get it.

Some lenders offer a special rate lock commitment that protects you from rising rates and allows you to get a lower rate if rates fall. Lenders often charge a larger fee for this kind of commitment. If you think that rates may go down, ask your lender if it offers this kind of commitment.

Within three business days from when you file an application, lenders are required by truth-in-lending laws to mail you a disclosure of the annual percentage rate (APR) for your loan. You also will receive a booklet prepared by the U.S. Department of Housing and Urban Development called *A Homebuyer's Guide to Settlement Costs* and an estimate of your settlement costs.

Verification

Assembling a loan package with all of the required documents is the most time-consuming step in the application process. All the key statements that you have made on your loan application must be verified and documented (see Figure 1.6). After you have submitted an application, the lender's loan processor assigned to your case will:

- Order a credit report and appraisal
- Mail letters to your employers asking them to verify your salary and commissions
- Mail letters to your banks asking them to verify your account balances
- Gather and prepare the other documents necessary to complete the loan package

Some requested documents are returned quickly; others must be requested a second or even a third time. When you are asked to provide a document, do so as quickly as possible. Your failure to give lenders what they need promptly can give them cause to cancel your lock-in agreement or even deny you credit.

FIGURE 1.6   Step 4: Verification of Documents

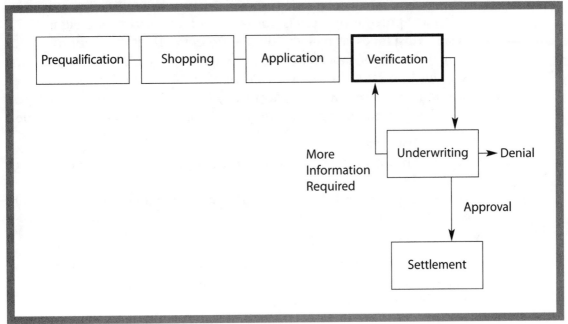

Alternative Documentation. Most lenders offer loan programs that shorten the time-consuming process of gathering written verifications from your employers, creditors, and banks. Instead of requiring all the letters listed previously, they accept substitute documents that provide them with sufficient proof of your income and assets. In place of a written verification of your salary, they require copies of two or three of your most recent paycheck stubs and a verbal confirmation of your employment and income from your employer. In place of a verification of your bank deposits, they require copies of two or three of your most recent bank statements. Alternative documentation loans can save considerable time and effort.

The loan officer who takes your application and the loan processor who assembles the necessary documentation generally do not have the authority to approve your loan. They simply gather information for others who will make the yes-or-no decision.

Underwriting

The approval process is known as *underwriting* (see Figure 1.7). In some instances, as many as three different entities must approve your loan: the lender's underwriter, a mortgage insurance company (for loans with an LTV ratio greater than 80 percent), and the lender's investor (for large loans requiring preapproval).

The underwriting procedure can yield one of four possible outcomes:

1. Approval
2. Approval with conditions (e.g., approval subject to the sale of the applicant's old home)
3. Application returned for additional documentation and resubmission
4. Denial of credit

When your loan is approved or approved with conditions, the lender will issue a commitment letter and begin preparations for *settlement* (also known as *closing*).

FIGURE 1.7   Step 5: Underwriting—the Approval Process

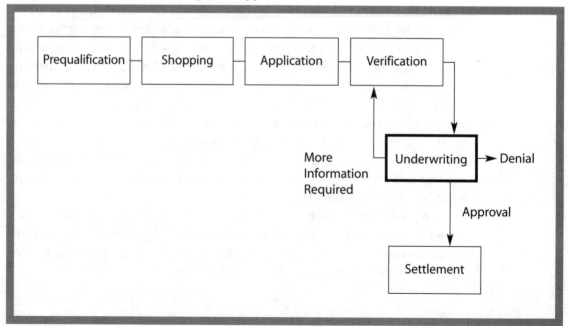

If the underwriter needs additional information before approving your loan, the entire package is returned to the loan processor. The processor will gather the additional documents and resubmit the package to underwriting.

If you are turned down and denied credit, the lender must issue a letter stating the reason for denial. If you were denied credit because of adverse information in a credit report, you have the right to inspect a summary of the report issued by the credit reporting agency, challenge inaccuracies, and request that the credit agencies make corrections.

Usually, your loan application is approved (or disapproved) by someone who has never met or even talked with you; the decision is based on the documents in your file. To some people, this depersonalization of the credit approval process is offensive and even emotionally upsetting. Some lenders, especially smaller banks and savings-and-loan associations, offer more personalized service. If personalized service is very important to you, ask lenders about their approval process when shopping around for a loan.

Important Note: The industry is in the process of combining the application-verification-underwriting steps of getting a mortgage by using huge computer systems developed by Fannie Mae, Freddie Mac, and some of the nation's very large mortgage lenders. They are called *automated underwriting* systems. Over 50 percent of loans processed today use automated underwriting systems. Because of their growing use, Chapter 2 contains a section describing them in detail.

Settlement (Closing)

Settlement is the procedure for funding the loan (see Figure 1.8). Several additional documents must be gathered or prepared for settlement:

- Deed (for home purchase, not refinance)
- Notes and addenda
- Deed of trust or mortgage (depending on your state) and riders
- Mortgage insurance certificate
- Title insurance policy (or binder)
- Survey (in most states)
- Homeowner's insurance policy
- Miscellaneous affidavits and agreements

FIGURE 1.8   Step 6: Settlement

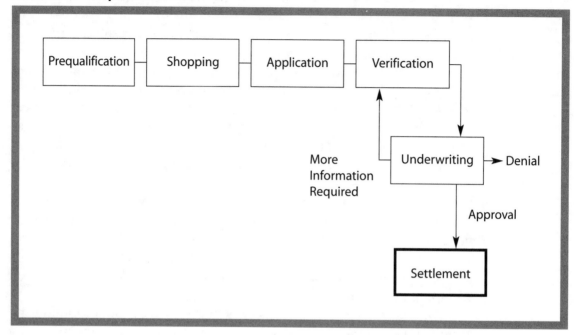

- Certificate of occupancy (newly constructed homes)
- FHA/VA documents (for FHA/VA loans)
- Uniform Settlement Statement (HUD-1)

Many costs are involved in closing a mortgage loan, and they vary greatly depending on the state, county, and metropolitan area. Figure 1.9 shows an example of the range of possible settlement costs.

M O R T G A G E   T I P

Comparison shopping can help you save money on title insurance, settlement attorneys, and homeowner's insurance.

FIGURE 1.9   Range of Settlement Costs (For a $100,000 Mortgage)

	Range	
Lender Fees		
Loan origination fee	$ 500	$ 1,000
Discount points	0	3,000
Appraisal and credit report	300	400
Inspection fee (new homes)	50	150
Underwriting fee	0	300
Document preparation/review fee	0	300
Tax service fee	0	85
Mortgage insurance	0	1,000
Title Charges		
Attorney's fees	$ 200	$ 500
Title insurance	300	400
Transfer tax (except refinances)	100	2,000
Recording tax	200	400
Miscellaneous Charges		
Survey	$ 0	$ 250
Termite inspection	50	150
Prepaid Expenses		
Odd days' interest	$ 0	$ 800
Homeowner's insurance	250	400
Real estate taxes	200	1,500
TOTAL	$2,150	$12,635

The lender charges the bulk of the settlement costs. Chapter 5, "Shopping for a Mortgage," tells you how to lower those costs. Title insurance, settlement attorneys, and homeowner's insurance costs are three other items where you can save money by shopping around.

The logistics of settlement—location, method, and disbursement of funds—vary depending on state law and local custom. Your lender, attorney, or real estate agent can explain how settlements are transacted in your area and can estimate your costs. Settlement of a refinance mortgage is generally less complicated and less expensive because no transfer of title is involved.

Newly Constructed Homes

If the home that you are buying is under construction when you apply for your mortgage, the settlement process will be somewhat more complicated than the process for an existing home. After your house has received its occupancy permit, your lender will inspect the house to make sure that it has been finished according to plans. The lender may require additional finish work or repairs before funding your mortgage.

Frequently, homebuyers want to move into a new home before it is completely finished. (They may have to vacate their apartment or old house.) Some lenders will not settle until the house is 100 percent complete. Often, they will hold back some of the mortgage until the house is completed. For example, a lender may fund only $90,000 of a $100,000 mortgage, pending completion of landscaping, a garage, or a finished basement. When a lender holds back funds, a homebuyer often can hold back payment to the builder. *Holdbacks* protect both the lender and the homebuyer from builders who fail to complete all the work that they promised. These holdbacks are also known as *completion escrows.*

2

Qualifying for
a Mortgage Loan

Before making a mortgage loan, a lender spends from $500 to $800 putting together a package of documents for its underwriters and loan committee. Based on these documents and on a set of nationally accepted standards, the lender decides whether to approve the loan application.

As many as *half* of all mortgage loan applicants fall in the gray area where loan approval decisions must be made. For example, first-time homebuyers will stretch their income to buy the largest home that they can afford. Before spending the $300 to $400 to apply for a mortgage, you should have a good idea whether you qualify for the loan amount that you want. If you get turned down, you may lose your application fee and, worse, you may lose the opportunity to buy the house you want.

Even if you are seeking only to refinance an existing mortgage, you could have trouble qualifying. Some of the nationally accepted qualification standards have changed in the past few years, and these changes may affect you. If your income has dropped since you got your last mortgage, you may have trouble refinancing, *even with the same lender.* If you have had any recent credit problems or if you have been delinquent on your current mortgage payments, this also may disqualify you.

If you have any doubts about your ability to qualify for the mortgage amount that you want, this chapter tells you what you can do to help you qualify yourself.

This chapter explains in detail all of the factors that mortgage lenders look at to assess your creditworthiness. Today, most of this process is manual, but the industry is now using computers more than ever. Computerized *automated underwriting* looks at the same factors as the manual process, but in a different way. For this reason, the last section in this chapter takes a look "under the hood" of these computer systems that are becoming so important.

National Standards

The majority of lenders today process and underwrite loans according to generally accepted national standards. These standards are dictated by Wall Street investors and government agencies who invest in mortgages or insure them against default. These investors are known as the *secondary mortgage market.* Knowing their standards will help you choose a mortgage and a lender.

Within the context of these standards, a lender has some leeway to be lenient and flexible, or strict and even picayune. If, after reading through this chapter, you have concerns about qualifying for the loan amount that you want, shop for a lender that is flexible.

What does a lender look at before saying "yes" (or "no")? The lender looks at the following:

- Each applicant's monthly income and expenses
- Each applicant's credit history
- Property appraisal
- Source of cash for down payment and settlement costs
- Each applicant's employment history

What Are Your Monthly Income and Expenses?

The first question that lenders must ask is "Can you afford the monthly payments on this new mortgage?" To find the answer, they examine your current income and expenses plus the cost of the new mortgage, and they apply mathematical formulas to see if you can afford the payments. Government loans (FHA/VA) and conventional loans use different formulas. Chapter 4, "Choosing the Right Type of Mortgage," explains the differences between government and conventional loans.

Conventional Loans

For conventional loans, lenders make two calculations that compare your income and mortgage expenses. These calculations determine your housing ratio and debt ratio. Your *housing ratio* (also known as *front ratio* or *top ratio*) is your total monthly mortgage payment (your payment of principal, interest, taxes, and insurance, or PITI) divided by your total monthly income (see Figure 2.1). Your *debt ratio* (also known as *total obligations ratio, back ratio,* or *bottom ratio*) is the sum of your total monthly mortgage payment and other monthly debt payments divided by your total monthly income (see Figure 2.2). If your ratios are too high, the lender may decide to deny your application. If you can demonstrate your ability to carry greater debts, the lender may allow you to exceed national standards, but usually not by very much. These ratios are very important. You can use the Do-It-Yourself Prequalification Worksheet in Appendix C to calculate your own ratios. Figure 2.3 is a sample worksheet.

FIGURE 2.1   Housing Ratio

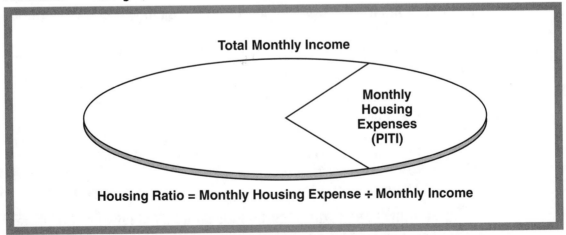

Total Monthly Income

Monthly Housing Expenses (PITI)

Housing Ratio = Monthly Housing Expense ÷ Monthly Income

FIGURE 2.2   Debt Ratio

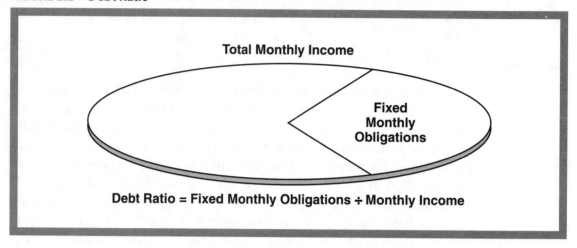

Total Monthly Income

Fixed
Monthly
Obligations

Debt Ratio = Fixed Monthly Obligations ÷ Monthly Income

Your monthly housing expenses include:

- Mortgage principal and interest payments
- Monthly cost of homeowner's insurance and flood insurance (if required)
- Monthly mortgage insurance payment (if any)
- Annual real estate tax divided by 12
- Monthly condominium or homeowners association dues

Your monthly housing expenses do not include utilities, telephone bills, etc.

For all applicants, whether or not married, your monthly income includes:

- Gross monthly salaries (pretax, not take-home pay)
- Commissions
- Bonuses
- Investment income (dividends, interest and rent)
- Pension or trust income
- Alimony or child support (that you receive, not pay)

Monthly income does not include anticipated raises or unsubstantiated estimates of future commissions and bonuses. It also does not include investment income on bank accounts or other assets that will be

FIGURE 2.3   Do-It-Yourself Prequalification Worksheet (For Conventional Loans)

Purchase Price	$ 115,000 (A)
Desired Mortgage Amount	$ 100,000 (B)
Term of Mortgage	30 years
Mortgage Rate	10.0%
Loan-to-Value Ratio: (B) ÷ (A) =	87.0% (C)
GROSS MONTHLY INCOME	$4,000.00 (D)
Mortgage Principal and Interest Payment	
(Payment Factor: 8.7757) × (B) =	$ 877.57
Annual Real Estate Taxes ÷ 12 =	+ 110.21
Homeowner's Insurance Premium ÷ 12 =	+ 25.00
Mortgage Insurance: (B) × .00025 =	+ 25.00
Homeowner/Condominium Association Dues	+_____
MONTHLY HOUSING EXPENSE	$1,037.78 (E)
Car Payments	+ 250.00
Alimony/Child Support Payments	+ 225.00
Credit Card/Charge Account Payments	+ 50.00
Other Loan Payments	+_____
FIXED MONTHLY OBLIGATIONS	$1,562.78 (F)

HOUSING RATIO (E) ÷ (D) = 25.9%

DEBT RATIO   (F) ÷ (D) = 39.1%

used for your down payment. It does include the salaries and other income of both husband and wife for two-income families.

All claimed income must be verified. The lender will send a letter to your employers to confirm your earnings or for alternative documentation loans, the lender will call your employers. Lenders may reduce your estimates of future income from commissions if you do not have at least a two-year history of consistent earnings that support those estimates.

Investment, pension, and trust income also must be verified. Lenders will ask for copies of stock certificates, brokerage account statements, and pension or trust documents. If you own a rental property, some lenders will assume a 25 percent vacancy rate when calculating the property's cash flow, unless you show them a long-term lease. In almost all cases, lenders deduct some amount for maintenance and repairs to the rental property.

Your fixed monthly obligations include:

- Monthly housing expense (from housing ratio in Figure 2.1)
- Car payments
- Student loan payments
- Alimony or child support (that you and/or your coapplicant(s) must pay)
- Credit card or charge account payments
- Other loan payments (including loans for which you have cosigned or guaranteed, *even if you don't make the payments on those loans*)

As with your income, your lender will require documentation on your debts. Installment loans (such as car loans) with ten or fewer monthly payments (six payments for FHA and VA loans) remaining do not have to be included in your fixed monthly obligations, but you still must disclose them to your lender.

If you or your coapplicant(s) are paying (or receiving) alimony or child support, you must provide a copy of the divorce decree. Even if you are not paying alimony or child support, many lenders require a copy of the divorce decree to prove that you are not obligated, especially if there are minor children involved.

The maximum allowable housing and debt ratios depend on your lender, the type of loan, the property, and the loan amount. For purposes of prequalification, you should use a maximum housing ratio of 28 percent and a maximum debt ratio of 36 percent (28/36). These are the generally accepted standard ratios that most lenders use. Some lenders use ratios of 30/38, especially with very large loans, some adjustable-rate mortgages (ARMs) are available with ratios of 40/40, and higher ratios are available on various new affordable-housing programs, but these vary by locality.

An underwriter, who is the lender's employee evaluating your credit application, is not tied completely to strict standards. Offsetting factors will be taken into account. If you can add further explanation to your income or expense situation that will make your numbers look better, by all means do so. However, document your claims in writing if possible.

In the sample Do-It-Yourself Prequalification Worksheet in Figure 2.3, Mr. and Mrs. Homebuyer's housing ratio is 25.9 percent, and their debt ratio is 39.1 percent. National standards for a 30-year, 87 percent LTV ratio loan are 28 percent for the housing ratio and 36 percent for the debt ratio. A strict lender could turn them down because their debt ratio is too high. A more lenient lender would accept these ratios if other aspects of their credit package were acceptable.

Self-Employment. You are considered self-employed if you own a 25 percent or greater interest in the business that employs you. If you fit this definition, you will have to supply the following additional documentation:

- Signed copies of your two most recent personal federal income tax returns with all applicable schedules
- Signed copies of your two most recent federal *business* income tax returns, if your business is a corporation, S corporation, or partnership
- A year-to-date profit and loss statement, if the loan application is dated more than 120 days after the end of the business's tax year
- A balance sheet for the previous two years, if the business is a sole proprietorship with significant business assets, has employees other than the owner and his or her spouse, and regularly prepares separate business financial balance sheets
- Your written permission to request copies of your tax returns for the past two years from the IRS

The stability of your income is very important to mortgage lenders. For salaried employees, lenders look at your job history for at least the past two years. For self-employed borrowers, they look at the profitability and cash flow of your business for the past two years in addition to your individual income. If you have started a business within the past two years, or if your business was unprofitable for one or both of the past two years, this presents a problem for most mortgage lenders.

Limited Documentation Loans. Some lenders *do not require any verification of income information* if your down payment is 30 percent or greater. Some charge a slightly higher interest rate for these special

> ## MORTGAGE TIP
>
> Some lenders do not require any verification of income information if your down payment is 30 percent or greater.

loans. If you are self-employed or your personal finances are complicated by unverifiable sources of income, and you can afford to make a large down payment, you should definitely look into these "low doc" or "easy doc" loans. This will help you avoid the hassle of verifying all of your finances. You will still be required to disclose your income, but the verification requirements will be minimal.

Note that these limited documentation loans are much less common than they were just a few years ago. In addition, for audit pur-

> ## MORTGAGE TIP
>
> Qualification Formulas:
>
> - The income/debt qualification formulas are important factors in determining whether your loan will be approved.
>
> - Although important, the ratios are not absolute. Some lenders are strict, but others are more flexible.
>
> - FHA/VA formulas allow you to qualify for a larger loan than the conventional loan ratios.
>
> - Use the Prequalification Worksheet in Appendix C to prequalify yourself, or have a loan officer prequalify you.

poses, lenders required signed authorization to obtain your tax records from the IRS.

Government Loans

Federal Housing Administration (FHA). The FHA calculates ratios using the same method that is used for conventional mortgages. The FHA's standards, however, are more lenient than those of conventional loans. Its maximum housing and debt ratios are 29/41.

Department of Veterans Affairs (VA). The VA uses two methods of calculating a borrower's ability to afford a mortgage: a maximum 41 percent debt ratio (and no housing ratio) and a calculation to determine *residual income*. Residual income is the amount of money you have left after paying your mortgage, and other housing expenses. Figure 2.4 shows an example of that calculation.

The VA guidelines for required residual income depend on your family size, the requested loan amount and the region of the country

FIGURE 2.4   VA Residual Income Qualification Example

Monthly Gross Income:	$4,000
Less federal taxes	(503)
Less state taxes	(250)
Less Social Security or federal retirement	(306)
Plus nontaxable income	100
Total Net Take-Home Pay	$3,041
Less debt/fixed payments	(525)
Less property tax	(110)
Less insurance	(25)
Less homeowners association/condominium dues	
Less utilities	(165)
Less maintenance	(50)
Available for Principal and Interest	$2,166
Less P and I payment ($100,000 at 10%)	(878)
Residual Income	$1,288

where you are buying a home. (For example, a family of four living in the northeast and seeking a $100,000 loan would need a residual income of $1,025 per month.) In the following example, residual income of $1,288 would be large enough to qualify a family of four for a VA loan.

What Is Your Credit History?

The second question that lenders must ask is "Have you repaid your past debts in a timely fashion?" To find this answer, the lender orders a mortgage credit report from a local credit bureau. A *credit bureau* collects information from retailers, banks, finance companies, mortgage lenders, and a variety of public sources on all consumers who use any type of credit—credit cards, car loans, mortgages, personal loans, and charge accounts. The information collected is stored in nationwide computerized *credit repositories.* Credit reports can be generated from credit repositories in minutes for a minimal cost. These reports, also known as *in file reports,* may not always contain the latest information on your credit standing. These computers track payment histories on more than 200 million accounts.

Credit Scoring. An increasingly important factor in determining an applicant's creditworthiness is credit scoring. A *credit score* is based on a statistical analysis of your credit history, and it is generally included as part of your mortgage credit report. It is called your FICO score, and the methodology for scoring was developed by the Fair Isaac Corporation. The FICO score ranges from 400 to 900. The higher your score, the better your credit rating. Borrowers with a credit score over 750 are very unlikely to default on a mortgage. Borrowers with a credit score of less than 600 are far more likely to default on a loan, and those with a low credit score will have to pay more for their mortgage, more discount points, and higher rates.

The factors that go into determining your credit score are:

- Your *history of past payments* (including public records that pertain to your credit: bankruptcies, liens, lawsuits, and judgments)
- The *amount of outstanding credit* that you have (the balances on your credit cards and other loans compared with the credit limits for those loans)

- The *age* of your open credit card and charge accounts
- The number and type of *recent credit inquires* that have been made into your credit data that suggest that you are seeking additional loans or credit cards
- The *mix of different types of credit* that you have outstanding (car loans, charge cards, mortgages, etc.)

The relative importance of these factors in calculating a FICO score is shown in Figure 2.5.

It is very important to know how good your credit score is before you apply for a mortgage. You often see ads offering to sell you a copy of your credit report, but the report does not always include a copy of your credit score. You can get a copy of your credit report, credit score, and full description of the factors that were key in determining your personal score on the Internet at <www.myfico.com>. This Web site also has a very complete description of credit scoring written for consumers.

The charts in Figures 2.6 and 2.7 show the national distribution of credit scores and the likelihood of serious delinquency by credit score.

Borrowers with scores less than 600 have a 50 percent or greater chance of being 90 days late on at least one of their loans over a two-year period. On the other hand, borrowers with scores over 700 have

FIGURE 2.5   Factors That Determine Credit Score

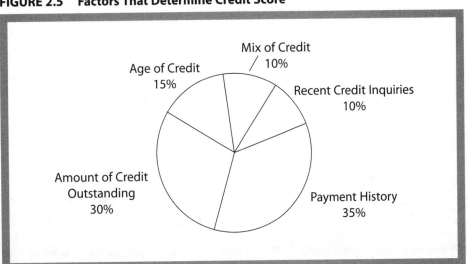

FIGURE 2.6   National Distribution of FICO Scores

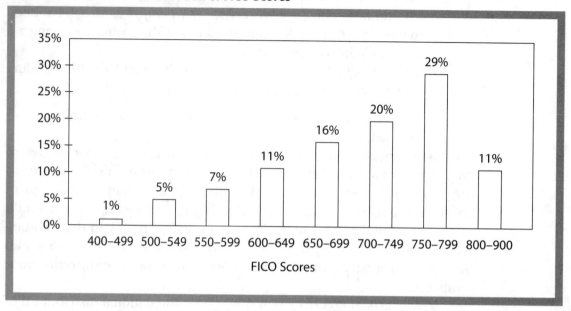

FIGURE 2.7   Average Delinquency Rate by FICO Score

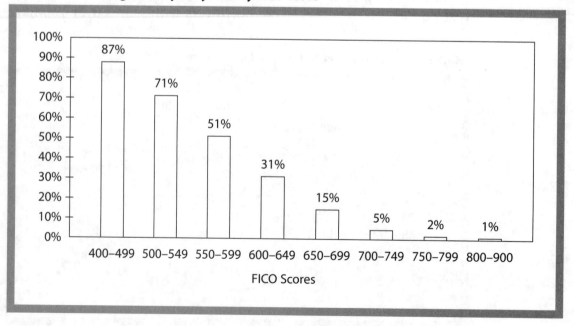

less than a 5 percent chance of being 90 days late. Credit scores are very accurate predictors of future delinquencies, and this is why your credit score is so important when you apply for a loan.

You can raise your credit score. If you have had a history of late payments, liens, repossessions, and other serious credit problems, it will take a few years of spotless credit to raise your score, but the following actions can help:

- Make sure that all of your accounts are current, and do not miss any payments. Even if you only pay the minimum amount, that is much better than skipping a payment. The longer that you stay current, the better your score.
- Pay down your credit card debt. If you have too many credit cards, it lowers your credit score. Do not get cards that you do not need. Do not close out cards that you do not use; that will not lower your score. Do not move debt around. Pay it off.
- If you are a new borrower, do not open several accounts right away. Opening new accounts lowers your score. Older accounts raise your score.
- Applying for several loans at the same time will cause lenders to inquire about your credit status. Multiple inquiries can lower your score. Ordering your own credit report does not affect your score.

The best way to maintain a good credit score is to use credit responsibly. Do not get loans or credit cards that you do not need. When you do get loans or credit cards, make your required payments on time.

Mortgage Credit Reports. The credit bureau begins preparing your mortgage credit report by searching the national computer files and its own files for information on you (and your spouse or coborrower, if applicable). In addition to searching their existing files, they obtain the latest information about your credit by making inquiries by telephone and letter specific to the information on your mortgage application.

The primary focus of your credit report is your credit history. For each of your bank and automobile loans, credit cards (whether you have used them recently), charge accounts, school loans, leases, and business and mortgage loans, a line of descriptive information will appear on your credit report, such as:

- Creditor's name
- Type of account (installment, credit card, charge account, automobile loan, etc.)
- Account number
- Date opened
- Maximum allowable balance, "high" credit balance, current balance and past due amount (if any)
- Required monthly payment
- Payment history

The payment history is of critical importance to your lender's underwriter. For each account listed, it shows how many times you were more than 30/60/90+ days late in making your required monthly payment. It also shows your usual payment patterns, whether you almost always pay on time or are usually late 30, 60, or 90 days. It also reports any repossessions, credit workouts, and accounts fully paid.

In addition to reporting on your credit history, the mortgage credit report verifies some of the noncredit information that you disclose on your mortgage application as well:

- Employment history for at least the past two years (employers, job titles, income, if available)
- Residency information for at least the past two years (address, landlord, and rental or mortgage payment history)
- Public record information (lawsuits, legal judgments, marriage or divorce, tax liens, bankruptcy, and foreclosures)

Failure to disclose credit problems or answer all of the related questions on your mortgage application fully is a sure way to be rejected.

Although the lender charges you for a credit report as part of your application fee, you will not have a chance to look at your credit report. As mentioned in Chapter 1, you do have the right to inspect a summary of the credit report, challenge any inaccuracies and request that the credit agencies make corrections. You can get a consumer version from any of the three repositories:

1. Equifax, 800-685-1111, <www.equifax.com>
2. Experian, 800-311-4769, <www.experian.com/consumer>
3. Trans Union LLC, 800-888-4213, <www.transunion.com>

The cost of a credit report is about $8.95, or $12.95 if it includes your credit score. If you believe that there is a mistake in your credit reports, or if you have been turned down for a loan, you can get a free copy of your credit report from any of the above companies.

Most lenders are strict on credit problems. Some do not make mortgage loans to people who have had a previous foreclosure or bankruptcy. Others require two or more years with a clean credit record, following such a major credit problem. If you have had credit problems, disclose them to the loan officer and ask about the lender's policies prior to application.

Many lenders will require you to submit a written explanation of any detrimental comments that appear on your credit report. For example, "Explain why you were a month late on two MasterCard payments the past year," or "Why did you miss a mortgage payment two years ago?" Although these requests may seem a little picky and may be somewhat irritating, a simple explanation such as "I was on vacation" or "I misplaced the bill" usually will be enough for minor credit discrepancies like these examples.

Moderate tardiness on paying bills usually will not disqualify you for a mortgage. But when combined with tight qualifying ratios and a small down payment, chronic credit problems may cause lenders to turn down your application. It may cost you additional points or a higher rate.

Property Appraisal

The third question that a lender must ask is "How much is the property worth?" An *appraisal* is necessary to ensure that a lender does not lend more on a property than its value. Most lenders hire an outside appraiser who:

- Inspects the property
- Compares it to nearby comparable properties sold recently
- Determines its value based on the sale prices of those comparable properties
- Submits a report to the lender

Unlike your credit report, you are entitled to receive a copy of the appraisal report if you paid for it and if you request a copy in writing. Most lenders now provide a disclosure notifying you that you are entitled to a copy. Some lenders routinely provide a copy of the appraisal to the applicant when the report becomes available. If you want a copy of the appraisal, be sure to make arrangements with the lender at the time that you are submitting your application.

National standards govern the content, format, and valuation methodology of residential appraisals. Whether you are applying for a government-insured loan or a conventional loan (see Chapter 4), your appraisal format will be based on requirements developed jointly by the Federal Housing Administration (FHA), the Department of Veterans Affairs (VA), Federal National Mortgage Association (Fannie Mae), and Federal Home Loan Mortgage Corporation (Freddie Mac). The FHA and VA continue to require certain additional information for their appraisals in the form of addenda included with the appraisal report. Some small local lenders may have their own special requirements, but most lenders follow the national requirements.

The national standards govern not only the format for appraisals; they also specify the appraiser's qualifications and credentials. In addition, most states now have enacted (or are in the process of enacting) appraiser licensing requirements for appraisers evaluating properties located within those states. Most lenders deal only with appraisers whose work they know and trust. Appraisers are required to have a certain amount of training and experience before their valuations are acceptable to mortgage lenders and investors.

Valuation Methods. Appraisers use three different methods to value residential properties: the *market value approach,* the *replacement cost approach* and, for investment properties, the *income approach.* Using these three different methods, an appraiser will frequently come up with slightly different values for the property. Using judgment and experience, the appraiser reconciles the difference and assigns a final appraised value.

The *market value approach* is the most important valuation method in appraisal because a property is worth only what a buyer is willing to pay and a seller is willing to accept. The market value is based on the actual sales prices of nearby similar homes that sold recently. These are known as *comparable sales.*

Appraisal reports are very detailed. (See Appendix G for copies of the Fannie Mae/Freddie Mac forms.) For the property being appraised (the *subject property* in appraisal terminology), they include:

- *General information.* Legal description, title restrictions (if any), real estate taxes, and zoning information.
- *Site description.* Lot size and shape, availability of public utilities, improvements such as sidewalks, curbs and gutters, and streetlights.
- *Neighborhood analysis.* Includes population density (urban, suburban, rural), development growth and other changes, price stability (rising, falling, or stable), availability of public amenities (schools, shopping, transportation, recreation, police and fire protection, employment), and nearby land use (single-family homes, apartments, commercial).
- *Home description.* Size, design, construction materials, number and type of rooms, appliances, adequacy of heating/cooling/plumbing, and overall quality of workmanship.
- *Other factors affecting value.* Garage or carport, swimming pool, and other improvements.

In addition, the appraiser must report on obvious construction problems such as leaking roofs, termite damage, dry rot, and exterior and interior damage that affect the salability of the property. If construction problems do exist, most lenders require that they be repaired prior to the sale or before the entire loan amount is fully disbursed. This is intended to protect the lender, but it also protects the buyer from problems that might not otherwise be recognized.

To value the property, the appraiser reviews the details of recent comparable home sales near the subject property. Those properties most similar to the subject property are used for comparison, detail by detail: size, date of sale, location, site, design, quality of construction, age, condition, heating and cooling, and other relevant improvements.

The appraiser adjusts the price of each comparable sale (up or down) depending how it compares (better or worse) with the subject property. He or she then reconciles the different prices to determine the market value of the property.

As an additional check on the value of the property, the appraiser also estimates the replacement cost for the property. Replacement cost is determined by valuing a vacant lot and determining the cost to build a house of similar size and construction. Finally, he or she reduces this cost by an age factor to reflect deterioration and depreciation.

It is very common for the appraised value on a property to be exactly the same as the amount of your sales contract. This is not a coincidence, nor does it indicate malfeasance on the appraiser's part. Your sales contract is the most comparable sales transaction there is. It represents what a buyer is willing to offer for the subject property and what the seller is willing to accept. Only when the comparable sales differ greatly from your sales contract will the appraised value be very different.

In the mid-1980s, appraisals caused problems for consumers in two ways. First, many appraisers were unable to keep up with the heavy work load that lower interest rates caused. Some had backlogs as long as two months, delaying loan approvals. Second, in some areas of the country where home prices were rising rapidly, appraised values were lower than asking prices. In the early 1990s, low appraisal values often caused problems for homeowners who wished to refinance. This often occurred when the homeowner had used maximum financing (e.g., 95 percent LTV) to acquire the property and the value of the property had not appreciated enough to refinance (most lenders will not refinance a home for more than 90 percent LTV). It also occurred in situations where the value of the property dropped since the time the property was acquired, or was last refinanced. If you are purchasing a home and the appraised value comes in lower than the purchase price, you may have to increase your down payment to qualify for the mortgage. Ask your real estate agent for advice on local appraisal conditions.

Source of Cash for Down Payment and Settlement Costs

The fourth question that lenders must ask is "Do you have enough money to close the sale and where are you getting it?" (This does not usually apply to refinancing.) Lenders require verification of deposits, gift letters, and other written evidence of funds available for settlement. These are necessary because of past frauds in which sellers or real estate agents loaned money to buyers "under the table" to facilitate a higher selling price or to circumvent lenders' qualification standards. Some lenders even require homebuyers to show where they got the money for the deposit shown in the sales contract, particularly if the case available is marginal, or very close to the total amount needed for settlement or if there have been large deposits to your accounts within the last few months.

Employment History

The two largest causes of mortgage foreclosure are divorce and unemployment. A lender cannot anticipate divorce, but employment history is reviewed. The final question that a lender must ask is "Will your future income be stable enough to meet monthly mortgage payments?"

The ideal employment history from a lender's perspective is several years of employment with a well-known, prosperous company, or a few job changes with increases in salary and responsibility. A lender may require a borrower with a spotty employment history to give an oral or written explanation. Usually, employment history will affect a lender's decision only when there are other problems with the application, such as a bad credit report or tight qualification ratios. Conversely, an excellent employment history—stability, promotions, and raises— often can overcome tight qualification ratios.

What If There Is a Skeleton in the Closet?

One-third to one-half of all mortgage loan applications do not precisely fit the guidelines described in this chapter. Nevertheless, more than 90 percent of mortgage loan applications are approved. An application can be turned down for a variety of reasons:

- Not enough income to support the loan payments or too much outstanding debt already
- Past credit problems
- An undesirable property or low appraisal value
- Insufficient cash to close
- A poor or limited employment history

M O R T G A G E   T I P

Before applying for a loan, do everything that you can to make sure that your application will be approved.

Although some things are outside of your control, the best advice is "Before applying, do everything that you can to make sure that your application will be approved."

If after reading this chapter, you are confident that your income, assets, credit history, and employment history fall well within national qualification guidelines, go on to Chapter 4. If not, or if you have a skeleton in the closet, Chapter 3 provides useful techniques to help you overcome qualification problems. Think of these as "skeleton keys." Few qualification problems cannot be solved if they are addressed early enough in the application process.

Automated Underwriting

Traditional underwriting is a system based on rules—thousands of rules! Fannie Mae, Freddie Mac, and the other investors who buy mortgages have set the rules. This chapter describes many of the important rules that lenders must follow. Mortgage lenders must devote several bookshelves to the manuals that govern what they must do before approving a mortgage. There are literally thousands of pages of rules that lenders must know and follow to properly prepare all of the paperwork for your mortgage. The cost of doing this paperwork ranges from $1,000 to $2,000 per loan depending on the complexity of a borrower's credit situation and how efficient the lender is at gathering the necessary information.

Automated underwriting computer programs are based on statistics. They use some of the same rules that are in the manuals, but not all. They are statistic models that compare data about loan applications to data about several hundred thousand loans that were made over the last several years. These computer systems predict how likely it is for your loan to be repaid based on how loans with the same characteristics have done in the past.

Over half of the mortgage applications in 2001 were submitted to an automated underwriting system. In a few years, automated underwriting will largely replace traditional underwriting. Fannie Mae's automated underwriting system is called Desktop Underwriter and Freddie Mac's automated underwriting system is called Loan Prospector.

Automated underwriting computers make the decision on whether you will be approved for the mortgage that you apply for. They also tell the lender what documentation is needed, such as bank statements or pay stubs.

Of what immediate value are these computer programs to you? The primary benefit to automated underwriting is speed and convenience. If your lender is automated with software and hardware that allows it to submit your application to either Fannie Mae or Freddie Mac's automated underwriting programs, you can get your loan approval within a few minutes after completing your application interview and getting your data entered into your lender's computer. Many loan officers now carry laptop computers that let them enter your data during the interview.

Over 50 percent of the applications that are submitted to the automated underwriting programs get instant approvals. The other 50 percent are not necessarily denied, but the automated underwriting programs simply determine that additional information is necessary to make a decision and that human judgment is necessary.

Automated underwriting changes the way that you get a mortgage as follows:

- *Lower cost mortgages.* By eliminating paperwork, the cost is reduced by as much as $1,000. If your loan is approved with few paperwork requirements, your lender saves time and money.
- *Greater certainty of approval.* More borrowers are approved by automated underwriting systems than are approved by manual underwriting. Automated underwriting will sometimes approve loans that would be rejected by rules-based underwriting. Loan applications that fall outside the rules may be good loans, and

automated underwriting systems will bend the rules, whereas human underwriters are more reluctant to do so.

- *Faster approvals.* The traditional manual process of preparing and approving mortgage loan applications takes about three to six weeks. Automated underwriting returns an answer in minutes.

M O R T G A G E   T I P

When applying for your loan, ask your lender if it will submit your application to an automated underwriting system. If the lender says no, request that it do so, or perhaps seek another lender. Getting a fast approval takes a lot of worry out of the mortgage application process.

3

Overcoming Qualification Problems

You are not alone if you have some problems qualifying for a mortgage. As many as 25 percent to 50 percent of all mortgage loan applications do not precisely fit the guidelines described in Chapter 2. For example, the following are common problems:

- *Monthly income and expenses.* Lenders have very specific requirements on the types of income included for qualification purposes and the kinds of expenses that are counted in calculating ratios. Your income may not meet the lender's requirements, or you may have debts that the lender considers too high.
- *Credit history.* People have illness in their families, get busy with travel or simply forget to mail payments for bills that are due, resulting in late payments on their credit report. At a minimum, you will almost certainly have to explain any "blemishes" (late payments) that appear on your credit report.
- *Property appraisal.* Sometimes houses simply cannot be appraised for the amount of the sales price.
- *Source of cash for down payment and settlement costs.* Funds may come from sources that are unacceptable to traditional lenders.
- *Employment history.* People lose their jobs, start new jobs, get transferred and experience all types of other changes relating to

employment; these changes may adversely affect the lender's underwriting consideration.

The purpose of this chapter is to outline some of the problems that you might encounter when applying for a mortgage loan and to suggest some possible strategies to overcome them *before* you apply.

To illustrate how widespread problems from credit ratings alone can be, consider the national statistics in Figure 3.1 regarding types of credit accounts that may be delinquent (30 days *or more* late) at the end of any given month. These numbers represent percentages of total loans outstanding that are delinquent as of each month. Loans may be delinquent in one month but not the next, so the total number of loans that are delinquent at some time during the course of the term of the loan is likely much higher than these statistics indicate.

Also look at the following statistics on repossessions or foreclosures (by which the lender repossesses the secured property for nonpayment of the debt):

FIGURE 3.1   Percent of Loans Delinquent per Month

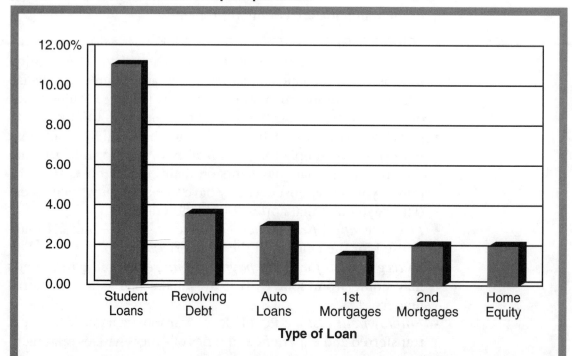

- Automobile loans—more than .08 percent per month or almost 1.0 percent per year
- Mobile home loans—more than .11 percent per month or more than 1.3 percent per year
- Marine financing (boat) loans—more than .12 percent per month or more than 1.5 percent per year
- Mortgages (first lien)—more than .1 percent per month or about 1.25 percent per year

These numbers represent percentages of total loans outstanding that result in repossession during the month. Vehicles may be repossessed more than once if the borrower makes up the delinquent payments, pays towing fees, etc., to bring the loan current. Mortgages in foreclosure do not necessarily indicate that the loan is "foreclosed." The process is full of legalities and takes several months (depending on the state in which the property is located) to complete. As with repossessed vehicles, loans may go into, and out of, foreclosure several times. Consequently, the number of mortgage loans that end up being actually "taken back" (property repossessed) by a lender is less than the numbers reported.

These numbers tell us that many people have less than perfect credit. In fact, almost everyone has some blemish on his or her credit report, whether because of an item lost in the mail, a forgotten payment or any number of other possible reasons. This does not mean that mortgage loans are not available; *it simply means that you must be more resourceful in presenting your case to the lender.*

Overcoming High Housing/Debt Ratios (Not Enough Income to Qualify)

Your ability to repay your mortgage is demonstrated by your *housing* and *debt ratios,* each of which is defined by the lender (see Chapter 2). If your ratios are too high, your application can be turned down. This section provides you with several solutions to the problem of high ratios.

Solution #1 Restructure Your Financing

If after prequalifying, you realize that your housing ratio and debt ratio are higher than the acceptable national standards, *choose a loan type that will lower your ratios.* The following chart shows how Mr. and Mrs. Homebuyer (whose ratios were calculated in the sample Do-It-Yourself Prequalification Worksheet in Figure 2.3) could have lowered their ratios by choosing a different type of mortgage and lowering the starting payment rate. (Fixed payment and adjustable-rate mortgage loans are discussed in Chapter 4.)

	10 Percent Fixed Payment	*9 Percent Temporary Buydown*	*8 Percent Adjustable-Rate Mortgage*
Housing Ratio	25.9 percent	24.1 percent	22.3 percent
Debt Ratio	39.1 percent	37.2 percent	35.5 percent

Buy Down the Interest Rate. If you have the available cash, consider paying additional points (or having the seller pay additional points) to reduce the interest rate.

MORTGAGE TIP

Lower your ratios by choosing a different loan type.

Obtain a Temporary Buydown. If you have the available cash, you can create your own buydown subsidy. The lender qualifies you on the "bought-down" rate, thus bringing your ratios within the guidelines. You also can have the seller fund your buydown, or you can obtain a "lender-funded" buydown. The lender funds the buydown by charging you a higher note interest rate to recoup the up-front expense of funding the temporary buydown, much as the lender might fund "zero-point" loans (see Chapter 6). This is attractive if you happen to be short of funds to close *and* have higher debt ratios.

Increase Your Down Payment. If you have enough available cash, increase your down payment to reduce the loan amount and bring your

```
┌─────────────────────────────────────────────────────────┐
│  ┌───────────────────────────────────────────────────┐  │
│  │            M O R T G A G E   T I P                │  │
│  └───────────────────────────────────────────────────┘  │
│                                                           │
│     Lower your ratios by increasing your down payment.    │
│                                                           │
└─────────────────────────────────────────────────────────┘
```

ratios into compliance with the guidelines (see below). Increasing your down payment also has other benefits. Lenders prefer large down payments. Mortgages with a 5 percent down payment are ten times more likely to go into foreclosure than loans with a 20 percent down payment. With a down payment of 20 percent, most lenders allow higher housing and debt ratios. Finally, a larger down payment can save you the cost of mortgage insurance, and your monthly mortgage payment will be lower.

	$15,000 Down Payment	*$20,000 Down Payment*	*$25,000 Down Payment*
Housing Ratio	25.9 percent	24.8 percent	23.1 percent
Debt Ratio	39.1 percent	37.9 percent	36.2 percent

Choose a Loan Type with More Lenient Qualification Ratios. FHA, VA, and nonconforming conventional loans may be easier to acquire because of their more lenient qualification ratios. (See Figure 3.2.)

Solution #2 Document Additional Income

Provide your lender with information about additional income that may have been overlooked or disallowed.

Self-Employment Income. Lenders generally will not accept self-employment income unless it has been stable and continuous for at least two years. This means that you have at least two years of tax returns to document the income. Exception: If you can demonstrate that you were successful in a similar business or activity prior to becoming self-employed (e.g., you were a salesperson and started your own market-

FIGURE 3.2 **Annual Income Required to Qualify for a $100,000 Mortgage at 8 Percent Interest for Different Mortgage Programs**

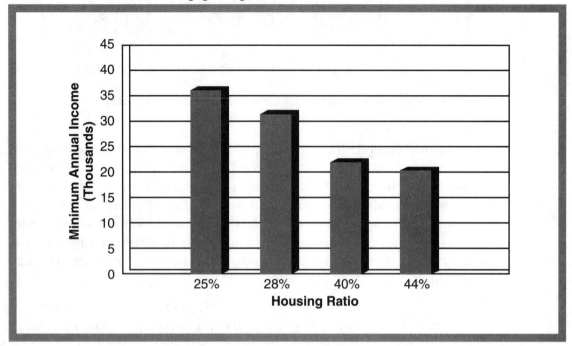

ing firm), the lender may consider a shorter term of self-employment. Even then, the lender probably will use an average of the two years' income unless the income for the most recent year is less than the previous year. In that case, the lender probably will use the lower of the two figures. If so, provide three or more years' tax returns (and an up-to-date profit-and-loss statement) to document that your self-employment income is cyclical and is not in permanent decline. If you can successfully argue this, the lender may be persuaded to use an average of your self-employment income over three or more years. If you are marginally qualified on the average of your self-employed income, you may persuade the lender to use your most recent year's income if you can demonstrate a consistent and significant upward trend (i.e., three years or more of increased earnings of at least 15 percent per year). Perhaps you can make another argument to support your case; for example, you just obtained a multiyear noncancelable contract and can document it from a large and stable customer over and above your ongoing business.

Commission Income. Generally, commission income is treated in about the same way as self-employment income. Provide documentation that your income is stable or increasing via your tax returns. If you are marginally qualified on the average of your commission income, you may persuade the lender to use your most recent year's income if you can demonstrate a consistent and significant upward trend (i.e., three years or more of increased earnings of at least 15 percent per year). Also, if you have a contract(s) in the present year that will significantly increase your income, you may receive favorable treatment. For example, Bob, a life insurance salesperson, generates commission in two ways: from sales of new policies during the current year and from *residuals,* or renewals of policies sold in previous years. If Bob continues to sell the same volume of policies each year, his income will continue to increase by the amount of the renewals of existing policies each year. In this case, a salesperson with a proven track record might qualify for a loan based on his most recent year's earnings rather than on an average of two or more years, *because of the probability of continued increasing income.*

Overtime Income. Income from overtime may be considered if you can document a full two-year history of consistent earnings for overtime income. Even if you cannot document two full years, it can be a strong compensating factor if you can demonstrate a year or more. You might persuade the lender to consider the overtime income if this income resulted from a year or more of overtime work and you can document that you will be required to continue working overtime in the foreseeable future.

Part-Time Income. This type of income may be considered if you can document a full two-year history of consistent earnings for part-time income. Even if you cannot document two full years, it can be a strong compensating factor if you can demonstrate a year or more.

Seasonal Income. This income may be considered if you can document a full two-year history of consistent earnings. Even if you cannot document two full years, it can be a strong compensating factor if you can demonstrate a year or more. If the income is from a regular source, such as a department store during the holiday season, or doing landscape work during the spring and summer, it is helpful to provide a letter from the employer indicating that you will be rehired for the next season.

Household Members' Income. Income earned by other members of the household will not be considered unless that individual is a party to the mortgage note. But you may be able to use the income of that person, such as an adult child living at home, as a compensating factor.

Tax-Free Income. This income can be "grossed up" to account for the tax-free status of that income. If you receive significant income from nontaxable *municipal bonds, VA benefits (other than education), child-support payments, certain types of retirement and disability income, or even food stamps,* the earnings from these types of income can be increased by an amount equivalent to taxable earnings.

Child-Support or Alimony Payments. These payments may be considered stable monthly income if there is a history of receiving these payments on a timely basis (and you can document it) and there is a likelihood that such payments will continue for at least three more years. If these payments are scheduled to end in less than three years but will last for a year or more, then this should be counted as a compensating factor.

Solution #3 *Document Compensating Factors*

Income is defined by mortgage lenders as *stable monthly income;* that is, income that can be documented for two previous years and can reasonably be expected to continue without interruption. Income that does not meet these strict guidelines, such as the income mentioned in Solution #2, may not be usable in calculating ratios, but it can be used as compensating factors allowing your lender to accept your application.

- *Probability of increased earnings.* This is a strong compensating factor if you happen to be a recent graduate and in a profession such as a lawyer, dentist, or physician. You can present earnings data of other professionals in your field to argue for favorable consideration.

- *Spotless credit.* If you have exemplary credit and you carry a heavy debt load, you can argue that you manage your financial affairs in a competent manner and that you will continue to do so when you own your own home. This argument is particularly strong if your overall monthly expenses will be about the same once you are in the house (i.e., your present housing expense is approximately the same as the proposed housing expense).
- *The tax advantages of home ownership.* Even if your overall housing expense increases with the new mortgage, argue that this increase is offset by the deductibility of mortgage interest for federal (and most states) income taxes. This is especially true for borrowers in higher tax brackets. When you factor income-tax savings, your overall housing expenses may be lower than what you are now paying if you are renting a house!

Solution #4 Get a Cosigner

Some lenders will relax their income qualification ratios if your rich uncle agrees to cosign (guarantee) your loan, for example. Without a cosigner, a lender may require that your monthly payment be less than 28 percent of your monthly income; with a wealthy cosigner, the lender may allow the monthly payment to be as much as 35 percent of your income and your debts 43 percent of your income. However, as a cosigner, your "rich uncle" will be required to go through all the processing and income verification hassles required for loan approval. You may not want to put your cosigner through that process. In addition, all the cosigner's debts will be included in the ratios, so be sure that the additional debt will be more than offset by the additional income before you bring the cosigner into the transaction.

Solution #5 Restructure Your Other Debt Obligations

If your housing ratio is low enough but your debt ratio is too high, *lower your monthly debt payments.* Your debt ratio equals your total monthly debt payments divided by your *stable monthly income* as defined by the lender. Consider the relationship between income and debt: *For each dollar of your monthly debt payments, you must generate three dollars of income to stay within mortgage lenders' guidelines.* Clearly, it is far more efficient (and usually easier) to reduce your debt than it is to increase your income.

- *Plan ahead; pay off your debts.* Before shopping for a home, make a sustained effort to reduce your overall debt burden. Pre-pay those items with the highest payment (relative to the balance due) first. This has the greatest impact on your debt ratios. While the lender is concerned with your overall debt burden, the total balance is not nearly so important as the monthly payment burden.
- *Consolidate or recast your debts.* Consolidate your debts well ahead of the time that you apply for your mortgage loan so that you can establish a payment history for the new debt, and your old debts will show as paid on your credit report. Keep in mind that your goal is to reduce your monthly payment in order to reduce your ratios, so opt for longer term, lower payments. If you don't reduce your overall monthly payment, you have not accomplished your goal. Exercise care when you consolidate *revolving debt,* such as credit cards and store credit accounts that have no fixed payment amount. You can consolidate your debts once or twice without creating problems. If you consolidate more than this, during a reasonable time span, you create a pattern of "running up" revolving debts followed by consolidations, resulting in an ever-increasing balance of outstanding debt. *Be prepared to explain the source of funds for paying off the debts as payoff dates are listed on the credit report.*

Overcoming a Bad Credit History

Disclose past credit problems to the loan officer before applying. One of the worst approaches to overcoming past credit problems is trying to hide them. Describe the steps that you have taken to solve those problems. The loan officer will know how strict his or her underwriters are with respect to credit problems. If your credit history would disqualify you with this lender, the loan officer should know and will give you advice.

Seek a Hard-Money Lender

If your past credit situation prevented you from qualifying for a mortgage from a traditional lender, you would have to seek out a "hard-money" lender. The stereotypical hard-money lender has been the fast-talking, polyester-clad salesperson with a burly bodyguard. Today, that is no longer the case. Many traditional mortgage lenders carry a line of mortgage products for customers with "less than perfect credit." These products are known as B-C-D loans. In most cases, lenders advertising B-C-D loans will be able to find a loan to overcome credit problems.

If your past credit problems are severe enough (bankruptcy, foreclosures, or unresolved lawsuits), you may want to see out a lender that specializes in loans for borrowers with credit problems rather than a traditional mortgage lender. *Hard-money lenders* do not use the national standards, and they find loans for people with credit problems. Their rates are quite a bit higher than traditional lenders, but they can lend money to people who have been turned down elsewhere. Beware of a lender that charges a large upfront fee (more than the $300 to $400 appraisal and credit report fee). As with all lenders, be sure to check the reputation of hard-money lenders. Check with your real estate agent and call the Better Business Bureau.

MORTGAGE TIP

Never, ever miss a mortgage or rent payment.

Wait Until You Reestablish a Good Credit Record

Depending on the nature of your past credit problems, it may be best to put off the purchase of a home until after you have reestablished a good credit record. The National Foundation for Consumer Credit (800-388-CCCS) is a nonprofit organization that can direct you to one of 617 local agencies. They can put you in touch with a local agency that will help analyze your finances and give you good advice about whether you're ready to buy a house. Generally, two years of clean credit is enough for conventional lenders. In reestablishing your credit, consider that although late payments should always be avoided, *some late payments are worse than others. Never, ever miss a mortgage or rent payment.* Be particularly sensitive to installment payments such as car payments, bank loans, student loans, and any government obligation (delinquent government obligations are important for FHA and VA loans). If you must be late on something, let the credit card or other revolving debt (except home equity loans) be the first to go.

Correct Mistakes Early

Occasionally, a dispute with a store over an incorrect billing or returned or damaged merchandise will show up as a detrimental comment on your credit report, even after the dispute has been resolved. If you have had such a dispute, tell your loan officer about it and request that the loan processor who is assembling the documents for your loan call you when your credit report is received. Provide the loan officer with documentation of the dispute. This includes dates and times of telephone calls and who you spoke with, as well as copies of letters you have written regarding the dispute. If the dispute is on the report, you can get it corrected right away.

If you are turned down by a lender, even if a mistake on your credit report was the cause, your rate lock-in commitment (see Chapter 5, "Shopping for a Mortgage") may expire before the mistake is resolved. *Correct mistakes on your credit report as soon as possible.*

Overcoming a Low Appraisal

The appraised value of the property (see Chapter 2, "Qualifying for a Mortgage Loan") is the one item over which you have the least control. However, you can affect or use to your advantage some things to compensate for weakness in another area.

Appraised Value Is Less Than the Purchase Price. Lenders use the *lesser* of the sales price or appraised value to determine the LTV ratio.

If you are attempting to get maximum financing or are just trying to avoid buying mortgage insurance, a low appraisal can be disastrous. If you are making a substantial enough down payment on the property so you will be unaffected by the appraised value, then it may not matter what the appraised value is, as long as you feel that the price fairly reflects the value that you perceive.

If you believe that the value is more accurately reflected in the sales price, you can appeal for a reappraisal of the property's value. To support the appeal, have your real estate agent provide data for comparable properties sold in the area within the previous six months.

- Consider the prices of the properties that are geographically closest to yours (much of a home's features can be changed, but relocating the house generally is not feasible).
- Consider houses that have similar lot sizes and square footage, the same number of bedrooms, similar floor plans, and amenities (such as remodeled kitchens, appliances, swimming pools, decks, balconies, landscaping, or particularly striking views).
- Consider the trend of prices; can you demonstrate that prices of similar homes have been increasing? If so, provide information, including newspaper clippings, information from the agent's database and (although weighted much less heavily) asking prices for homes currently on the market. Consider the sales cycle; are comparable homes being snapped up as soon as they come on the market, or do they take months to sell?

If you make a convincing argument, the appraiser may relent and give you a higher value. Be aware, however, that you are questioning the judgment of a professional, so be sure to have convincing information in hand before beginning this discussion. You might be allowed by your lender to *get a second appraisal,* but it too might come in low.

If you believe that the first appraisal is correct, that perhaps the value is less than the sales price, you might *negotiate with the seller to obtain a lower sales price.*

If the *appraised value is greater than the purchase price,* it does not affect the lender's valuation of the property for determining LTV ratio because the sales price then becomes the determining factor. If your loan application is weak in another area, however, it would be helpful to highlight the compensating factor that the property is of a greater value. Every positive feature that you can document about the transaction increases your chances of getting the mortgage.

Finding Sources of Cash for Down Payment and Closing Costs

Liquid assets, or *cash to close,* may come from a number of sources. Rules concerning sources of cash to close vary depending on the type of loan and the loan to value. FHA and VA are more flexible concerning sources of cash to close. The major agencies, Fannie Mae and Freddie Mac, are very strict about the minimum contribution from the borrower's own funds; at lower LTV ratios, they permit larger amounts from sources other than borrower's own funds. If you are short of cash to close (you should make this determination long before you ever sign a sales contract), you may be able to improve your position by doing one or more of the following:

- *Increase the sales price.* Consider that everything in the purchase transaction is negotiable. The amount of money that is *net* to the seller (how much money the seller gets after all expenses are paid) is the major concern for the seller. You can structure the transaction to meet the mortgage lender's guidelines, increase the loan amount and reduce your cash out of pocket. Here's how: Offer the seller a higher sales price, and have the seller pay your closing costs. Most mortgage lenders permit sellers to pay discount points, origination fees, buydown fees, and closing costs (except prepaid items, such as odd days' interest, insurance, and taxes) up to 3 percent of the "value" (the lesser of the appraised value or sales price) for loans more than 90 percent LTV and up to 6 percent of "value" for loans with an LTV or 90 percent or less. The seller gets the same net proceeds from the transaction, and you don't spend all your cash at the settlement table. (See Figure 3.3.) The downside is that the house may not appraise for the higher price; if it does, you will have a somewhat larger mortgage with somewhat larger monthly payments. If you are marginally qualified on the ratios, this could be detrimental.
- *Request* monthly *private mortgage insurance (for conventional insured loans).* Many private mortgage insurance companies

FIGURE 3.3   Increase the Sales Price to Conserve Cash at Settlement

	Borrower Pays All Closing Costs	Seller Pays $5,000 of Closing Costs
Sales Price	$100,000.00	$105,000.00
Points at 3 Percent	3,000.00	3,150.00
Closing Costs at 3 Percent	3,000.00	3,150.00
Total	$106,000.00	$111,300.00
90 Percent LTV Mortgage	(90,000.00)	(94,500.00)
Closing Costs Paid by Seller	0.00	(5,000.00)
Cash Required for Closing	$ 16,000.00	$ 11,800.00
Borrower's Available Cash	15,000.00	15,000.00
Borrower's Cash (Deficit) after Closing	($ 1,000.00)	$ 3,200.00
Net Cash to Seller	$100,000.00	$100,000.00

have recently introduced monthly mortgage insurance. Using monthly mortgage insurance can reduce your closing costs dramatically. Under the old plan, the first year's premium is required to be paid at settlement. Depending on the LTV ratio and the type of loan, this could result in a premium of .5 percent to 1 percent of the loan amount, or $300 to $600 for a $100,000 mortgage loan. With monthly mortgage insurance, you simply pay the first month's premium at settlement (approximately $35 in this example). This can result in a savings of approximately 90 percent of your mortgage insurance costs at the settlement table ($265 in this example). Although the monthly mortgage insurance premium is somewhat higher than annual mortgage insurance, it is well worth the cost if it makes the difference in whether you can own your own home.

- *Get a gift.* If you have a family member (or religious group, municipality, or nonprofit organization) who is willing to help with closing costs, that person can "give" you the money. A family member generally is defined as a close relative, and the amount that can be given is limited to amounts over the minimum 5 percent (of the sales price) contribution from your own funds unless the LTV ratio is 80 percent or less. The donor must sign a letter that specifies the amount and date of the gift; and indicate the donor's name, address, telephone number, and relationship to the borrower; and include a statement that *no repayment is expected.* A gift can be part of the minimum 5 percent down payment if the relative has lived with you for the previous 12 months and intends to continue to live with you in the new house. The mortgage lender will verify that the donor has the funds available to "give" and that the funds have been transferred into your possession. Under *no circumstances* can you be given a "gift" by a party to the transaction such as the real estate agent, seller, or builder.

- *Get a loan.* If you have assets that you do not wish to liquidate, you can borrow against those assets to meet your cash requirements. The key is that the borrowing must be *secured.* Unsecured loans are not permitted. Consider that repayment of the borrowed funds will be counted in your ratios and the debt will be included in your total debt.

- *Have the lender pay some or all of your settlement costs.* Many lenders now have programs known as "zero-point" or "zero-cost" loans. Zero-point loans pay all origination fees and discount points by charging a somewhat higher interest rate on the loan. Zero-cost loans pay origination and discount points as well as your closing costs (except prepaid costs). Again, this is accomplished by charging a higher interest rate so that the lender recoups costs over time. There are limitations to this if the lender is affiliated with a party to the transaction (for example, the seller is a builder and the builder owns the mortgage company or the mortgage company is owned by the real estate agent, or agent's company).

- *Have your employer pay part of your closing costs.* If your employer has a program by which it pays closing costs as an employee benefit, you may use these funds as part of your closing costs.

- *Sign up for a Community Homebuyer Program.* Both Fannie Mae and Freddie Mac (and many states) are encouraging lenders all over the country to participate in these programs. Special underwriting standards apply to these programs for first-time homebuyers. This permits you to contribute as little as 3 percent of your own cash, and in some cases you can borrow or get a grant for the entire down payment.

- *Investigate Community Reinvestment Act (CRA) opportunities.* Many banks now are focusing intense efforts to comply with Community Reinvestment Act (CRA) requirements. They are focusing their lending efforts in targeted neighborhoods in an effort to comply with the law. This often means that the mortgage lenders may have special programs in effect with relaxed underwriting standards to increase lending in targeted neighborhoods. Check with your local lenders to see whether this might apply to you.

- *Rent with the option to purchase.* If you have a signed agreement with the seller, you have rented the property for at least 12 months (and can document it with canceled checks or other means), you can apply the portion of the rent that is above the *market rent* (as determined by an appraiser) toward the down payment. Be aware that if the appraiser determines that the rent is below market, it will have the opposite effect and be treated as a sales concession, which is deducted from the price of the house.

- *Apply for programs for veterans.* You can get a VA guaranteed loan with 100 percent financing (90 percent financing for cash-out refinances), or you can apply for an FHA-insured loan (through its veterans' purchase program) with as little as $200 out-of-pocket cash.

Resolving Employment History Problems

Salaried employment for the two full years preceding the mortgage application is almost automatically considered unless the company (or industry) in which you work has special difficulties. Several common employment history problems include:

- *Employed for less than two full years.* If you were employed for less than two years and you were previously in school or in the military, then provide a copy of your diploma or military discharge papers.

- *Gaps or interruptions in employment.* Employment gaps or interruptions that extend beyond one month should be addressed in writing. Describe gaps in employment honestly but as favorably as possible.

- *Frequent job changes.* If you change jobs frequently to advance within the same line of work and you are successful in that work, then you should receive favorable consideration. Document your success in changing jobs or careers in a letter to the loan officer. If you do not demonstrate advancement (i.e., increased pay) when you change jobs or move from one line of work to another, however, the lender may view this as a negative, *unless* you can demonstrate that the changes in jobs were due to industry or economic changes over which you had no control. In fact, you can turn this into a plus by arguing that you were able to maintain your level of income despite widespread economic or industry changes.

4

Choosing the Right Type of Mortgage

In 1980, this chapter would have been very short. You could choose from only a few types of mortgages. Today, however, many are available. This chapter describes the mortgage products that are most popular and widely offered, and it gives the advantages and disadvantages of each type:

- Traditional 30-year, fixed-rate mortgages
- 15-year, fast-payoff mortgages
- Graduated-payment mortgages
- Growing equity mortgages
- Adjustable-rate mortgages
- Balloons, 3/1 ARMs, and Two-Steps
- FHA, VA, and conventional loans

Fixed-Rate Mortgages

Fixed-rate mortgages include not only the traditional 30-year loan that most people are familiar with but also 15-year loans, graduated payment mortgages, and growing equity mortgages. With all of these mortgages, your interest rate remains the same throughout the life of the loan.

Traditional 30-Year Mortgage

Its rate does not change, its payment does not change, and in 30 years, it is all paid off. It is the most popular mortgage, and when interest rates are less than 10 percent, most borrowers should get the traditional 30-year mortgage.

With a $100,000 30-year mortgage at 8 percent, you would pay $733.77 principal and interest (P&I) per month. A portion of the P&I payment is the interest on your loan. The remainder of the payment reduces the loan's outstanding principal balance, slowly repaying the entire loan. Loans that are repaid gradually over their life are called *amortizing loans.* The loan amortization chart in Figure 4.1 for a $100,000 loan at 8 percent shows the remaining principal balance over the life of the loan.

You repay very little principal in the early years. At the end of ten years, your remaining loan balance is still $88,000; at the end of 20 years, $61,000; at the end of 30 years, it is paid off. Appendix J contains amortization tables for loans with terms from 5 to 40 years and interest rates of 2 percent to 19 percent.

Advantages. The main advantage of the traditional fixed-rate mortgage is certainty that your rate, monthly principal, and interest payments will not go up. Your payment stays the same for 30 years.

Disadvantages. If overall interest rates go down as they did in the early 1990s, your rate on a traditional mortgage will not go down with them. To take advantage of lower interest-rate levels, you would have to refinance, and that may cost thousands of dollars. Many people who bought homes in the early 1980s with fixed-rate loans at 14 percent and 15 percent refinanced in early 1985 to new fixed-rate loans at 12 percent. Then they faced the prospect of paying even more to get the 10-percent loans being offered in 1986. In the early 1990s, lenders introduced *zero-point* and *no-cost refinance loans* that enabled many borrowers to refinance repeatedly without adding to their loan balances or being faced with extraordinary out-of-pocket costs. (See Chapter 8, "Refinancing," for a fuller discussion.) A fixed-rate loan is a two-edged sword: It is good when rates go up, but bad when rates go down.

FIGURE 4.1   Amortization Chart for a Traditional 30-Year, Fixed-Rate Mortgage

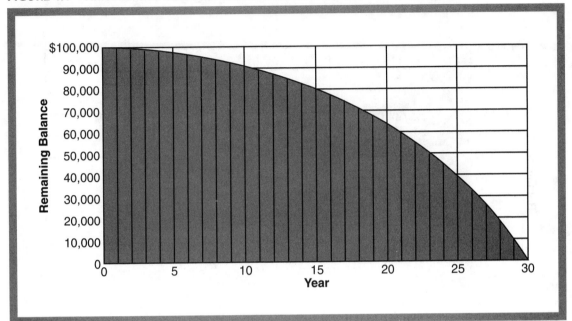

15-Year, Fast-Payoff Mortgage

The 15-year mortgage generally becomes popular when mortgage interest rates are lower, as consumers tend to refinance their 30-year fixed-rate mortgages with 15-year mortgages. It is just like a traditional 30-year loan except that its monthly payment is higher and it pays off in 15 years (see Figure 4.2).

Advantages. Because lenders get their money back sooner than with a traditional mortgage, they charge a slightly lower rate for 15-year loans. The difference varies from lender to lender, but if 30-year loans are offered at 8 percent, then you could expect 15-year loans to be at 7.75 percent.

Also, because you pay off the loan faster, you borrow less money for less time, and over the life of the loan you pay less total interest—more than 50 percent less (see Figure 4.3).

Like a 30-year fixed-rate loan, you have the security of knowing that your monthly principal and interest payment will not go up.

FIGURE 4.2   Amortization Chart for a 15-Year, Fast-Payoff Mortgage

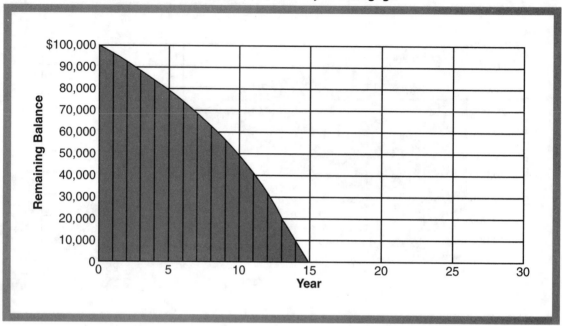

A 15-year mortgage is probably best suited for people who are planning to retire in 15 years and would like to "burn their mortgage" at their retirement party.

FIGURE 4.3   Comparison of a 30-Year and a 15-Year Mortgage:
Total Interest Payments over the Life of the Loan

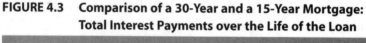

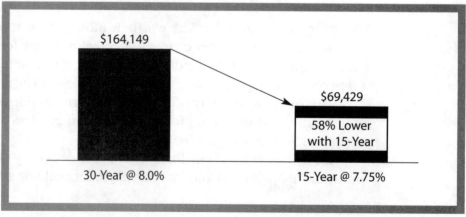

Disadvantages. Your monthly payment is much higher.

In the example in Figure 4.4, the monthly payment is 28 percent higher than that of a comparable 30-year loan. Because the monthly payment is higher, you must have a higher annual income to qualify for it.

In the example in Figure 4.5 (assuming the lender uses a 28-perent housing ratio), you would need to earn about 28 percent more to qualify for a 15-year loan. (See Chapter 2, "Qualifying for a Mortgage Loan," for a full description of housing and debt ratios.)

FIGURE 4.4   **Comparison of a 30-Year and a 15-Year Mortgage: Monthly Principal and Interest Payment**

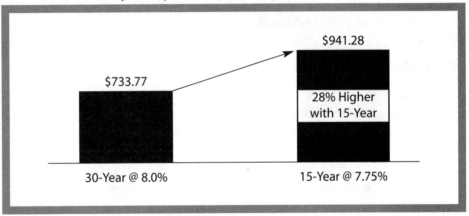

FIGURE 4.5   **Comparison of a 30-Year and a 15-Year Mortgage: Income Required To Qualify**

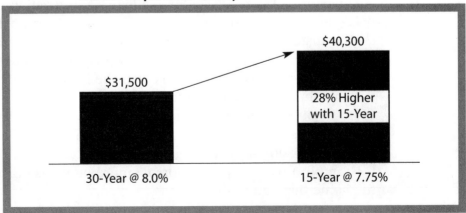

Although 15-year loans have been highly touted, many believe that 30-year loans are still better deals. With most mortgages today, you can make extra payments whenever you like to reduce your loan balance. Depending on the size and frequency of your extra payments, you will pay off your loan in much less than 30 years. For example, if you make 13 payments a year instead of 12, you will pay off a 30-year mortgage in about 20 years. With a 30-year loan, you have the flexibility of making the extra payments when you want to make them.

A 15-year mortgage can be thought of as a "forced savings plan." You put money into your mortgage that you might otherwise invest in stocks, bonds, or other real estate. Depending on your investment alternatives, you may have better ways to invest your money than paying off your mortgage.

Graduated-Payment Mortgage

A *graduated-payment mortgage (GPM)* is designed to be more affordable in the early years than the traditional mortgage. Its monthly payments start low and increase by a fixed percentage every year for five years.

The example in Figure 4.6 is a $100,000 graduated-payment mortgage at 8.75 percent. The starting monthly payment is $593.45 compared with $733.77 for a traditional mortgage. Its payment increases by 7.5 percent every year until it reaches $851.97 in the sixth year. From there on, it stays the same until paid off in 30 years.

The graduated-payment mortgage's amortization chart (see Figure 4.7) looks similar to the traditional loan's amortization chart, but it is different. For the first five years, the remaining loan balance goes up slightly instead of down like the traditional loan. This is called *negative amortization.* Negative amortization (see Figure 4.8) occurs when your monthly payment is too small to cover the interest due your lender, so the amount you pay goes up to cover the interest.

The outstanding principal balance of this graduated-payment mortgage reaches a maximum $104,050 at the end of the fifth year before starting back down again. Negative amortization is not inherently bad. It is simply a way for you to borrow more money so that you can buy the home that you want.

FIGURE 4.6   Example of Graduated Payments

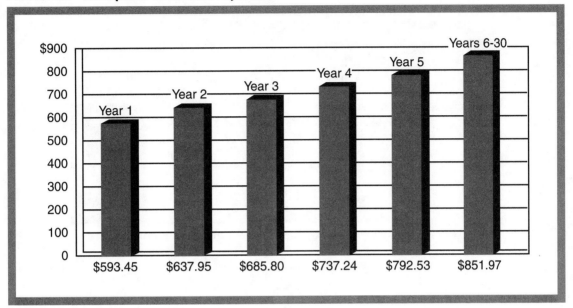

FIGURE 4.7   Amortization Chart of a Sample Graduated-Payment Mortgage

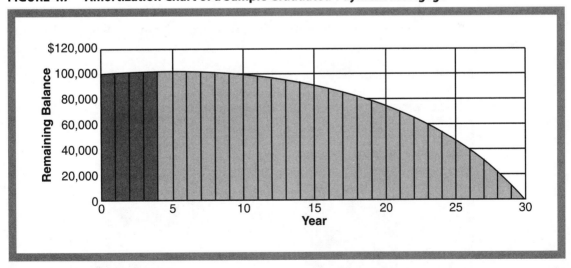

FIGURE 4.8   Question: With Negative Amortization, What Happens When Your Monthly Payments Are Too Small to Cover the Interest Due?

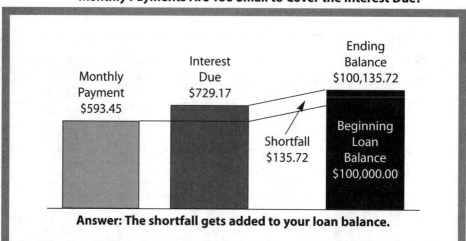

Answer: The shortfall gets added to your loan balance.

Advantages. The main advantage of the graduated-payment mortgage is affordability. Because of its low starting payments, you can qualify for a larger loan with less income.

In the example in Figure 4.9, you could qualify for a $100,000 loan with 20 percent less income. This mortgage form is ideally suited for

FIGURE 4.9   Comparison of a Traditional and a Graduated-Payment Mortgage (GPM): Income Required to Qualify

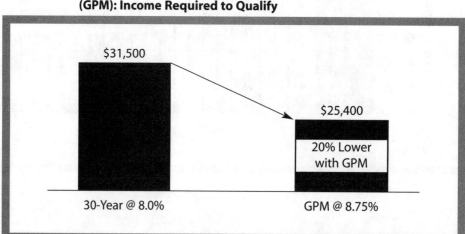

young homebuyers whose income will rise to meet the GPM's monthly payments through raises and promotions.

Disadvantages. First, lenders charge a slightly higher interest rate for GPMs. The rate for a graduated-payment mortgage is typically 0.75 percent to 1 percent higher than for a traditional mortgage.

Second, lenders usually require at least a 10-percent down payment with a GPM, compared with a minimum of 5 percent with a traditional mortgage.

Third, negative amortization, although not usually a problem, can be under certain economic conditions. If home values go down in your area, a GPM's loan balance may become larger than the home's reduced value. This also can happen with a 5-percent down payment loan. The real problem is not negative amortization, but the local economy.

Growing Equity Mortgage

A *growing equity mortgage* (GEM), also known as an *early-ownership mortgage,* is a graduated-payment mortgage whose payments continue to increase until the loan is paid off. They do not level off after the fifth year like those of a GPM (see Figure 4.10).

There are a wide variety of GEMs. Usually, the first year's monthly payments are the same as those of a traditional 30-year loan. They increase each year by a fixed percentage.

In Figure 4.10 (a $100,000 GEM at 7.75 percent), the first year's payments are $716.41. They go up 4 percent each year to $1,240.59 in the 15th year when the loan is paid off.

Advantages. Like a 15-year mortgage, a GEM is paid off quickly, and its interest rate is typically 0.25 percent to 0.50 percent less than that of a traditional mortgage. Also, as with a 15-year loan, you would pay less total interest over the life of the loan.

Unlike a 15-year mortgage, it is no harder to qualify for a GEM than it is to qualify for a traditional loan because of a GEM's lower starting monthly payment.

On balance, a GEM would be well suited to someone whose income is rising and who is planning to retire in about 15 years.

FIGURE 4.10   Example of Payments for a Growing Equity Mortgage

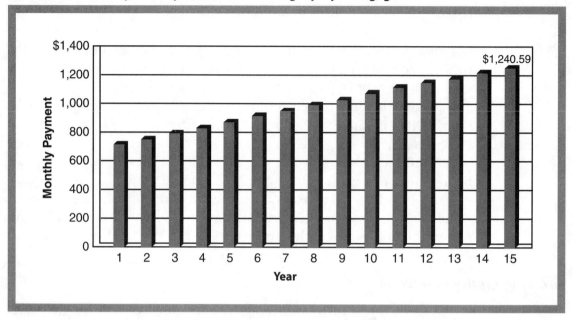

FIGURE 4.11   Amortization Chart of a Sample Growing Equity Mortgage

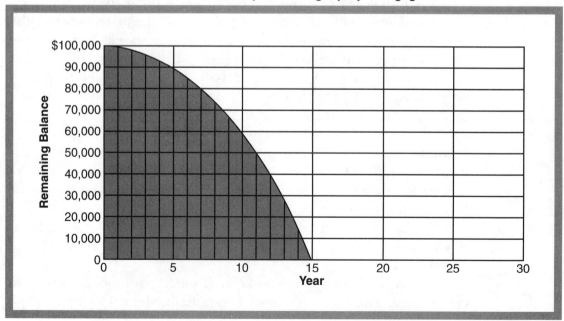

Disadvantages. With a GEM, the payments keep going up whether or not your income goes up with them. In the previous example, the payments increase by more than 70 percent over 15 years. For many people, family income keeps pace with the rising payments. For others, rising payments squeeze the household budget.

Adjustable-Rate Mortgages

Adjustable-rate mortgages (ARMs) became popular in the early 1980s when interest rates were much higher. When lenders were offering fixed-rate mortgages at 15 percent to 16 percent, more than 60 percent of homebuyers chose ARMs with interest rates starting at 12 percent to 13 percent. In 1986 and 1987, when rates were below 10 percent, most lenders reported that fewer than 15 percent of homebuyers were financing their homes with ARMs.

ARMs are good to consider when:

- You believe that rates are going to fall to levels much lower than they are today.
- You plan to keep your home for only two or three years, and an ARM looks less expensive in the short term.

If you have an ARM right now and are wondering whether to refinance to a fixed-rate mortgage, this section as well as Chapter 8 can help you decide what to do.

The obvious difference between an adjustable-rate mortgage and a traditional fixed-rate mortgage is that with an ARM, the interest rate goes up and down (see Figure 4.12). It changes according to a set formula every year or so for the life of the loan. Usually, your monthly payment goes up and down with the interest rate.

Basic and Optional Features

An ARM, much like an automobile, has some basic features and a number of options. This section covers the four basic features common to all ARMs and the four most common optional features.

FIGURE 4.12   Fluctuating Interest Rates with Adjustable-Rate Mortgages

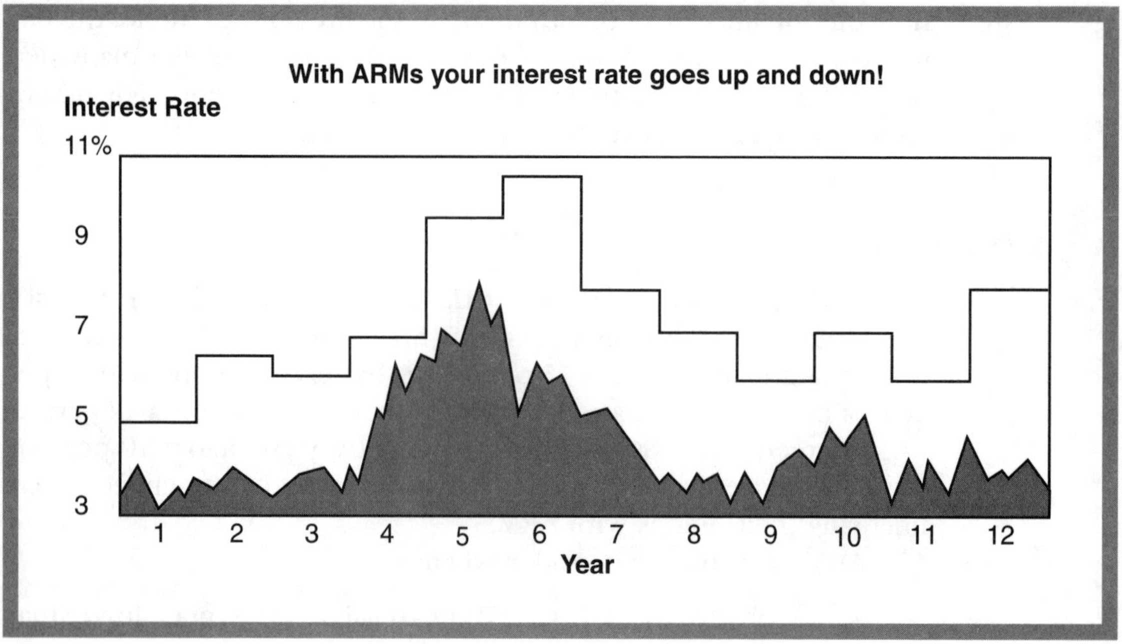

Basic Features

1. Index
2. Margin
3. Adjustment interval
4. Initial interest rate

Optional Features
1. Life interest rate cap
2. Periodic interest rate cap
3. Monthly payment cap
4. Convertibility to fixed-rate

Basic Features

Index. An ARM's interest rate goes up and down according to a nationally published index (see Figure 4.13). Your lender has no control over the index and cannot arbitrarily adjust your rate. Your rate is determined by the index.

FIGURE 4.13   How Index Affects Interest Rates of Adjustable-Rate Mortgages

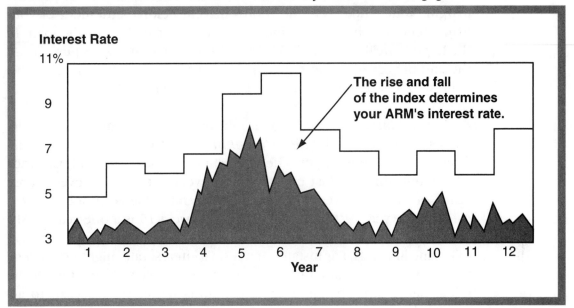

Different ARMs follow different indexes. The One-Year Treasury Bond Index is the most common ARM index. Other indexes are:

- Six-Month Treasury Bill Index
- Three-Year Treasury Bond Index
- Five-Year Treasury Bond Index
- 11th District Cost of Funds Index (COFI)
- National Cost of Funds Index
- Federal Home Loan Bank Board (FHLBB) Contract Rate Index
- London Interbank Offering Rate (LIBOR) Index

The two Cost of Funds indexes are better for consumers than the Treasury Bond and FHLBB indexes because they do not go up so quickly when overall interest rates rise. For example, in September of 1981 when the One-Year Treasury Security Index hit a high of 17.15 percent, the 11th District Cost of Funds Index (COFI) was only 12.325 percent. During the 1980s, the COFI was never higher than 12.70 percent. The current values of the most commonly used mortgage indexes frequently are reported in the business or real estate section of your newspaper.

Margin. Your ARM's interest rate is the sum of the index value plus the margin. Your lender sets the ARM's margin before settlement of your loan. Once set, the margin does not change for the life of the loan. In the hypothetical example in Figure 4.14, the margin is 2.75 percent. At the end of year 5, the index is 7.75 percent. So the rate for year 6 becomes 10.5 percent (7.75 percent plus 2.75 percent).

Adjustment Interval. The interest rate of an ARM changes at fixed intervals. This is called the *adjustment interval.* Different ARMs have different adjustment intervals. The interest rate of most ARMs adjusts once a year, but others adjust every month, every six months, every three years, or every five years. An ARM whose rate changes once a year is called a one-year ARM; the example in Figure 4.15 is a one-year ARM.

Sometimes the first adjustment interval is longer or shorter than following intervals. For instance, an ARM's interest rate might not change for the first three years, but then change once a year thereafter. Or the initial rate might change after ten months rather than a year, to accommodate the lender's accounting systems.

FIGURE 4.14   Relation of Margin to Adjustable-Rate Mortgages

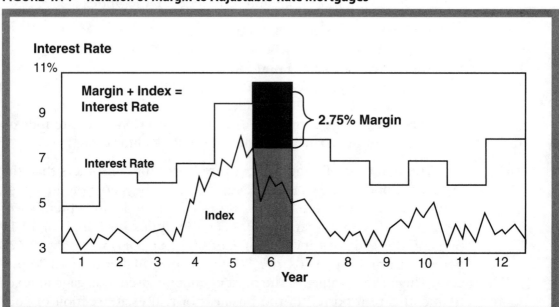

FIGURE 4.15   How the Adjustment Interval Works in Adjustable-Rate Mortgages

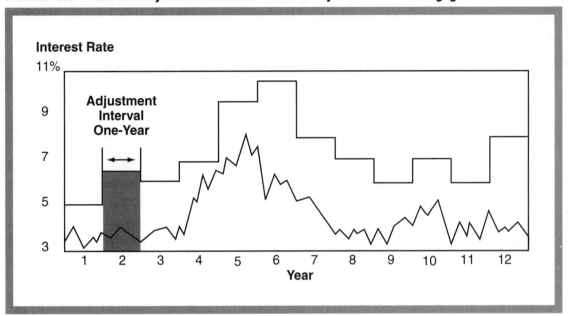

Initial Interest Rate. The final feature common to all adjustable-rate mortgages is the *initial interest rate.* This is the rate that you pay until the end of the first adjustment interval. The initial interest rate also determines the size of your starting monthly payment, which the lender usually uses to qualify you for the loan. Note that for loans with exceptionally low initial interest rates, the lender *may* qualify you at a higher rate, usually the fully indexed rate, or the second year maximum rate. The initial interest rate in Figure 4.16 is 5 percent.

Often the initial interest rate is lower than the sum of the current index value plus margin. When it is several percentage points lower, it is called a *teaser rate.* If your ARM starts with a teaser rate, your interest rate and monthly payment will increase at the end of the first adjustment interval unless your ARM's index goes down enough to offset the discounted teaser rate.

Optional Features. Most ARMs have consumer protection options that limit the amount that your interest rate and monthly payment can increase. They are called *caps.* The first type of cap that you want on

FIGURE 4.16   How the Initial Interest Rate Works in Adjustable-Rate Mortgages

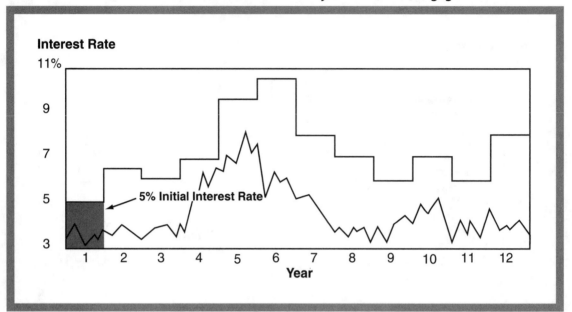

an ARM is the *life interest rate cap.* It sets the maximum and minimum interest rates that you can be charged for the life of the loan.

Life Interest Rate Cap. In the example in Figure 4.17, the life interest rate cap is 10 percent. In year 6, the index value plus margin equals 10.5 percent, but the life cap limits the rate increase to 10 percent. Even if the index went to 16 percent, as the One-Year Treasury Bond Index did in 1982, the interest rate of this ARM would still be limited to 10 percent.

Sometimes the life cap is quoted in percentage points over the initial interest rate. For example, a "5 percent life interest rate cap" means 5 percent over the initial rate, which in Figure 4.17 is 5 percent.

Periodic Interest Rate Cap. The second type of cap is the *periodic interest rate cap.* It limits the amount an ARM's interest rate can change from one adjustment interval to the next. In the example in Figure 4.18, the periodic interest rate cap is 2 percent. This means that the ARM's interest rate cannot go up or down more than 2 percent from

FIGURE 4.17   How the Life Interest Rate Cap Works in Adjustable-Rate Mortgages

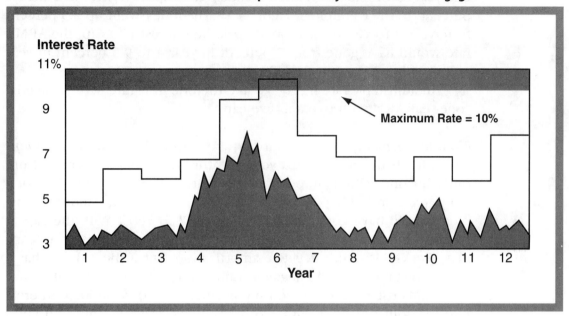

FIGURE 4.18   How the Periodic Interest Rate Cap Works in Adjustable-Rate Mortgages

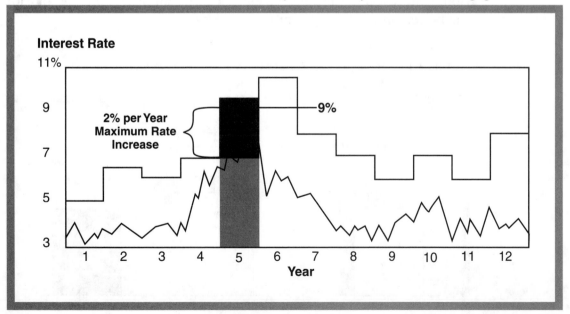

one year to the next, even if the index goes up or down more than 2 percent. In the example in Figure 4.13, the index went up 2.5 percent from year 4 to year 5. Without a periodic interest rate cap, the ARM's rate would have gone from 7 percent in year 4 to 9.5 percent in year 5. But with a 2 percent periodic rate cap, it goes to 9 percent.

An adjustable-rate mortgage like the one in Figure 4.18 is called a "one-year ARM with two and five caps."

Monthly Payment Cap. The third type of cap is the *monthly payment cap.* It limits the amount that your monthly payment can increase from one adjustment interval to the next. Figure 4.18 shows the effect of a 7.5 percent monthly payment cap. Without the cap, the monthly payment would have gone up $128 from $537 to $665. With the cap, it went up only $40 to $577 (see Figure 4.19). ARMs with payment caps may, like GPMs, incur negative amortization, but if the AM also has a life interest rate cap, the negative amortization will be minimal.

ARMs usually have a monthly payment cap or a periodic interest rate cap, but not both. Either of these caps provides you with good protection against extreme increases in your monthly payment. The monthly payment cap provides slightly better protection than the periodic interest rate cap, but through negative amortization, you pay for the better protection with more interest charges.

FIGURE 4.19   How You Can Benefit from a Monthly Payment Cap in Adjustable-Rate Mortgages

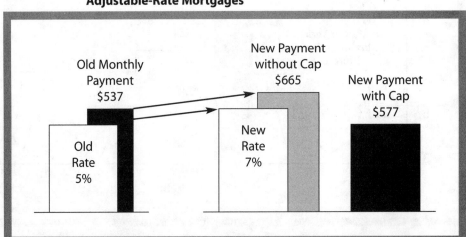

M O R T G A G E   T I P

Beware of ARMs with no caps! If you are looking for a long-term loan, get a fixed-rate mortgage or an ARM with caps.

Some of the ARMs offered in the early 1980s and some of the adjustable-rate second mortgages offered today have no caps! If a lender offers you an ARM with no caps, beware. If you plan to pay it off in a year or two, it probably will be no problem for you. But if you are looking for a long-term loan, get a fixed-rate mortgage or an ARM with caps.

Convertibility to Fixed Rate. The fourth optional feature, which can be a great benefit to consumers, is *convertibility* to fixed rate (see Figure 4.20). ARMs with this feature can be converted at the borrower's option to a fixed-rate mortgage without refinancing.

FIGURE 4.20   Convertibility to Fixed-Rate in Adjustable-Rate Mortgages

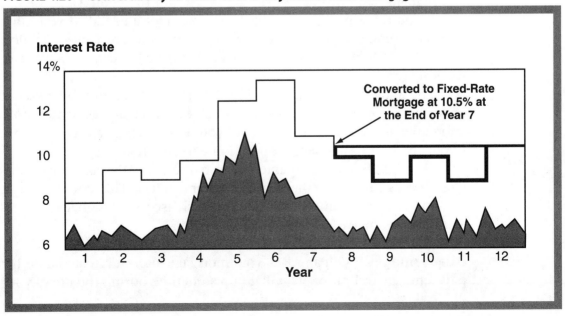

The terms of convertibility vary substantially from lender to lender. Some ARMS with this feature are convertible at any time, others only during the first five years and others only at the end of five years. The fixed-rate loan to which you can convert may not be a "market" rate at that time. Most lenders add a margin to the existing fixed rates for purposes of conversion, making a converted fixed rate somewhat higher than market rates. Terms of conversion are specified in the lender's disclosures and in the ARM note.

Lenders often charge a one-point fee for the convertibility feature, either at the inception of the loan, at the time of conversion or both. A good conversion feature is worth the additional fee. Most people who choose an ARM when rates are high prefer a fixed-rate mortgage. With a convertible ARM, they can wait until rates fall and convert to the fixed-rate loan that they really wanted in the first place.

Advantages and Disadvantages

Advantages. With adjustable-rate mortgages, your mortgage interest rate goes up and down. If rates are high and likely to fall, this is an advantage. If rates are low and likely to rise, this is a disadvantage. ARMs have some other attractive attributes, but interest-rate forecasts should be the major factor in deciding whether or not to get an ARM.

If you think rates are going down, consider an ARM. If you think rates are going up, get a fixed-rate mortgage. If interest rates stabilize or fall, an ARM will be less expensive than fixed-rate mortgages over the long term.

The initial interest rate of ARMs is typically 2 percent to 3 percent lower than traditional fixed-rate mortgages. ARMs are generally more affordable in the first two years, and you do not need so much income to qualify for an ARM as for a traditional fixed-rate loan.

Most ARMs are assumable (see Chapter 6, "Miscellaneous Mortgage Topics," for an explanation of assumability). This could make it easier to sell your home if interest rates increase to the high levels prevalent during the early 1980s.

Disadvantages. With an ARM, your mortgage interest rate and monthly payment can and probably will go up sometime during the life of your loan. In the hypothetical example, the ARM's initial 5 percent rate in year 1 rose to 10 percent in year 6. That kind of increase in rate would cause a 65 percent increase in your monthly payment even with all of the protective caps. Few household budgets can absorb that kind of mortgage payment increase without feeling a pinch.

In 1993, the One-Year Treasury Security Index (the most common ARM index) ranged from 3.25 percent to 3.60 percent. Over the ten years from 1981 to 1990, it has ranged from a low of 5.5 percent to a high of 17.2 percent. Overall interest-rate levels may go lower than they are today, but based on the past ten years, rates have a lot more room to go up than down. Predicting interest rates is difficult for even the most skilled economists. It is even more difficult if you are betting your mortgage payment on your predictions.

Important! Before you decide to get an ARM, be sure to get answers to the following three questions:

1. If interest rates (and the ARM's Index) stay at the same level as today, what will my monthly payment be after one year? Two years? Three years?
2. If interest rates (and the ARM's Index) rise precipitously, what will be the maximum monthly payment that I might possibly have to pay? Can I afford it?
3. Will there be negative amortization that increases my loan?

You need to answer question 1 because those are the payments you will most likely be making. Usually, these payments will be disclosed on your preliminary and final Truth-in-Lending disclosures provided to you by your lender.

You need to know the answer to question 2 because this is the worst-case scenario. If you keep your home for 30 years, rates will rise dramatically at least once or twice during that period. To calculate the maximum payment in a worst-case scenario, calculate the *maximum interest rate* (initial interest rate + life interest rate cap) and multiply your loan amount by the mortgage payment factor (found in Appendix I) for the maximum rate to determine the maximum payment.

You should feel comfortable that you can afford the expected payment increases (question 1) as well as the worst-case payment increases (question 2).

Special Mortgage Packages

In the late 1980s, three new residential mortgage variants were introduced (or reintroduced) on a national scale: "balloon loans," the Freddie Mac "Reset" and the Fannie Mae "Two-Step" ARM, and 3/1 ARM (also the 5/1, 7/1, and 10/1 ARMs). All of these loans have one feature in common: *For the first few years, their rates and payments are fixed.* After the initial period of three, five, seven, or ten years, their rates and payments change, but in a different way for each type of loan.

Advantages. Each of these loan types starts at a lower rate and monthly payment than a 30-year fixed-rate loan. The interest rate for a seven-year balloon will typically be 0.5 percent lower than a comparable 30-year fixed-rate loan. This makes it easier for you to qualify, and it makes the loan payment more affordable in the critical first few years of the loan. When compared with a normal ARM, these loans provide a longer initial period of stable rates and monthly payments.

Disadvantages. After the initial period of fixed rate and payments, the new rates and payments are uncertain. Some of the loans have caps to protect consumers from "payment shock." The balloon loans and some of the others have no protection.

Balloon Loans

A *balloon loan* is just like a traditional 30-year fixed-rate loan, *with one major exception!* At the end of five, seven, or ten years (depending on the balloon term), the loan becomes due and payable. A balloon loan amortizes just like a traditional fixed-rate loan. A $100,000 7.5-percent, seven-year balloon loan with 30-year amortization requires 83 principal and interest payments of $699.21 and a final payment of $91,958.51.

When it matures, you must pay it off in cash or refinance. Some balloon loans, *but not all,* require your lender to refinance the loan when it matures at the then current interest rates, assuming that you qualify for the new loan. You will have to pay closing costs again, and you may be required to provide all of the income, employment, and debt information that you supplied when you first applied for your loan. If you choose a balloon loan, be sure that you read and fully understand the conditions of your right to refinance.

Under what circumstances should you choose a balloon loan over a 30-year fixed-rate loan? The answer is *when you know for certain that you will be selling your home or refinancing before your balloon loan matures.* Even if you are sure that you will be selling or refinancing before your loan matures, try to find a balloon that requires your lender to refinance your loan just in case your plans change.

Two-Steps and Resets

Fannie Mae developed the *Two-Step loan,* while Freddie Mac developed the *Reset.* Both loans are really a type of adjustable-rate mortgage, but the rate adjusts only once in its 30-year term. For the first seven years (five years for the Freddie Mac Reset), called the *initial period,* the rate is fixed at the note rate that is quoted to you. At the end of the initial period, the rate is adjusted like every other ARM by adding a specified margin to an index. The new rate and monthly principal and interest payment then remain the same for the remaining 23 years or 25 years. At the end of the 30 years, the loan is fully amortized. These loans are sometimes referred to as a "7/23" or "5/25."

The Two-Step and the Reset have the advantage of a lower initial rate like a balloon, but they do not require you to refinance at the end of the initial period as you would with a balloon loan. This makes the Two-Step and the Reset more desirable than a comparable balloon.

The Two-Step and Reset loans are appropriate for someone who wants a fixed-rate loan but is willing to trade a little bit of future uncertainty to get a lower and more affordable initial monthly payment.

3/1 ARMs

A *3/1 ARM* is a one-year ARM with an initial adjustment interval of three years. For the first three years, the rate and monthly payment are fixed. At the end of three years and annually thereafter, the rate and payment are adjusted as they are for a one-year ARM. There are also 5/1, 7/1, and 10/1 ARMs with initial adjustment periods of five, seven, and ten years, respectively.

When interest rates for fixed-rate loans are too high for you to qualify for your desired loan amount, and you want a loan that will provide a level payment for at least the first few years, the 3/1, 5/1, or 7/1 ARMs could be right for you. Their initial rates will be lower than a fixed-rate loan for easier qualifying, and their payments will remain the same for a few years, giving you a fixed amount for which you can budget.

As with other ARMs, make sure that you have answered the questions "What will my payments be if rates stay where they are today?" and "What is the maximum monthly payment amount?"

FHA, VA, and Conventional Mortgages

To support home ownership for veterans and low- to moderate-income families, the federal government's Department of Veterans Affairs (VA) and Federal Housing Administration (FHA) have mortgage loan programs. About 20 percent of residential mortgages carry a government guaranty or insurance. In the mortgage industry, they are called *government loans*. The other 80 percent are called *conventional loans*. Government loans are described in the following sections.

Government Loans

Advantages. FHA loans and VA loans have several advantages to the consumer over conventional loans:

- Lower interest rates (often 0.5 percent lower)
- Easier qualifying requirements (more lenient qualification formulas than conventional loans)
- Lower down-payment requirements (FHA: 2 percent to 3 percent; VA: no money down to $240,000)
- Assumable loans

Both FHA and VA loan programs include 30-year and 15-year fixed-rate, level-payment loans, one-year ARM loans with 1/5 caps, and graduated-payment mortgages.

Disadvantages. FHA and VA loans carry some restrictions and disadvantages:

FHA

- In 2001, the maximum loan amount for an FHA-insured single-family loan ranged from $144,336 (in lower-cost areas) to $261,609 (in high-cost areas), and up to $291,650 for Alaska and Hawaii. FHA loan limits are set annually for each county or metropolitan area in the country. They are listed on the FHA Web site.
- In 2001, the FHA mortgage insurance premiums were lowered for all types of loans. The up-front fee paid at closing is 1.5 percent of the loan amount. The annual premium paid as part of your mortgage payment depends on the LTV and term of your loan. Figure 4.21 details the premium structure as of 2001.
- They are not available for non-owner-occupied investment properties or vacation homes except for certain refinances of existing FHA-insured loans.

VA

- In 2002, the maximum loan amount for a VA-guaranteed loan was $240,000.
- To get a VA loan, you must be a qualifying veteran, the unmarried widow of a veteran, a Public Health Service Officer, or an

FIGURE 4.21   FHA Mortgage Insurance Premiums (MIP) as of Jan. 1, 2001

30-Year Term Mortgages		
LTV Ratio	**Up-Front Fee***	**Annual Fee****
All	1.5%	0.5%
15-Year Term Mortgages		
LTV Ratio	**Up-Front Fee***	**Annual Fee****
90% and higher	1.5%	0.25%
89.9% and lower	1.5%	none

*If you repay your mortgage before five years, you get a pro-rated refund.
**The annual fee is dropped after the mortgage is paid down to 78 percent LTV.

active-duty serviceman (with 181-day service). Check with the VA with questions on eligibility.

- Presently, the VA Funding Fee is as much as 3 percent of the loan amount, depending on your down payment, whether you are a veteran of active duty military service or a reservist with at least six years of service and whether this is a first-time use of the VA-guaranteed loan program. As of 2001, the VA loan guaranty fees were as follows:

Loan Type		Active Duty Veteran or	National Guard/ Reservist
Purchase/construction	0% down	2.000%	2.750%
	5% down	1.500	2.250
	10% down	1.250	2.000
Regular refinance (cash out)		2.000	2.750
Rate reduction refinance		0.500	0.500
Second or subsequent use (other than rate reduction refinance or purchase/construction with at least 5% down)		3.000	3.000

- VA loans are not available for investment properties or vacation homes.

Because of their lower rates and assumability, VA loans are better deals for consumers than conventional loans. (However, if you are making a down payment of 20 percent or more, the VA guarantee fees, which are charged regardless of loan-to-value ratio, may make a VA loan more expensive than a conventional loan. If you are making a down payment of less than 20 percent, a VA loan probably will be less expensive.)

Mortgage companies make more than 85 percent of the nation's FHA and VA loans. So if you decide to get a government loan, concentrate your shopping effort on mortgage companies.

Conventional Loans

The federal government also affects the market for *conventional mortgages.* Two federally chartered government agencies, Fannie Mae and Freddie Mac, buy mortgages from lenders. These two agencies supply more than 70 percent of the nation's mortgage money and directly affect mortgage rates for conventional loans.

Congress has set some restrictions on the mortgages that Fannie Mae and Freddie Mac can buy. The most critical restriction is the maximum loan amount. For 2002, it is as follows:

No. of Units	Maximum Loan Amounts for Conforming Loans	
	Continental U.S. and Puerto Rico	Alaska, Guam, Hawaii, and Virgin Islands
1	$300,700	$451,050
2	$384,900	$577,350
3	$465,200	$697,800
4	$578,150	$867,225

Conventional loans that Fannie Mae and Freddie Mac are allowed to purchase are called *conforming loans*. Conventional loans that are too large for these government agencies are called *nonconforming loans* or *jumbo loans*. Jumbo loans have higher interest rates than conforming loans, typically 0.5 percent to 1 percent higher. Jumbo loans also have higher down-payment requirements, especially for loans larger than $300,000.

Other Mortgage Programs

In addition to the traditional 30-year and 15-year fixed-rate mortgages, adjustable-rate mortgages, and balloon mortgages, other less common mortgage programs are available. These include state and local subsidy programs, reverse annuity (sometimes known as reverse equity) mortgages, mortgages insured by the Rural Development Service, and biweekly mortgages.

State and Local Housing Finance Authorities

There are thousands of public housing programs developed by state and local governments that promote home ownership. Most of the programs are targeted at:

• First time homebuyers (or homebuyers who have not owned for at least three years)

- Low and moderate income homebuyers
- Teachers, policemen, firemen, and other municipal employees
- Neighborhood redevelopment

The programs differ widely from state to state and from county to county. The benefits to a homebuyer may include:

- *Lower mortgage rates.* $1/2$ percent to 1 percent lower than prevailing market rates.
- *Tax breaks.* For example, first time homebuyers in Washington, D.C., may get a $5,000 tax credit.
- *Low-cost housing.* Teachers and police officers can buy a home for half-price from the FHA in selected neighborhoods.
- *Easier qualifying and lower down payments.*

If you think that you fall into one of these categories, getting your mortgage or your home through one of these programs might mean even greater savings than shopping through normal mortgage channels. Appendix L (Internet Resources) lists the Web site addresses for state housing finance authorities. Many counties also have subsidized housing and subsidized mortgage programs. Call your local government to find out if there is a program that might benefit you. Appendix L also has the Web site addresses for two associations of housing finance authorities.

Reverse Annuity Mortgages

The Federal Housing Administration insures reverse annuity mortgages. The program is for elderly individuals (62 and over) who own their home free and clear (without a mortgage) but need additional income for day-to-day living expenses. Under this program, borrowers do not receive the entire principal balance at settlement but receive periodic payments of principal during the term of the loan up to a maximum insurable amount as defined by the FHA. The amount may increase by 1/12th of the expected annual appreciation (of the property) each month. Interest on the principal advanced and FHA's annual mortgage insurance are added to the outstanding balance on a monthly basis. When the total outstanding principal balance reaches the maximum insurable by FHA, payments of principal cease. If the value of the home is not sufficient to pay off the outstanding loan amount when the borrower dies, FHA will not attempt to collect the balance from the heirs to the estate. If the value of the home is greater than the loan balance, the remainder of the proceeds is available to the estate. However, in some cases, there is an equity sharing arrangement: The lender shares in a percentage of the appreciation of the property if the value is greater than the loan balance. The program has not proven to be very popular among borrowers, and lenders who are authorized to lend under this program are limited. See your local lender for details.

Biweekly Mortgages

Payments are due on a biweekly basis (every two weeks) rather than once a month. The payment is calculated by dividing the monthly payment by two. Because payment is collected every two weeks, you make an extra month's payment every year, thus substantially speeding up the amortization of your loan. In addition, with a true biweekly mortgage, the loan is amortized on a biweekly basis, so the impact of the payment schedule is actually much greater than just making an extra payment each year. Most biweekly mortgages require that the biweekly payment be deducted directly from your checking account by the lender. If you had insufficient funds in the account under certain circumstances, the loan would revert to a normally amortizing mortgage.

Be aware, however, that some third parties will offer to convert your existing traditional mortgage to a biweekly mortgage by collecting the payments on a biweekly basis and forwarding them to your mortgage lender. This offer is not such a good deal. Although an extra monthly payment is made each year, the loan does not actually amortize on a biweekly basis and the third party charges a fee for the service, which may cost more than the savings in interest over the term of the loan. You would probably be better off by making an extra mortgage payment on your own each year in this scenario.

Rural Development Service Mortgages

Because it is sometimes difficult to find a mortgage in rural areas of the country, the U.S. Department of Agriculture offers mortgage programs through its Rural Development Service (RDS), formerly called the Farmers Home Administration. RDS loans are primarily for low-cost housing and made to low-income borrowers. The average loan size is well below $100,000. The RDS has a direct lending program in which it is the lender, and it has a guarantee program in which loans are offered through traditional banks and mortgage companies. Highlights of the programs are as follows:

- RDS loans are only available in rural areas as defined by the U.S. Census Bureau.
- Like VA loans, the LTV ratio can be up to 100 percent (no money down).
- Borrower income generally must be no greater than 80 percent of the median income for the area in which the property is located.
- Like VA loans, the RDS charges an up-front fee (2 percent in 2002), but no monthly fees like FHA.
- The interest rates on the loans that RDS makes directly are subsidized slightly. Usually they are $\frac{1}{2}$ to $\frac{3}{4}$ percent lower than market rates.
- The amount of money available each year for these loans is limited. It is set in concert with the federal budget process.

Choosing the Right Type of Mortgage for You

For most people, a conventional 30-year traditional mortgage is the right choice. It is by far the most popular. It also makes a good benchmark for making comparisons with other types of loans. The type of loan that you choose depends on your needs. The chart in Figure 4.22 summarizes the characteristics that you might be looking for in a mortgage and matches loan types to those characteristics.

Not all loans are readily available for all loan amounts and all loan-to-value ratios. Figure 4.23 summarizes the limitations for various types of loans.

The Mortgage Data Form described in Figure 5.3 in Chapter 5, "Shopping for a Mortgage," will help you determine how large a mortgage you need and your loan-to-value ratio. Chapter 2, "Qualifying for a Mortgage Loan," will help you determine how large a loan you qualify for and if you need a loan type that makes qualifying easier. In addition to using all of this information, you can consult a loan officer of a mortgage company, bank, or savings-and-loan association for help in choosing the right type of loan.

FIGURE 4.22   Comparing Different Types of Mortgages to 30-Year Fixed Rate

| | Fixed-Rate Mortgages | | | | | | FHA/ |
| | Level Payments | | | Graduated Payments | | | |
	30-Year	15-Year	Balloons	GPMs	GEMs	ARMs	VA
Lower Rates	0	+1	+1	−1	+1	+2	+1
Easier Qualifying	0	−2	+1	+2	0	+2	+1
Fast Payoff	0	+2	−1	0	+2	0	0
Low Down Payment	0	0	0	−1	0	0	+2
Low Initial Monthly Payment	0	−2	0	+2	0	+2	0

Legend: −1 = unfavorable   0 = similar to 30-yr.
        −2 = even less favorable compared   +1 = more favorable
           to 30-yr. fixed-rate mortgage   +2 = much more favorable

FIGURE 4.23   Restrictions on Different Types of Mortgages

| | Conventional Loans | | | Government Loans | |
	Traditional	GPMs	ARMs	FHA	VA
Maximum Loan Amount	No maximum	Difficult to find over $250,000	No maximum	$144,336 to $291,650, depending on region	$240,000
Maximum Loan-to-Value Ratio (LTV)	• 97% (special programs) • lower for refinance • lower for larger nonconforming loans • lower for second homes and investor loans	• 90% or less	• wide variation in loans offered	• 98.75% if sales price equal to or less than $50,000 • 97.65% if sales price exceeds $50,000 up to $125,000 • 97.15% if sales price exceeds $125,000	• No down payment required

5

Shopping for a Mortgage

When shopping for a mortgage, your goal should be twofold: First, shop to make price comparisons (see Figure 5.1). A recent survey showed that in major metropolitan markets, mortgage interest rates vary by 0.375 percent to 0.50 percent for exactly the same product. That difference amounts to $350 a year on a $100,000 mortgage. The price difference also can show up in the points lenders charge. The same survey showed differences as large as 2.5 points for the same product at the same rate, as much as $2,500 on a $100,000 loan!

Second, look for a lender with a reputation for integrity and service. Although most lenders stand behind their commitments and provide good service, there have been instances when consumers did not get what they bargained for. Ask your agent, your attorney, or the Better

FIGURE 5.1   The Process of Shopping for a Mortgage

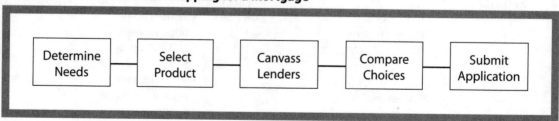

Determine Needs — Select Product — Canvass Lenders — Compare Choices — Submit Application

Business Bureau about the reputation of a lender before submitting an application.

Determine Your Needs

Before you start telephoning lenders, you should have a firm idea of the product that you are going to inquire about. Rates and the availability of mortgages depend on the following factors:

- Loan amount
- Loan type
- Occupancy (Is the home to be used as a primary residence, second home, or investor property?)
- Loan-to-value ratio
- Purpose of loan (for a home purchase or refinance?)

Mortgage Data Form

The first step in shopping for a mortgage is documenting precisely what you need (see Figure 5.2) so that you can answer some of the basic questions lenders will ask you.

A sample Mortgage Data Form in Figure 5.3 includes most of the information that you should have at your fingertips for your initial contact with lenders. Appendix D has a blank form for you to fill out.

In the example in Figure 5.3, Mr. and Mrs. Homebuyer need a $107,500 mortgage to purchase a home for $125,000. The home will be their primary residence, and the LTV ratio will be about 86 percent. (They already have prequalified for this loan amount at prevailing interest rates.)

FIGURE 5.2   Step 1: Determine Your Needs

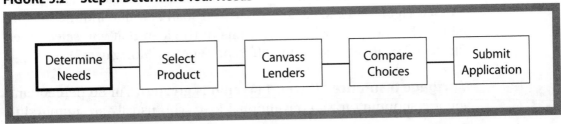

FIGURE 5.3   Sample Mortgage Data Form

Contract Purchase Price (Home Purchase) or Estimated Value (Refinance)	$125,000 (A)
Estimated Closing Costs: 6% × (A) for Purchase or 4% × (A) for Refinance	+ 7,500 (B)
Estimated Total Funds Required: (A) + (B)	$132,500 (C)
Cash Available (Purchase) or Equity (Refinance): (A) − Old Mortgage Balance	− 25,000 (D)
Estimated Mortgage Amount: (C) − (D)	$107,500 (E)
Estimated Loan-to-Value Ratio: (E) ÷ (A)	86.0% (F)

Type of Loan

☐ FHA
☐ VA
☒ Conventional
  (☒ Conforming or ☐ Jumbo)

☒ Level Payment (Traditional)
☐ Graduated Payment
  (☐ 5% or ☐ 7.5% payment increase)
☐ Adjustable-Rate Mortgage (ARM)
☐ Growing Equity Mortgage (GEM)

Term

☒ 30 Years
☐ 15 Years

Occupancy

☒ Primary Residence
☐ Vacation (Second) Home
☐ Investment

Select the Mortgage Product

The topics in Chapter 2, "Qualifying for a Mortgage Loan," Chapter 4, "Choosing the Right Type of Mortgage," Chapter 7, "Investor Loans" and Chapter 8, "Refinancing," all affect the type of mortgage that you select. Read through them and make your selection before calling lenders (see Figure 5.4). Make sure that your loan amount and the loan-to-value (LTV) ratio fall within the limits of the loan that you select. (See Figure 4.23, "Restrictions on Different Types of Mortgages.")

Mortgage Insurance. If your LTV ratio is greater than 80 percent and you are shopping for a conventional loan, you usually are required to

FIGURE 5.4   Step 2: Select the Mortgage Product

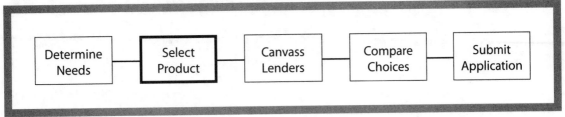

pay a mortgage insurance premium (MIP) each month as part of your monthly payment (see Chapter 6). Monthly mortgage insurance premiums vary from 0.25 percent to 0.50 percent of the original loan amount depending on LTV ratio, loan type, and loan amount. These premiums increase your effective interest rate by the rate of the premium.

Some lenders self-insure by charging a slightly higher mortgage rate instead of requiring mortgage insurance. To compare their rates to lenders who require mortgage insurance, you must add the mortgage insurance premium rate to the rate to get the effective rate. If none of the lenders that you canvass self-insures or your LTV is 80 percent or below, you can ignore the cost of mortgage insurance.

Temporary Buydown. If you plan to use a temporary buydown to help in qualifying, you must ask about the cost when you do your rate shopping (see Chapter 6). Different lenders charge different amounts for the same buydown plans, just as they charge different rates for the same loans.

Canvass Lenders

It is difficult, if not impossible, to find the "best deal" in town. Many lenders change their posted rates daily. No lender has the best rates all the time, and a lender with the lowest rates in one type of mortgage may have high rates in another type. Despite the difficulties involved with shopping for a loan, there is no better way for you to save money than telephoning lenders and comparing rates (see Figure 5.5). The Internet now has many sites with current mortgage interest rates, both nationally and locally. (See the section in Chapter 6 called

FIGURE 5.5   Step 3: Telephone Lenders and Compare Rates

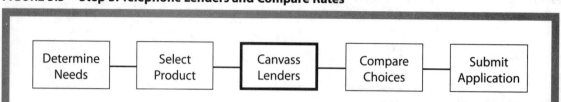

"Mortgage Lending on the Internet" for additional advice, and see Appendix L for some Internet sites to visit.)

Whom to Call

Some large metropolitan areas may have as many as 150 mortgage lenders; smaller markets, as few as a dozen. In most areas, calling every lender in the telephone book would be impractical, but calling 15 to 20 lenders should result in significant savings.

If only a dozen lenders are in your area, call them all. If there are 150, how do you choose the 15 or 20 to canvass?

In some metropolitan areas, there are Mortgage Rate Reporting Services that poll lenders for their rates and publish a weekly report, some Boards of REALTORS® maintain a list of mortgage rates on their Multiple Listing Service computers, and many newspapers publish a list of mortgage rates in their real estate section. Ask your agent or check with the local newspaper to find out if there is a rate reporting service in your area. You can also select a mortgage broker, explained later in this chapter.

Because interest rates change frequently, the weekly listings often are out-of-date by the time they are published. However, some lenders' rates are consistently lower than average, and other lenders' rates are consistently higher. The value of the rate reporting services is to help you select the 20 lenders to canvass.

If there is no rate reporting service in your area, you will have to rely on your real estate agent, your attorney, your friends, and the Yellow Pages. Mortgage companies make more than half of the nation's mortgage loans. Commercial banks now make more than 25 percent, and savings-and-loan associations less than 20 percent (see Figure 5.6). This is an almost complete reversal from the situation of only a few years ago,

FIGURE 5.6   Who Makes Mortgage Loans?

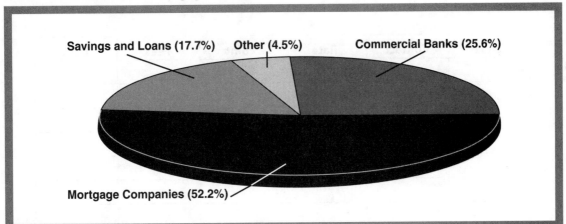

when more than half of all mortgage loans were originated by savings-and-loan associations and commercial banks were only "bit" players.

If you are refinancing or have a mortgage on a home that you are selling, call your current mortgage lender first. Some lenders will give special deals to existing borrowers. Second, call the banks where you have checking and savings accounts. They may not be active in the mortgage market, but if not, they can be another source of advice on who the most competitive lenders are.

Mortgage companies make 85 percent of the FHA- and VA-insured loans. If you are shopping for an FHA or VA loan, limit your search to mortgage companies. If you are shopping for a conventional loan, call several savings-and-loan associations, several mortgage companies, and a few banks. If you are self-employed or own a business, your commercial bank may give you a subsidized mortgage rate as an incentive to keep your commercial accounts.

Shopping Lists

Appendices E and F have shopping lists for you to use while calling lenders for their rates: One list is for fixed-rate loans and one is for ARMs. Figure 5.7 shows you a blank fixed-rate shopping list.

Try to make all your telephone calls to lenders within one or two days. If you spread the calls out over a week's time, the rates will have

FIGURE 5.7   Fixed-Rate Loan Shopping List

Lender	Contact	Rate	Point	Fees	Lock

changed by the time you have finished canvassing all the lenders on your list. Also, plan to submit an application immediately after you have canvassed the lenders. Again, if you wait a week, the rates may have changed.

Some lenders may give you two or three quotes for the same loan but with different combinations of rate and points. Write them all down and decide which is best later.

If you are refinancing, be sure to ask the lender for a loan with just one or two points so that your payback period will be short. Most lenders will be able to quote several combinations of rate and points.

If you are buying a home and do not have much cash for the down payment and closing costs, you should also ask for a loan with low points. This will reduce your closing costs and the cash required to buy the home.

Locking In a Rate

In most markets, lenders will allow you to lock in the quoted rate and points that are available when you submit your application. Usually, lock-in commitments are good for a period of 45 to 60 days. Even if interest rates increase while your loan is being processed and approved, the lender will close your loan at the lower rate that you locked in earlier. If rates have fallen, most lenders still will expect you to close the loan at the lock-in rate.

Problems arise when lenders are unable to process and close a loan within the lock-in commitment period. In 1993, for example, lenders were flooded with loan applications from homebuyers and homeowners seeking to take advantage of low interest rates. Many lenders, appraisers, title companies, and settlement attorneys had a 90- to 120-day backlog. Lenders were unable to close loans within 60 days. Many homebuyers' lock-in commitments expired, and they were forced to close their loans at higher rates. During periods of exceptionally high loan volume, some lenders may temporarily stop offering lock-in commitments.

Question: If you cannot lock in the low interest rate that you find by canvassing lenders, what value is there is shopping around?

Answer: Lenders with below-average rates today are more likely to have lower rates in three months than lenders with higher rates today. If lenders in your area are not offering lock-in commitments, the value of shopping will be diminished but not lost. Just as discount stores have lower prices than full-service department stores, some lenders have lower-than-average mortgage rates on an ongoing basis.

Question: Are lock-in commitments free?

Answer: In most markets, lenders will not charge a nonrefundable fee for locking in your rate if you are purchasing a home, but in some markets they will. It is not uncommon for lenders to charge a lock-in fee for refinance loans. Some lenders will charge one-half to one full point more for a loan with a 60-day lock-in commitment. Others will factor the cost of commitments into the interest rate and number of points that they charge.

Some lenders offer a 120-day lock-in commitment for a nonrefundable up-front fee. This might be attractive to you if you cannot settle for three or four months, but would like to lock in a low interest rate.

Even when a lock-in commitment is available and the lender will be able to close your loan within the lock-in period, you may not want to lock in a rate. If you feel strongly that interest rates are falling, you may want to wait until closing to set your rate. If so, do not lock in a rate.

Mortgage Brokers

In some areas of the country, mortgage brokers will take your application and find a lender for you. They provide a very useful service. They know which lenders have the most competitive rates and which lenders have the most relaxed underwriting standards. Generally, they can do a better job of shopping than a consumer who does not have the time to do it thoroughly.

However, many lenders do not accept application packages from mortgage brokers, and others will tack on an additional fee to their ordinary rates to pay the broker's commission. Some brokers will add their own fee on top of that.

Bottom Line on Mortgage Brokers. If a mortgage broker with a good reputation can get you a loan at a lower price than you can find yourself, use him or her.

Compare Your Choices

The next step after canvassing lenders is to compare your options (see Figure 5.8).

Question: After you have made your telephone calls and filled out the shopping list, how do you select one loan and lender from among the many choices?

Answer: By process of elimination.

The price that you pay for a loan is a combination of rate, points, and fees. Price comparisons are tricky, and unfortunately there is no way to make good comparisons without resorting to some arithmetic. Comparing the prices to choose a lender is a four-step process:

FIGURE 5.8   Step 4: Compare Your Choices

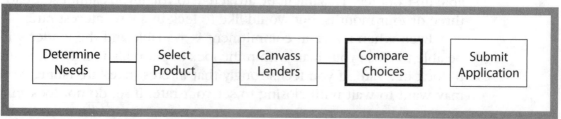

1. Sort your list of loans by rate and points.
2. Eliminate the obviously high-priced loans.
3. Calculate effective rate for remaining loans.
4. Choose a low rate loan from a reputable lender.

When you have completed your telephone calls, you will have a list of 15 to 25 loans. To make the example in Figure 5.9 simpler, we have listed just eight of them.

Figure 5.9 shows the loans in the same order as they came from the shopping list. Note that the rates are expressed as decimals rather than fractions. This makes the arithmetic easier. Use the following conversion table if lenders quote rates in fractions:

$$8 = 8.000$$
$$8\tfrac{1}{4} = 8.250$$
$$8\tfrac{1}{2} = 8.500$$
$$8\tfrac{3}{4} = 8.750$$
$$8\tfrac{1}{8} = 8.125$$
$$8\tfrac{3}{8} = 8.375$$
$$8\tfrac{5}{8} = 8.625$$
$$8\tfrac{7}{8} = 8.875$$

FIGURE 5.9   Sample Shopping List: Gather Information

Fixed-Rate Loan Shopping List

Lender	Contact	Rate	Point	Fees	Lock
ABC Mortgage Co.	Joe Reilly	8.125%	4.00	$300	60 days
ABC Mortgage Co.	Joe Reilly	8.000	4.75	300	60 days
Amer. Home Mortg. Co.	Sue Clifton	8.000	5.00	250	45 days
1st Home Savings Bank	Bill Wilson	8.250	4.25	250	60 days
1st Home Savings Bank	Bill Wilson	8.625	1.00	250	60 days
Hometown S&L	John Smith	8.375	2.00	300	60 days
First National Bank	Kathy Johns	8.375	3.00	350	60 days
First Federal S&L	Lynn Barrs	8.500	2.00	250	45 days

First, after you have finished canvassing the lenders, sort your list of quotes by rate and then points (see Figure 5.10). You usually will find that the mortgages with the lowest rates will have the most points.

The next step is to eliminate the loans whose rates and points are obviously higher than other loans on the list (see Figure 5.11). This will cut down the amount of arithmetic required.

Eliminate loans that have the same rate as another loan on your list and more points. In the example that follows, American Home Mortgage Company's loan at 8 percent plus five points is higher priced than ABC Mortgage Company's loan at 8 percent plus 4.75 points, and First National Bank's loan is one point higher than Hometown S&L.

Also eliminate loans that have a higher rate than another loan on your list and the same number or more points. First Federal S&L's loan at 8.5 percent plus two points is higher priced than Hometown S&L's loan at 8.375 percent plus two points so it, too, can be eliminated. First Home Savings Bank's loan at 8.25 percent plus 4.25 points is higher priced than ABC Mortgage Company's loan at 8.125 percent plus four points because both its rate and points are higher.

FIGURE 5.10   Sort Your List

Fixed-Rate Loan Shopping List

Lender	Contact	Rate	Point	Fees	Lock
ABC Mortgage Co.	Joe Reilly	8.000%	4.75	$300	60 days
Amer. Home Mortg. Co.	Sue Clifton	8.000	5.00	250	45 days
ABC Mortgage Co.	Joe Reilly	8.125	4.00	300	60 days
1st Home Savings Bank	Bill Wilson	8.250	4.25	250	60 days
Hometown S&L	John Smith	8.375	2.00	300	60 days
First National Bank	Kathy Johns	8.375	3.00	350	60 days
First Federal S&L	Lynn Barrs	8.500	2.00	250	45 days
1st Home Savings Bank	Bill Wilson	8.625	1.00	250	60 days

FIGURE 5.11   Begin Narrowing Your List

Fixed-Rate Loan Shopping List

Lender	Contact	Rate	Point	Fees	Lock
ABC Mortgage Co.	Joe Reilly	8.000%	4.75	$300	60 days
~~Amer. Home Mortg. Co.~~	~~Sue Clifton~~	~~8.000~~	~~5.00~~	~~250~~	~~45 days~~
ABC Mortgage Co.	Joe Reilly	8.125	4.00	300	60 days
~~1st Home Savings Bank~~	~~Bill Wilson~~	~~8.250~~	~~4.25~~	~~250~~	~~60 days~~
Hometown S&L	John Smith	8.375	2.00	300	60 days
~~First National Bank~~	~~Kathy Johns~~	~~8.375~~	~~3.00~~	~~350~~	~~60 days~~
~~First Federal S&L~~	~~Lynn Barrs~~	~~8.500~~	~~2.00~~	~~250~~	~~45 days~~
1st Home Savings Bank	Bill Wilson	8.625	1.00	250	60 days

Making the Arithmetic Easier

The third step is to convert the rate and points for the remaining loans into their effective rate. Calculating the effective rate precisely requires a computer or financial calculator, but you do not need to be that precise to compare loans. The following formula works well for people who plan to keep their loan for 7 to 12 years:

Interest rate + (Points ÷ 6) = Effective rate

For example, the effective rate for ABC Mortgage Company's 8 percent plus 4.75-point loan is: 8.0 percent + (4.750 points ÷ 6) = 8.792 percent. (Note: This formula does not work with adjustable-rate mortgages.)

If you plan to keep your home for more than 12 years, divide the points by 8 instead of 6. If you plan to stay for 4 to 6 years, divide the points by 4. If you plan to stay 1 to 3 years, divide the points by the number of years.

The final step is choosing a low rate from a reputable lender. In the previous example, Hometown S&L has the lowest effective rate at 8.708 percent (see Figure 5.12). In the case of a tie, you can use fees

FIGURE 5.12   Select Reputable Lender with Lowest Effective Rate

Fixed-Rate Loan Shopping List

Lender	Contact	Rate	Points	Effective Rate	
ABC Mortgage Co.	Joe Reilly	8.000%	4.75	8.792	
~~Amer. Home Mortg. Co.~~	~~Sue Clifton~~	~~8.000~~	~~5.00~~	~~$250~~	~~45 days~~
ABC Mortgage Co.	Joe Reilly	8.125	4.00	8.792	
~~1st Home Savings Bank~~	~~Bill Wilson~~	~~8.250~~	~~4.25~~	~~$250~~	~~60 days~~
Hometown S&L	John Smith	8.375	2.00	8.708	
~~First National Bank~~	~~Kathy Johns~~	~~8.375~~	~~3.00~~	~~$350~~	~~60 days~~
~~First Federal S&L~~	~~Lynn Barrs~~	~~8.500~~	~~2.00~~	~~$250~~	~~45 days~~
1st Home Savings Bank	Bill Wilson	8.625	1.00	8.792	

as a tiebreaker, but in any event check a lender's reputation before submitting your application, and make sure that the lender can process and close your loan during the rate lock-in period.

Comparing ARMs

Comparing adjustable-rate mortgages is much more difficult than comparing fixed-rate loans. ARMs have so many different features that it is impossible to develop a simple formula for deciding which loan is best.

For ARMs, the interest rate is determined by the index, margin, points, fees, starting rate, and periodic and life interest rate caps. Without knowing what future interest rate levels will be, you have no sure way to know what the loan rate will be.

However, you should consider these critical elements:

- The maximum rate (life rate cap)
- The index and margin
- The points and initial rate
- The possibility of negative amortization

The maximum rate is especially important because it will determine the maximum monthly payment that you would have to make if high interest rates return. The monthly payment for a $100,000 mortgage is $878 at 10 percent versus $1,029 at 12 percent. The critical question with an ARM is "How much monthly payment can you afford?"

With ARMs, your interest rate is adjusted yearly (or periodically depending on the adjustment interval). The new rate is determined by adding the margin to the new index value. If two ARMs have the same index (most use the One-Year Treasury Security Index), then the loan with the lower margin is the lower rate loan.

With ARMs, points and initial rate are often traded one-for-one. For example, a lender might offer a choice of the same ARM with an initial rate of 9 percent plus two points or 8 percent plus three points. This is similar to a temporary buydown (see Chapter 6, "Miscellaneous Mortgage Topics"), but there is a difference. If the periodic and life interest rate caps are keyed to the initial rate (i.e., two and five caps), the maximum second-year payment and the life rate cap will be 1 percent lower for the loan at 8 percent plus three points than for the loan at 9 percent plus two points.

Before choosing an ARM over a fixed-rate mortgage, compare the current index value plus margin (i.e., 3.54 percent One-Year Treasury Index + 2.75 percent margin = 6.21 percent) to the current fixed-rate (i.e., 8.25 percent). The difference (2.04 percent) is the interest rate savings that you would get by choosing an ARM if interest rates were to remain the same. You should weigh this savings against the risk that the ARMs' rate could increase to its maximum (i.e., 10 percent) if rates rise to high levels again. If you select an ARM loan that includes the possibility of negative amortization, you should consider the effect of interest being added to your original loan amount.

Submit Your Application

After you have made your choice, move quickly to submit your application (see Figure 5.13). Rates can change daily! If you are canvassing lenders on Wednesday and Thursday, plan to submit your application on Friday. When you call to set up an appointment for the

FIGURE 5.13   Step 5: Submit Your Application

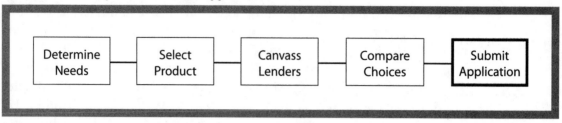

application interview, reconfirm the rate, points, and fees that you were quoted, and try to get an oral commitment to hold that price.

Review Chapter 1, "The Application Process," so that you bring all the necessary documentation with you to the interview. All borrowers (e.g., both husband and wife) must sign the loan application, and some lenders require all borrowers to attend the interview.

Final Note on Shopping. After you have applied for the loan, your lender probably will ask you for some additional documents or information. Make a log of when you received those requests, and respond quickly (keep track of when you responded). If your lock-in period expires and your lender tries to renege, you will have documentation to show that you complied with all requests.

6

Miscellaneous Mortgage Topics

In this chapter, various mortgage topics will be covered, including:

- Assumability
- Buydowns
- Late payment charges
- Mortgage insurance
- Mortgage lending on the Internet
- New developments in mortgage lending
- Prepayment penalty
- Second mortgages
- Tax deductions

Assumability

During the early 1980s when interest rates were very high, many homebuyers shopped for homes with an *assumable mortgage*. A loan is assumable if the lender will allow a new borrower to replace the old borrower (see Figure 6.1). Rather than finance the home purchase with a brand-new loan at 15 percent or 16 percent interest, for example, a buyer would make a larger down payment and take over the responsibility of making the payments on the seller's old 9 percent or 10 percent loan.

FIGURE 6.1   Assumability

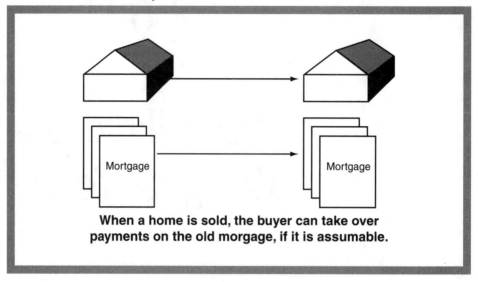

**When a home is sold, the buyer can take over
payments on the old morgage, if it is assumable.**

Having a low rate, an assumable mortgage during periods of high
interest rates gives a seller a definite advantage in selling a home. By assuming a loan, the buyer pays less interest and lower monthly payments.
Closing costs are lower, and often the buyer can avoid going through
the qualification process.

Assumability is an attractive feature to have on your mortgage, but it
is not important unless (1) interest rates rise and (2) you are forced to sell
your home when rates are much higher. If you are choosing between
two mortgages that are identical in price and all other respects, except
that one is assumable and the other is not, choose the assumable loan.

Generally, FHA loans, VA loans, and ARMs are assumable, and conventional fixed-rate loans are not assumable. (You can assume a VA loan
even if you are not a veteran.)

Loans that are not assumable have a due-on-sale clause in the mortgage note. A *due-on-sale clause* states that the loan is due and payable
if the property is sold. If a mortgage is assumable, it will have a clause
describing the conditions of assumption—assumption fee (typically
one point), buyer qualification, and processing requirements. If you are
assuming a loan or getting a new mortgage that is assumable, read the
conditions of assumption.

Assuming a Loan versus Getting a New Loan

If you are buying a home that has an assumable mortgage, here are some questions to ask:

- Will the lender charge an assumption fee? How much?
- What is the outstanding balance of the old loan? Is it large enough? How much cash will I need?
- If it is not large enough, will the seller be willing to take back a second mortgage?
- What are the rates and costs of a second mortgage? From the seller? From a lender?
- Would the combined monthly payments and interest of the old mortgage plus a new second mortgage be more or less than those of a new first mortgage?

There is no simple formula or rule of thumb to help decide whether or not to assume an old loan. However, the following example shows how an assumption can be much better than a new loan.

Example: Mr. and Mrs. Homebuyer are purchasing a $125,000 home, and they have $30,000 is cash to cover the down payment ($25,000) and closing costs (about $2,000, plus points). They have the option of assuming an existing loan with a balance of $73,000 or getting a new first mortgage.

Option 1: Assume Old Loan

Old first mortgage:

- $85,000 original balance, $73,000 remaining balance
- 7 percent first mortgage with one-point assumption fee
- 20 years remaining on 30-year term
- Monthly principal and interest payment: $565.61

New second mortgage:

- $25,000 at 10 percent fixed-rate plus one point
- 15-year term
- Monthly principal and interest payment: $268.65

FIGURE 6.2   Assumption versus New Mortgage

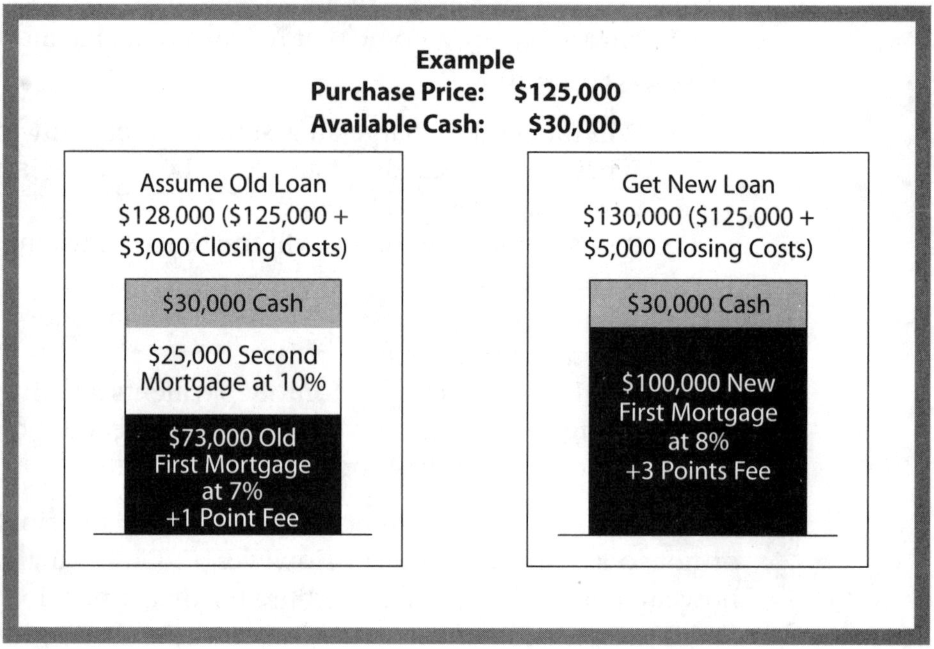

Example
Purchase Price: **$125,000**
Available Cash: **$30,000**

Assume Old Loan
$128,000 ($125,000 +
$3,000 Closing Costs)

$30,000 Cash

$25,000 Second
Mortgage at 10%

$73,000 Old
First Mortgage
at 7%
+1 Point Fee

Get New Loan
$130,000 ($125,000 +
$5,000 Closing Costs)

$30,000 Cash

$100,000 New
First Mortgage
at 8%
+3 Points Fee

Option 2: Get New Loan

New first mortgage:

- $100,000 at 8 percent fixed rate plus three points
- 30-year term
- Monthly principal and interest payment: $733.76

By assuming the existing loan, Mr. and Mrs. Homebuyer would save $2,000 in points. The assumption fee is one point ($730), and the second mortgage lender charges one point ($250) for a total of $980, versus $3,000 in points for a new first mortgage. The monthly payments for assuming the old loan are $100 per month higher. But because the interest rate on the old mortgage is only 7 percent, the interest charges are $80 per month lower. More of the payments are going toward principal and less toward interest. By paying just 15 percent or $100 per month more in their monthly payments, Mr. and Mrs. Homebuyer would pay off their mortgages faster and save more than $80,000. (See Figure 6.3.)

FIGURE 6.3   Comparison of Monthly Payments and Total Payments

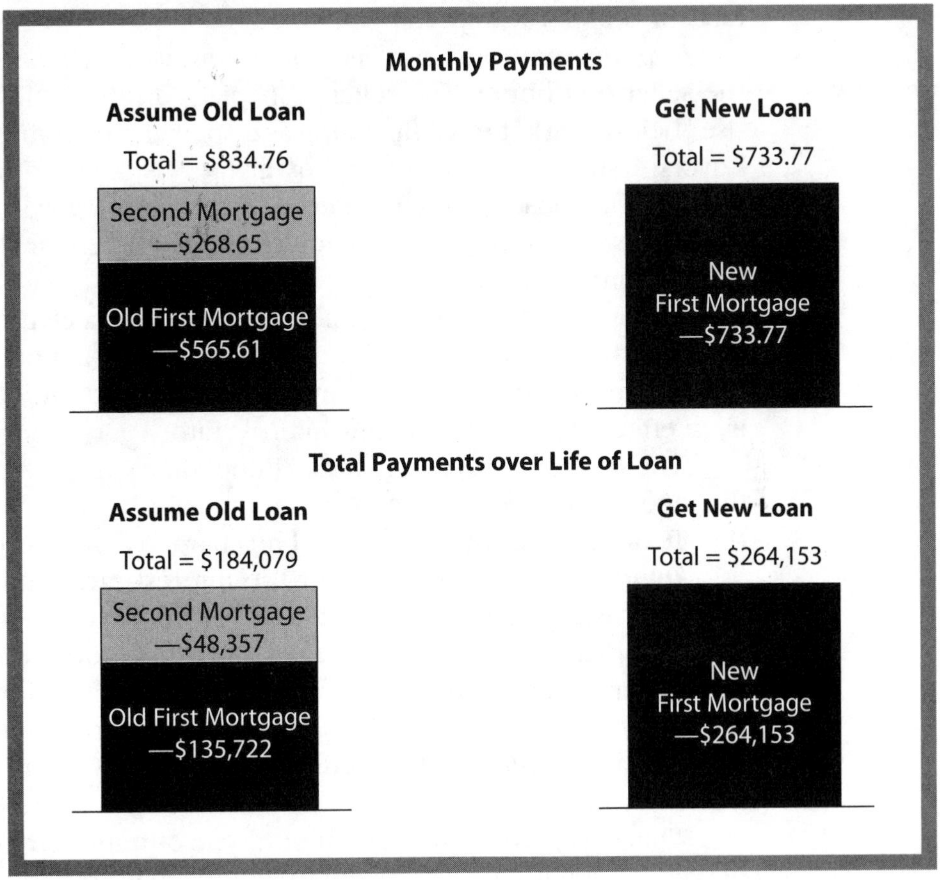

Option 1: $565.61 × 240 months + $268.65 × 180 months = $184,079
Option 2: $733.76 × 360 months = $264,153

In this example, assuming the old loan would be far better than getting a new mortgage.

Buydowns

A *buydown* is a method of lowering the interest rate of a mortgage by paying additional points. There are two types of buydowns: permanent and temporary. A *permanent buydown* lowers the interest rate for the life of the loan, and a *temporary buydown* lowers the interest rate for the first few years.

A permanent buydown is most often used as a sales incentive by the seller of a home. The seller (especially a homebuilder) will advertise "below market rate" financing as a special inducement to would-be buyers. Usually, the cost of the lower rates is factored into the asking price of the house. (Large builders also have other ways of offering low rates. They often can negotiate lower rates with lenders because of the large volume of loans.)

In negotiating to buy a home, you may write a clause into the sales contract that requires the seller to pay up to a certain number of points for your mortgage. This is common with FHA and VA loans. The seller is, in effect, buying down your interest rate.

The cost of a buydown varies depending on the type of loan and the lender. To lower the interest rate of a 30-year loan by 1 percent for the life of the loan, you usually will be charged from six to eight points.

Temporary buydowns lower the interest rate (and monthly payment) for the first few years of a loan. Temporary buydowns are used like a graduated payment mortgage to help a borrower qualify for a higher loan amount than his or her income would allow with a level payment mortgage. Unlike GPMs, there is no negative amortization with a temporary buydown. The additional points pay for the lower initial interest rates.

The 3-2-1 buydown is a common type of temporary buydown. A 9 percent loan with a 3-2-1 buydown would have a 6 percent rate for the first year, 7 percent for the second year, 8 percent for the third year and 9 percent for years 4 through 30.

The example in Figure 6.4 is a $100,000 3-2-1 buydown. Monthly payments start at $599.55 and rise to $804.63 by the fourth year. Using a 3-2-1 buydown, a homebuyer can qualify for an approximately 25 to 30 percent larger loan. However, the cost of a 3-2-1 buydown is usually five and a half to six additional points, a big increase in closing costs.

Another popular temporary buydown is the 2-1 buydown. It reduces your interest rate 2 percent in the first year and 1 percent in the second year. It does not cut your initial payment as much as the 3-2-1 buydown, but it costs only about half as much (about three points).

A buydown is an expensive way to reduce your initial payments, but you can use two methods to offset the up-front costs of a buydown.

FIGURE 6.4   3-2-1 Temporary Buydown

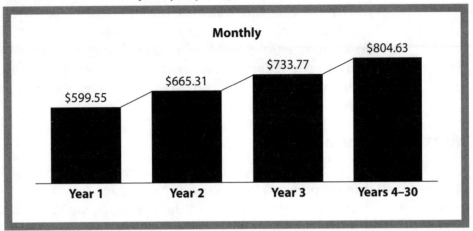

First, negotiate to have the seller pay for some or all of the buydown costs. It is very common for homebuilders to pay buydown costs for buyers. Second, your lender may allow a "buyup" in the loan's base interest rate to offset the cost of the temporary buydown. For example, if the market rate for a 30-year fixed-rate loan is 8 percent plus two points, you might expect to pay five points for an 8 percent rate with a 2-1 buydown. Some lenders will offer an 8.5 percent rate with a 2-1 buydown for two points. The first year rate would be 6.5 percent, the second-year rate would be 7.5 percent, and the remaining payments would be at a rate of 8.5 percent.

Late Payment Charges

If you fail to make your monthly mortgage payment by the 15th of the month, lenders add a late charge to your payment. A typical late charge is 5 percent of your monthly payment of principal and interest, that is, $36.69 for being late on the $733.77 monthly payment for a $100,000, 8-percent loan. The late charge for FHA-insured and VA-guaranteed loans is no more than 4 percent of the payment of PITI.

In shopping for and comparing loans, the late charge is not something that you should be concerned with. But the late charges will be disclosed in the truth-in-lending statement that you receive after submitting your application. Review the late-charge clause for the loan that you have selected and calculate the cost of being late with your payment.

Many banks and savings-and-loan associations will allow you to set up an automatic monthly withdrawal from a savings or checking account to pay recurring bills such as mortgage payments. By setting up such a withdrawal, you can avoid the hassle of late charges entirely.

Mortgage Insurance

If your down payment is less than 20 percent (LTV ratio greater than 80 percent), you must buy mortgage insurance. *Mortgage insurance* insures the lender, not the borrower, against default and foreclosure. If a borrower defaults on his or her payments and the property is foreclosed, the mortgage insurance company must repay the lender all or a portion of its losses.

[Note: Do not confuse mortgage insurance with mortgage life insurance. *Mortgage life insurance* is an optional life insurance policy that you can buy from your lender or your insurance agent. It pays off your mortgage in the event of your death.]

Although mortgage insurance primarily benefits the lender, it does allow homebuyers to purchase their home with a low down payment. The borrower pays the mortgage insurance premium (MIP).

There are three types of mortgage insurance, or loan guaranty: (1) FHA mortgage insurance, (2) VA loan guaranty, and (3) private mortgage insurance (PMI). FHA loans are insured by the Federal Housing Administration, and VA loans are guaranteed by the Department of Veterans Affairs. Both are agencies of the federal government. Conventional loans are insured by private mortgage insurance companies.

The terms, conditions, and premium charges for mortgage insurance have changed several times since the early 1980s, particularly for PMI. For up-to-date details on specifics such as maximum loan amount, LTV ratio, mortgage types, and premiums, you must talk to a lender.

Financing Mortgage Insurance

For conventional loans, there are two ways to pay for private mortgage insurance: (1) by adding a small premium amount to each monthly

FIGURE 6.5   Three Types of Mortgage Insurance

	FHA	VA	PMI
Maximum Loan Amount	$291,650 or less depending on region	$240,000	No set maximum; varies with LTV
Maximum LTV Ratio	98.75% to 97.15%	100%	97%
Mortgage Types Available	15- and 30-year fixed, ARMs and GPMs	15- and 30-year fixed, ARMs and GPMs	All mortgage types
Insurance Premium/ Guaranty Fee	See table in Chapter 4	Up-front fee— 1.25% to 3.00% of loan amount	See table in Appendix A
Features	• Easier to qualify • Assumable loans	• Easier to qualify • Assumable loans • Must be veteran	

payment (*renewable plan,* or annual plan) or (2) by paying a larger, one-time, or single, premium at settlement. The *single premium plans* fall into two categories: *refundable premiums* and *nonrefundable premiums.* Refundable premiums cost more up-front, but you get a refund of the unused premium if you pay off the loan early. If you are planning to keep your mortgage for only a few years, the pay-by-month plan is probably the best deal. If you are planning to keep your mortgage for several years, look into a one-time premium. Most lenders will let you add the cost of mortgage insurance to your loan amount so the up-front premium does not increase your closing costs; however, your monthly payment will increase to reflect the larger loan.

Financing the one-time mortgage insurance premium has one additional benefit. Mortgage insurance premiums are not a valid income-tax deduction, but if you finance the one-time premium, the interest that you pay on the slightly larger loan amount is deductible. In addition, you can see in Figure 6.6 that the total monthly payment is somewhat less when premiums are financed rather than paid monthly. The

FIGURE 6.6   Monthly Payments for Different Mortgage Insurance Plans

	Renewable Mortgage Insurance	Refundable Single Premium	Nonrefundable Single Premium
Loan Amount	$100,000.00	$102,650.00 (includes financed premium)	$102,000.00 (includes financed premium)
Principal and Interest Payment (at 8%)	$733.37	$753.21	$748.44
Mortgage Insurance Premium	$29.17	N/A	N/A
Total—Principal, Interest, and Mortgage Insurance	$762.54	$753.21	$748.44

disadvantage is that financed mortgage insurance cannot be canceled unless you pay off the mortgage.

With the FHA MIP and the VA funding fee, you do not have the same flexibility that you do with conventional loans. As with conventional mortgage insurance, you may choose to pay the VA funding fee or up-front portion of MIP in cash or finance it. Note that with most FHA-insured loans you still must pay monthly MIP in addition to the up-front premium.

Discontinuing Mortgage Insurance Premiums

If you have a conventional loan with private (renewable or monthly) mortgage insurance or an FHA loan with monthly PMI, your mortgage insurance payments will stop automatically when your LTV declines to 78 percent as a result of your normal monthly payments. Because each monthly payment contains a small amount of principal repayment, every month, your outstanding loan balance goes down. As your loan balance goes down, so does your LTV. An 8 percent, 30-year loan at 90 percent LTV will take 10 years and seven months to amortize down to 78 percent. An 8 percent, 30-year loan at 95 percent LTV will take 12 years and ten months. Your lender is required by federal regulations to notify you and to cancel your mortgage insurance payments.

If you make additional principal payments, that also reduces your LTV, but you must ask your lender in writing to cancel your mortgage insurance when your LTV is below 78 percent. They are not required to cancel it automatically. If you have had a history of late payments, they may have the right to deny your request.

For conventional loans, you can request cancellation of PMI when your LTV reaches 80 percent through normal amortization. If you have made your payments on time for the last two years, your lender is required to cancel it.

If the value of your home increases, your LTV goes down. With conventional loans, the law allows you to submit a new appraisal to your lender showing that your home is more valuable. You must pay for your own appraisal. If the recalculated LTV is less than 78 percent, you can request cancellation of your mortgage insurance. Again, if you have had a history of late payments, they may have the right to deny your request.

Example: Mr. and Mrs. Homebuyer purchase a $110,000 home with a $10,000 down payment and a $100,000 mortgage. Their LTV ratio is 91 percent, and they must get mortgage insurance. Their annual premium would be $440 per year. In a few years, the value of their home has gone up to $140,000, and they have reduced their mortgage balance through monthly payments to $97,000. Their new LTV ratio would be 69 percent. Their lender will allow them to discontinue the PMI premiums versus $250 for a new appraisal. The $250 reappraisal would save them $440 a year.

Mortgage Lending on the Internet

Thousands of mortgage lenders now have Internet Web sites (also called home pages), and use the Internet to advertise their products and their companies to technology-savvy consumers. The Internet can serve as your Yellow Pages. You can use it for comparison shopping. You can find free computer software to help you better understand your mortgage options. There is a vast amount of information about mortgages and the mortgage lending process available on the Internet. You can even apply for a mortgage online.

Unfortunately, the Internet is not organized like an encyclopedia. It is barely organized at all. Every site on the Internet has an address and to go to a site, you must first get the address. And companies change their addresses frequently. Appendix L contains Internet addresses for several useful mortgage industry sites. (These addresses may change, and they may not be valid when you try to go to them.) Internet search engines such as Yahoo and Google will list hundreds of mortgage-related sites.

Online Interest Rate Comparisons

Shopping for a mortgage is the best way to save money. The Internet is a great place to look first. Several sites listed in Appendix L give current prevailing interest rates, both nationally and locally. You can get a very good picture of prevailing rates before you make your first phone calls to local lenders. Do not limit your search to the Internet. Local lenders may have lower rates than the national lenders advertising on the Internet.

Because a lender has a fancy, sophisticated site on the Internet, do not assume that their rates will be better than your local lender. Just as local lenders have very different rates, so do companies doing business on the Internet. Although there are real bargains to be found on the Internet, there are also higher than average rates.

Interest rates are subject to local variations. They tend to be higher in smaller markets than in large urban areas, and they tend to be higher in areas with less competition. For a lender to do business in your area, it must be licensed by the state. If you are looking at the rates quoted by a lender on the Internet, be sure that it does business in your state. Otherwise, the rates may not be applicable to your search.

Finding a Lender on the Internet

There are two types of mortgage lenders you can find searching the Internet. The first type is what you would find if you went to your local Yellow Pages: traditional lenders with local branch offices who advertise on the Internet. It might be a national company with offices all over the country, or it might be a small lender with only one or two offices. The second type of mortgage lender does not have local offices.

It does the entire mortgage application process over the phone through toll-free numbers. Whether you choose to apply with a local lender or the new breed of long-distance lender, make sure to check their references.

Appendix L lists several sites where you can find both national and local lenders. It also has a few listings for specific lenders. This is not a recommendation of those lenders, but just some examples of different types of mortgage lender Internet sites.

Mortgage Calculation Tools

There are numerous free mortgage calculation tools available on the Internet. Some are built into the Internet sites where they are located, and others are small programs you can download, install and run on your computer.

Appendix L lists several sites with calculation tools for homebuyers. Tools available include:

- Rent or buy?
- Refinance?
- How much can I afford?
- Loan payment calculator
- Tax savings

A very diverse and complete list (33 different calculators) is at the FinanCenter.com <www.financenter.com>.

Fannie Mae, Freddie Mac, and FHA also have calculation tools on their Web sites.

Applying for a Mortgage Online

There are several sites that ostensibly allow consumers to apply for a mortgage online. Most of these online applications are very unsophisticated forms that gather a little bit about you and do not constitute a full mortgage application. Most of these online applications will precipitate a phone call from a loan officer or will be followed up with a full application package in the mail.

There are a few sites where you could fill out an entire Fannie Mae/Freddie Mac loan application (Form 1003) online. Unfortunately, the application is too long and complicated, and the Internet is too slow to make online applications practical or desirable.

New Developments in the Mortgage Lending Industry

The fourth edition of *The Mortgage Kit,* written in 1997, had three topics in this section on new developments in the mortgage lending industry: automated underwriting, credit scoring, and cost-based pricing. Since then, automated underwriting and credit scoring have been widely adopted by the industry. So, in this fifth edition, they have been expanded and moved into Chapter 2, "Qualifying for a Mortgage Loan."

At the Mortgage Bankers Association Annual Convention on October 7, 1997, Leland Brendsel, Chairman and CEO of Freddie Mac, the country's second largest investor in mortgage loans, said: "Today we stand on the brink of a technological revolution in the way people buy homes, in the way lenders make loans, and in the way America finances home-ownership." He also said, "By the year 2000, I predict that 100 percent of our mortgage purchases will be priced according to projected costs."

In fact, technology (automated underwriting and credit scoring) is changing the way that lenders make loans. However, cost-based pricing (predicted by Brendsel for 2000) is still a part of the future and is therefore relegated to this section on new and emerging developments.

Cost-Based Pricing

The costs involved in making and servicing a loan depend on the borrower's creditworthiness, the amount of down payment that they make, and the type of loan that they choose. For a long time, lenders have charged higher prices for loans with greater risk. Borrowers that want a lower down payment have to pay mortgage insurance premiums. The higher the LTV, the greater the risk and the higher the mortgage insurance premium to offset that risk. Borrowers with poor credit ratings must pay much higher interest rates than prime credit borrowers. These are examples of *cost-based pricing*.

Today's cost-based pricing is not as discriminating as it could be or as it will be in the future. Today, a borrower with a FICO score of 650 making a 20 percent down payment will get the same rate as a borrower with a FICO score of 800 making a 50 percent down payment. Although both of these loans are good loans by most standards, the second loan is safer than the first.

The automated underwriting programs of the future will look at all of the relevant factors in an applicant's loan application and assign a risk factor. Based on the risk factor and the loan type, a price will be quoted for that specific loan application. In the future, there may be as many combinations of prices for mortgages as there are today for cars.

Prepayment Penalty

Some lenders charge you a fee for paying off your mortgage early, called a *prepayment penalty.* If your loan has a prepayment penalty clause, your lender will disclose it in the truth-in-lending statement that you receive shortly after submitting your application. A typical prepayment penalty clause charges borrowers a three-point fee on the remaining principal balance if they repay their mortgage within the first three years of the loan.

In the 1970s, prepayment penalties were more common than they are today. If you are planning to move, refinance, or pay off your new loan within three years, however, ask your lender whether or not you will be charged a prepayment penalty before submitting an application. Because of the huge refinancing volume during the early 1990s, there is much talk among lenders about reinstituting prepayment penalties.

Recently, lenders have introduced a new type of prepayment penalty clause. It penalizes borrowers who refinance their mortgages in the first few years of their loan, but it does not penalize borrowers who pay off their mortgage because they sell their homes. This new prepayment penalty clause protects lenders from customers who swap mortgages every time rates drop but protects borrowers who must pay off their loans because they are selling their homes.

Second Mortgages

A *second mortgage,* just as its name suggests, is a second loan secured by the same property as a first mortgage. There are two reasons why you might want a second mortgage:

1. First, if you are buying a home, a second mortgage can help supplement your cash for your down payment and closing costs, especially if you are assuming a low rate but small first mortgage (see section on "Assumability"). (See Figure 6.7.)
2. Second, if you are refinancing to "take cash out" of your property, a second mortgage or home equity loan often is cheaper than replacing your first mortgage (see Chapter 8, "Refinancing").

Higher Rates, Shorter Terms

To lenders, second mortgages are riskier than first mortgages. In the event of default and foreclosure, the second mortgage lender gets paid off only after the first mortgage lender is paid in full. Because of this additional risk, lenders usually charge a higher rate for second mortgages than for first mortgages.

Most first mortgages have terms of 15, 25, or 30 years. Second mortgages typically have terms ranging from 5 to 15 years.

Combined Loan-to-Value (CLTV) Ratio

If you have a $125,000 home and a $100,000 first mortgage, the loan-to-value ratio for that mortgage is 80 percent ($100,000 ÷ $125,000).

FIGURE 6.7   How a Second Mortgage Can Help You Supplement an Assumed First Mortgage

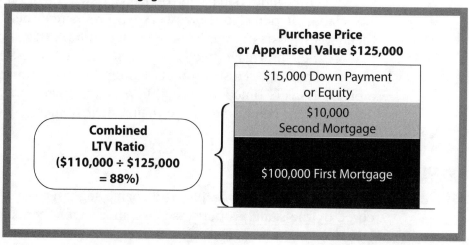

Purchase Price or Appraised Value $125,000

$15,000 Down Payment or Equity

$10,000 Second Mortgage

$100,000 First Mortgage

Combined LTV Ratio ($110,000 ÷ $125,000 = 88%)

If you also have a $10,000 second mortgage in addition to your first mortgage, your combined LTV ratio is 88 percent ([$10,000 + $100,000] ÷ $125,000). Your *combined LTV (CLTV)* ratio is the sum of all your mortgages divided by the value of your home.

When making a second mortgage loan, lenders will restrict your CLTV ratio. Depending on loan type, occupancy, and purpose, the maximum CLTV will range from 70 to 90 percent. The rate for this type of second mortgage is typically 2 percent to 3 percent higher than the rate for a 15-year first mortgage. If your CLTV ratio is more than 80 percent, you should expect the rate for your second mortgage to be 3 percent to 6 percent higher than a 15-year first mortgage.

Balloon versus Fully Amortizing Second Mortgages

With a traditional first mortgage, a portion of each payment that you make reduces your loan balance, and by the time you reach your last monthly payment, you have fully paid off your loan. This is called a *fully amortizing loan.* Some second mortgages are also fully amortizing.

Others, however, come due with a large portion of their principal balance still unpaid. These loans are called *balloon loans,* and the final principal payment is called a *balloon payment.*

Example:

- $25,000 second mortgage at 10-percent interest
- 7-year term with 30-year amortization schedule
- $219.40 monthly principal and interest payment
- $23,881 balloon payment due at the end of seven years

In the previous example, you would have paid off only 4 percent of your $25,000 loan by the time it comes due in seven years. The advantage of a balloon loan is a lower monthly payment. The monthly payment of a fully amortizing $25,000 seven-year loan at 10 percent would be $415.03 versus $219.40 for the balloon loan.

Purchase-Money Mortgages

When the seller of a property makes a mortgage loan to the buyer, it is called a *purchase-money mortgage.* Usually, the seller "takes back" a second mortgage to facilitate the sale when a buyer cannot meet the amount required for the down payment and closing costs. Purchase-money mortgages often are made in conjunction with an assumed first mortgage. Typically, a seller will loan you money at a better rate than a traditional lender.

Home Equity Lines of Credit (HELOCs) and Debt Consolidation Loans

Consumer borrowing through credit cards, installment loans, and personal loans is at an all-time high. Many consumers are saddled with tens of thousands of dollars of debt on credit cards with interest rates of 18 percent or more. A whole new class of second mortgage loans and mortgage lenders has appeared to help consumers get out from under their credit card debt. These loans have interest rates that are much higher than traditional first mortgages but are usually much lower than interest rates charged on credit cards.

There are no standard loan types for these second mortgage products. Some are like credit card debt and in fact can be accessed with credit cards or checks. Others are fixed rate, amortizing loans and balloon loans. Many lenders will now lend up to 125 to 135 percent of a home's value. An LTV ratio of 125 percent is unheard of in traditional mortgage lending.

The only common feature among these loans is that they all are secured by a lien on the borrower's home. Unlike credit card debt, if the borrower fails to repay these loans, the lender can foreclose on the borrower's home.

Most consumers who need a high rate debt consolidation loan should seek financial advice from a qualified financial adviser or from one of the many nonprofit or government consumer counseling services (call 800-388-CCCS for a counseling agency near you).

Tax Deductions

One of the enduring benefits of home ownership is the federal tax deduction for interest and real estate taxes. On a home with a $100,000 mortgage, the deductions will total about $8,000 per year, and depending on your tax bracket, they will reduce your federal taxes by $1,200 to $3,200. This amount will decrease as you pay down the loan or, if you have an ARM loan, may go up in the event your interest rate increases.

The Tax Reform Acts of 1990 and 1993 changed the rules governing the deductibility of interest, and the regulations are particularly complicated when you purchase a home or refinance your mortgage. The Internal Revenue Service's Publication 545, *Interest Expense,* describes when and if interest, fees, points, and other charges relating to your mortgage are deductible. The rules for home purchase are different from refinancing, and the rules for FHA/VA loans are different from conventional loans. Consult with an accountant, tax attorney, or an IRS adviser for the proper way to file your taxes, especially for the year that you get a new mortgage. (See Figure 6.8.)

FIGURE 6.8 Tax Deductible Interest and Points, First Year, 8-Percent Mortgage

Taxes You Paid (See page A-1.)	5	State and local income taxes	5		
	6	Real estate taxes (see page A-2)	6		
	7	Other taxes. List—include personal property taxes ▶	7		
	8	Add lines 5 through 7 . . . . ▶			8
Interest You Paid (See page A-2.)	9a	Home mortgage interest and points reported to you on Form 1098	9a	9,969 93	
	b	Home mortgage interest not reported to you on Form 1098. If paid to the person from whom you bought the home, see page A-3 and show that person's name, identifying no., and address ▶	9b		
Note: Personal interest is not deductible.	10	Points not reported to you on Form 1098. See page A-3 for special rules	10		
	11	Investment interest. If required, attach Form 4952. (See page A-3.)	11		
	12	Add lines 9a through 11 . . . . ▶			12

7

Investor Loans

Over the past ten years, individuals and real estate partnerships have purchased thousands of residential units—single-family homes, town houses, and condominium units—as investments. Most of these purchases were financed with what the industry refers to as an *investor loan.* An investor loan is a mortgage on a one-unit to four-unit residential property that will be rented by the owner to others. If the owner plans to live in one unit and rent out the other units, it is called an *owner-occupied property;* otherwise it is called *non-owner-occupied.*

This chapter covers the requirements for getting a mortgage on a small (one-unit to four-unit) residential investment property. It does not cover the advisability of making such an investment, and it does not cover the financing of large commercial properties or larger apartment buildings.

In 1984, some of the nation's major mortgage lenders and mortgage insurers began having delinquency and default problems on investor loans. These problems climaxed in 1985 when Equity Programs Investment Corporation (EPIC), a purchaser of 20,000 residential investment properties, declared bankruptcy.

The entire mortgage industry and especially the $100-billion Fannie Mae responded to these problems by tightening their underwriting guidelines and charging an additional premium of 0.25 percent to 0.50

percent interest rate for investor loans. The FHA has eliminated its investor loan programs entirely for non-owner-occupied properties. As a result, it is much more difficult to get an investor loan today than it was before the problems of the mid-1980s.

Fannie Mae Guidelines

Not all lenders follow Fannie Mae's underwriting guidelines for investor loans, but understanding Fannie Mae's guidelines will give you a good idea of the kinds of issues that all lenders consider before making an investor loan. If you have not already read Chapter 2 on qualifying for a loan, go back and read it before continuing with this chapter. That will help you better understand the following examples.

Prequalification for Investment Properties

When applying for a mortgage on your primary residence, you must *qualify*. You must have enough income to cover your housing expenses and other debt obligations according to industry standards.

When applying for a mortgage on a small residential investment property, you still must qualify according to the same standards; in addition, you must submit a detailed pro forma Operating Income Statement, Fannie Mae Form 216, on the investment property that you are buying. Also, your appraiser must submit comparable rent information using Fannie Mae Form 1007 for single-unit investment properties or Fannie Mae Form 1025 for two- to four-unit properties. (See Appendix G for Fannie Mae's instructions on completing these forms.)

Qualifying for an owner-occupied investor loan is different from qualifying for a non-owner-occupied investor loan. The two examples that follow illustrate the difference. In both examples, John Q. Investor is buying a four-unit property for $250,000. His income is $5,000 per month (before buying the property), and his only other debt obligation is a $300 monthly car payment.

Example 1: Mr. Investor buys the property and occupies one of the four units as his primary residence.

Details of Purchase

Price	$250,000.00
Down payment	50,000.00
Mortgage amount	200,000.00
Loan-to-value ratio	80.0%
Mortgage rate	8.5%
Monthly payment (PITI)	$1,952.41

Each unit will rent for $500 per month, with a vacancy rate of 6 percent and a monthly operating expense of $100. (Some lenders assume a 25-percent vacancy rate for underwriting purposes. This makes it much harder to qualify.)

Summary Operating Income Statement
(Three Rental Units)

Monthly rental income	$1,500.00
Vacancy allowance at 6%	−90.00
Effective gross income	$1,410.00
Monthly operating expense	−300.00
Operating Income	**$1,110.00**

When qualifying as an owner-occupant, you use the entire mortgage payment to determine your housing expense ratio, even though you are living in only one of the units. The operating income (before PITI) is added to your income.

Owner-Occupied Qualification Example

Monthly income (before purchase)	$5,000.00
Operating income from rental units	+1,110.00
Gross monthly income	$6,110.00
Monthly housing expense (PITI)	1,952.41
Monthly car payment	+300.00
Fixed monthly obligations	$2,252.41

HOUSING RATIO: 32.0%   DEBT RATIO: 36.9%

Because industry standards call for ratios of 28/36 or lower, Mr. Investor *would not qualify for the loan in this example,* if held to these Fannie Mae standards.

Example 2: Mr. Investor buys the property and rents out all four units for investment income.

Details of Purchase

Price	$250,000.00
Down payment	75,000.00
Mortgage amount	175,000.00
Loan-to-value ratio	70.0%
Mortgage rate	8.5%
Monthly payment (PITI)	$1,753.93

As in the first example, each unit will rent for $500 per month with a vacancy rate of 6 percent and a monthly operating expense of $100. When the purchaser of an investment property will not be occupying one of the units, an additional calculation is required. The monthly payment is deducted from the operating income to determine net cash flow.

Summary Operating Income Statement (Four Rental Units)

Monthly rental income	$2,000.00
Vacancy allowance at 6%	−120.00
Effective gross income	$1,880.00
Monthly operating expense	−400.00
Operating Income	$1,480.00
Mortgage payment (PITI)	−1,753.93
Net cash flow	**$−273.93**

When qualifying for a non-owner-occupant, you use your existing residence to determine your housing ratio, not the investment property. For this example, assume that Mr. Investor has the same $5,000 per month income as in the first example. The mortgage on his residence is $125,000, and his mortgage payment (PITI) is $1,281.55. If the projected net cash flow from the investment property is positive, it is added to the income for qualifying. If negative, it is added to the debt obligations. In this example, the net cash flow is a negative $273.93 per month, so it is added to his debt payments.

Non-Owner-Occupied Qualification Example

Gross monthly income	$5,000.00
Monthly housing expense (PITI)	$1,281.55
Monthly car payment	300.00
Net cash flow from real estate investment	−273.93
Fixed monthly obligations	$1,855.48

HOUSING RATIO: 25.7%   DEBT RATIO: 37.2%

Because industry standards call for ratios of 28/36 or lower, Mr. Investor *might not qualify for the loan in this example* because his debt ratio is too high, if held to these Fannie Mae standards.

Supporting Income and Expense Projections

Fannie Mae's operating income statement that you (or the appraiser) must fill out is long and detailed, but both the appraiser and the underwriter will review each income and expense item on it before your loan is approved. If an appraiser or underwriter makes adjustments to your projections, most likely he or she will lower the rental income or increase projected expenses. These adjustments will reduce the debt service coverage ratio and net cash flow projections. They may disqualify the loan.

Whenever possible, support your income projections with documentation. Submit copies of leases to support rent projections and utility bills for expenses. Submit prior years' operating statements ("Schedule E" from prior year's tax returns) if they are available. Well-documented projections will have fewer adjustments.

Fannie Mae Restrictions for Investor Loans

In addition to tightening up its qualification requirements, Fannie Mae has increased the amount of down payment that you must make to purchase an investment property.

- *Owner-occupied properties.* Minimum 10 percent down payment for two-unit properties (90 percent LTV), and 20 percent for three- to four-unit properties (80 percent LTV).

- *Non-owner-occupied properties.* Minimum 30 percent down payment (70 percent LTV).

For borrowers with very good credit scores, Fannie Mae will allow higher LTV ratios for both owner-occupied and non-owner-occupied investment properties. Have your lender submit your application to Fannie Mae's Desktop Underwriter automated underwriting system.

M O R T G A G E   T I P

Whenever possible, support your income projections with documentation. Submit copies of leases to support rent projections and utility bills for expenses. Submit prior years' operating statements ("Schedule E" from prior year's tax returns) if they are available. Well-documented projections will have fewer adjustments.

Note: The previous examples used Fannie Mae's minimum down payments. Other lenders are willing to make investor loans with smaller down payment requirements.

- *Limited "cash out" refinance loans.* Fannie Mae limits the amount of cash that you take out of a refinancing transaction on investor loans. You can increase your loan amount to pay off your old mortgage, cover closing costs, and pay off second mortgages and lines of credit, but you can put 1 percent of the new loan amount into your pocket. And the new loan is still limited to 70 percent LTV for non-owner-occupied properties and 75 percent for owner-occupied properties.
- *No ARM loans.*
- *No temporary buydowns.*

These restrictions, plus a maximum loan-to-value ratio of 70 percent and a limited cash out provision for refinances, substantially reduce investors' flexibility. Two major advantages of investing in real estate are leverage and tax shelter. The 70-percent maximum LTV ratio reduces leverage, and the limited cash out restriction for refinancing makes it difficult for an investor to liquidate an investment without selling the property and incurring capital gains tax and sales costs.

- *Maximum of five mortgaged units.* Some investors buy as many properties as their incomes allow. Fannie Mae now limits a borrower to five mortgaged properties. Properties may include any combination of single-family, second homes, or one- to four-unit properties that are *financed.* Under this restriction, you could have no more than four investment properties plus your residence that are *financed through any lender.*

FHA Guidelines

The FHA no longer insures mortgages on non-owner-occupied properties. It still will insure mortgages on owner-occupied two- to four-unit properties. The maximum mortgage amounts, which change annually, are as follows (for 2002)*:

2 units	$334,863
3 units	$404,724
4 units	$502,990

*The up-to-date limits are available on the Internet (see Appendix L).

In areas of the country with lower housing costs, the maximum FHA mortgage amounts will be lower than these amounts.

Assuming an FHA Loan as an Investor

FHA loans are assumable. (See Chapter 6, "Miscellaneous Mortgage Topics," for an explanation of assumability.) As an investor, you may find a property that you would like to buy that has an existing FHA mortgage. Whether you may assume the loan as a non-owner-occupant depends on when the loan was made initially:

137

- FHA loans closed on or after February 15, 1989, may not be assumed by a non-owner-occupant investor.
- FHA loans closed from February 5, 1988, through February 14, 1989, may be assumed by a non-owner-occupant investor, but the loan must be paid down to 75 percent of the original acquisition cost or appraised value (new appraisal required).
- FHA loans closed prior to February 1, 1986, may be freely assumed. No credit check or income qualification is required unless the original borrower wants to be released from liability.

Assuming an older FHA loan is one of the best ways to acquire an investment property because of the high LTV (hence leverage) and generally lower interest rates. When looking for investment properties, ask your real estate agent to look for properties with older FHA loans in place.

8

Refinancing

Why Refinance?

A *refinance mortgage* is a financing of a property in which property ownership is not transferred. A refinance mortgage pays off existing mortgages, if any, may pay some or all closing costs, and may even return equity (cash out) to the owner of the property. There are many reasons why you might want to refinance your home mortgage, but all of those reasons fall into three general categories:

1. Saving money by paying lower interest rates
2. Borrowing more money
3. Restructuring (changing from one type of mortgage to another)

You may want to do all three. This chapter covers the important issues for all three of these categories, and it will direct you to other chapters that you should read before beginning the process of refinancing your home.

Saving Money

Mortgage interest rates have gone up and down more sharply over the past 20 years than they had previously since World War II.

Today, however, rates are much lower than they were in the mid-1980s (see Figure 8.1). If your mortgage rate is 1 to 2 percent higher than current rates, you probably can lower your monthly mortgage payment and *save thousands of dollars in interest by refinancing your old mortgage.*

Refinancing to save money is like making an investment. The cost of refinancing is the amount of your investment, and the interest you save is the return on your investment. However, during the boom refinancing years of 1992 and 1993, zero-point and no-cost refinance loans came into vogue. These creative refinance programs eliminate cost as a consideration in refinancing. Lenders can offer these programs by charging a somewhat higher interest rate than they would if you were paying points and closing costs. Lenders recover their costs by selling your loan into the secondary market at a premium. In other words, investors looking to get a higher return on their investment will pay more for a higher interest rate loan than for a lower interest rate loan.

FIGURE 8.1   Mortgage Interest Rates

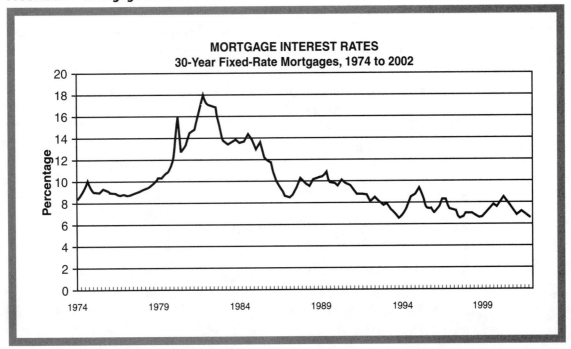

Although there is no hard and fast rule, the relationship between interest and discount points is generally about 6 to 8 discount points for each percent of interest rate. For example, a lender might fund up to $3,000 of closing costs on a $100,000 loan for a borrower in exchange for an additional one half percent interest rate over the current market rate.

Before investing your time and money to refinance your home mortgage, you should answer three questions:

1. How much money will I save?
2. How much will it cost me to refinance?
3. Are the savings large enough to justify the costs?

Calculating Your Savings

Figure 8.2 illustrates that by lowering your interest rate by as little as 2 percent on a $100,000 mortgage, you can lower your monthly mortgage payment by more than $140. The lower monthly payment is a direct result of paying less interest.

The table in Figure 8.3 shows the difference in the monthly payments on a $100,000 loan for different combinations of interest rates. For example, if you lower the rate on a $100,000 loan from 9 percent to 6 percent, you lower the monthly payment by $205.07.

FIGURE 8.2   How a 2 Percent Difference in Interest Rates Can Lower Your Monthly Payments

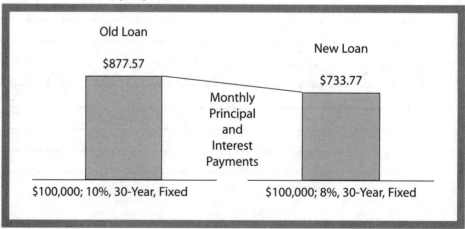

FIGURE 8.3   Example of Potential Monthly Payment Savings after Refinancing (for a $100,000 30-Year Mortgage)

Old Interest Rate	New Interest Rate				
	7.0%	6.5%	6.0%	5.5%	5.0%
9.0%	$139.32	$172.55	$205.07	$236.83	$267.80
8.5	103.61	136.85	169.36	201.12	232.09
8.0	68.46	101.70	134.21	165.98	196.94
7.5	33.91	67.15	99.66	131.43	162.39
7.0	n/a	33.23	65.75	97.51	128.48

In both Figures 8.2 and 8.3, the loan amount is $100,000. If your mortgage is $50,000 (or $75,000 or $175,000), you can adjust the examples to more closely fit your situation by multiplying the monthly payment and interest rate savings shown in the examples by .50 (or .75 or 1.75 as appropriate). A Do-It-Yourself Refinance Worksheet in Appendix H will help you estimate your savings and decide whether to refinance. Three worksheet examples follow in this section.

Refinancing lowers the principal and interest portion of your monthly payment. (See the "Introduction" for an explanation of the elements of your monthly mortgage payment.) Occasionally, there are some other small changes because of adjustments to your homeowners insurance premium and your mortgage insurance premium. However, these changes rarely will be large enough to affect your refinancing decision.

Cost of Refinancing

Refinancing your mortgage may cost anywhere from 2 percent to 6.5 percent of your loan amount. On a $100,000 loan, this would be from $2,000 to $6,500. Remember the settlement costs that you paid when you first bought your home? When you refinance, you have to pay most of these costs again. The cost of refinancing your mortgage depends on several factors:

- The lender and loan that you choose,

- The cost of settlement services in your area and
- The recording fees charged by your local government.

The largest cost items in refinancing are the points and other fees charged by your lender. Those fees generally range from 1 percent to 4.5 percent of your mortgage amount. All other costs combined range from only 1 percent to 2 percent of the total mortgage amount.

Some mortgages have a prepayment penalty clause that requires the borrower to pay a fee for repaying the mortgage before a specified period of years. (See Chapter 6, "Miscellaneous Mortgage Topics.") If your *old mortgage* has a prepayment penalty clause and you refinance it before the specified period is over, consider that fee an additional cost of refinancing. A typical prepayment penalty clause might charge from 1 percent to 3 percent of your loan amount if you repay your loan

---

M O R T G A G E   T I P

Problem—High cost of refinancing:

- Points

- Processing fees

- Appraisal, credit report

- Title policy update

- Recording tax

- Lawyer

- Real estate tax and hazard insurance escrows

Solution—Increase the loan amount or get a "no-cost" loan to cover the cost.

in less than three years. Read your current mortgage note to see if it has a prepayment penalty clause. If it does, you may want to wait until the prepayment penalty period is over before refinancing.

Few people are willing or able to reach into their pocket for $2,000 to $6,500 to save $150 a month, even if they know it is the smart thing to do. Usually, it is not necessary to pay out of pocket more than a few hundred dollars to refinance. You simply increase your mortgage amount to cover the cost of refinancing, or if your lender offers it, obtain a zero-point or no-cost refinance. Your cash outlay should be minimal.

Important Exception. Many lenders will not refinance a loan for more than 90 percent of appraised value. (The LTV ratio for the new loan must be 90 percent or less.) If your existing loan has a 90 percent or greater LTV ratio, you may have to pay some or all of the refinancing costs in cash. If this situation applies to you, try the following:

- When you are shopping for lenders, explain your situation to them and ask if they have products that will solve the problem.
- Shop for an FHA or VA loan if possible (both allow LTV ratios greater than 90 percent).
- Consider a zero-point or no-cost loan to minimize out-of-pocket expenses.
- If homes in your neighborhood have increased in value and your old loan is more than two years old, your lender will recalculate the LTV ratio for the new loan based on the new, higher appraised value.

FIGURE 8.4   Adding Refinancing Costs to Your Mortgage Balance

Refinancing Costs:	$ 2,220
Old Loan Balance:	+$ 99,637
New Loan Amount:	$101,857

Deciding Whether to Refinance

The industry rule of thumb—"refinance when you can lower your interest rate by 2 percent or more"—no longer is correct. It may make sense for you to refinance even if you lower your rate by only 0.5 percent. (See Figure 8.5.)

On the other hand, if you plan to move in a year or two, you might be better off not refinancing. It makes sense to refinance if you can recover your costs and make a decent return on your investment before you plan to sell your home or pay off your mortgage.

The time necessary to recover your costs is called the *payback period.* Determining the length of the payback period is the critical calculation that you must make before deciding whether to refinance. The Do-It-Yourself Refinance Worksheet helps you to estimate your payback period.

Should you refinance? To answer this question, you must know:

- Your current mortgage rate and amount
- The mortgage rate for a new loan
- Your approximate refinancing costs
- About how long you plan to stay in your home

In the example in Figure 8.6, the old mortgage rate is 10 percent, and the new mortgage rate is 8 percent. The estimated refinancing costs are about $2,300, and the annual interest savings are about $1,700. So

FIGURE 8.5   Higher Appraised Value Allows Higher Loan Amount

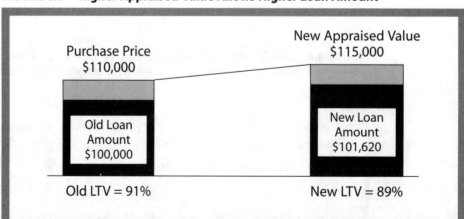

FIGURE 8.6   Sample Do-It-Yourself Refinance Worksheet

Do-It-Yourself Refinance Worksheet A

Old Mortgage

Initial mortgage amount	$100,000.00	(A)
Age of mortgage (years)	1.00	(B)
Old interest rate	10.00%	(C)
Remaining principal balance (Factor from table 0.994)	$ 99,400.00	(D)

New Mortgage

Estimated refinancing costs		
Points 1.00 % × (D) =	$ 994.00	
Fees	700.00	
Other costs 0.60 % × (D) =	596.00	
TOTAL COSTS	$ 2,290.00	(E)
Estimated new mortgage amount (E) + (D) =	$101,690.00	(F)
New interest rate	8.00%	(G)

Interest Savings

Interest (old loan) (C) × (D) =	$ 9,940.00	(H)
Interest (new loan) (F) × (G) =	−8,135.20	(I)
SAVINGS	$ 1,804.80	(J)

Payback Period

Payback period in months 12 × (E) / (J) =	15 months	

it takes only a year and four months to recover the costs of refinancing. (The savings over 30 years would grow to $36,000.) Unless you had plans to move in less than two years, refinancing would make good sense in this situation.

Figure 8.7 is the same as Figure 8.6 except that the old mortgage rate is 9 percent instead of 10 percent. The difference between the rates is just 1 percent, but you would still recover your refinancing costs in just three years.

FIGURE 8.7   Sample Do-It-Yourself Refinance Worksheet

Do-It-Yourself Refinance Worksheet B

Old Mortgage

Initial mortgage amount	$100,000.00	(A)
Age of mortgage (years)	1.00	(B)
Old interest rate	9.00%	(C)
Remaining principal balance (Factor from table 0.993)	$ 99,300.00	(D)

New Mortgage

Estimated refinancing costs		
Points 1.00 % × (D) =	$ 990.00	
Fees	700.00	
Other costs 0.60 % × (D) =	590.00	
TOTAL COSTS	$ 2,280.00	(E)
Estimated new mortgage amount (E) + (D) =	$101,589.00	(F)
New interest rate	8.00%	(G)

Interest Savings

Interest (old loan) (C) × (D) =	$ 8,937.00	(H)
Interest (new loan) (F) × (G) =	−8,127.00	(I)
SAVINGS	$ 809.00	(J)

Payback Period

Payback period in months 12 × (E) / (J) =	34 months

For most people, it would make sense to refinance with a three-year payback period. This example illustrates a weakness in the industry's 2-percent rule of thumb.

In Figure 8.8, the lender is charging no points for the new loan instead of one point, *and* the lender is picking up all the costs. The costs of refinancing are $2,220, but the lender is picking up all the costs. In this example, the savings are less, $621 compared to $809 in Figure 8.7, but the payback is *immediate*.

FIGURE 8.8   Sample Do-It-Yourself Refinance Worksheet

Do-It-Yourself Refinance Worksheet C

Old Mortgage

Initial mortgage amount	$100,000.00	(A)
Age of mortgage (years)	1.00	(B)
Old interest rate	9.00%	(C)
Remaining principal balance (Factor from table 0.993)	$ 99,300.00	(D)

New Mortgage

Estimated refinancing costs		
Points 0.00 % × (D) =	$ 0.00	
Fees	0.00	
Other costs 0.00 % × (D) =	0.00	
TOTAL COSTS	$ 0.00	(E)
Estimated new mortgage amount (E) + (D) =	$ 99,300.00	(F)
New interest rate	8.375%	(G)

Interest Savings

Interest (old loan) (C) × (D) =	$ 8,937.00	(H)
Interest (new loan) (F) × (G) =	−8,316.00	(I)
SAVINGS	$ 621.00	(J)

Payback Period

Payback period in months 12 × (E) / (J) =	0 months

Businesspeople and financiers often use payback periods to rate investments—the shorter the payback period, the better the investment.

This is also true with refinancing. A shorter payback period is better. Even if you have to pay a slightly higher interest rate, choose a loan with few points over one with many points. You will be shortening your payback period.

In Figure 8.9, loans A, B, and C from Figures 8.6 to 8.8 are all approximately the same cost. (A loan priced at 9 percent plus one point

FIGURE 8.9   Payback Period

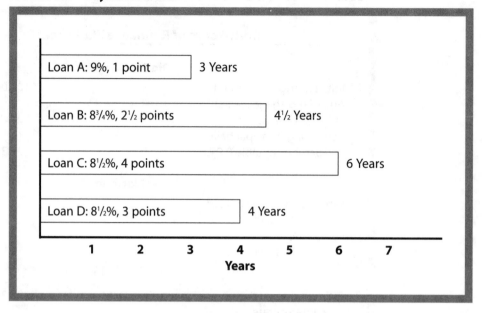

costs about the same as 8.75 percent plus two and a half points or 8.5 percent plus four points. See "Introduction.") If you were purchasing a home, these three loans would be essentially equivalent, but if you were refinancing an old 10 percent loan, loan A would be far superior to loans B and C. Its payback period would be only three years compared with four and a half years for loan B, and six years for loan C.

Loan D is a lower cost loan than loan A, but for this refinancing transaction, its payback period is a year longer. If you were planning to move within five or six years, loan A still would be better even though its rate is 0.50 percent higher than loan D. Only after seven years would the lower overall price of loan D begin to provide better savings for you than loan A.

When you are shopping for a loan to refinance your current mortgage, ask lenders for a loan with no more than two points. *The fewer points, the better.*

M O R T G A G E   T I P

Refinancing to save money:

- Lowering your interest rate by as little at 1 percent can save you thousands of dollars.

- You do not start saving money until after you have recovered the costs of refinancing. Do not refinance if you plan to move soon.

- Shop for a mortgage with few or no points even if it has a slightly higher rate. This will shorten your payback period and start your savings faster.

- A prepayment penalty is a hidden cost of refinancing. Check your mortgage note for such a clause.

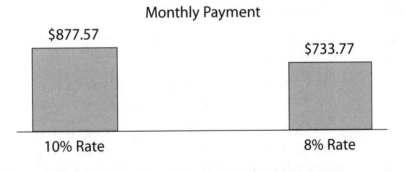

Monthly Payment

$877.57   10% Rate $733.77   8% Rate

Borrowing More Money

If you bought your home in the early 1980s, it probably is worth more today than you paid for it. At the same time, you have been paying off your old mortgage.

The *equity* that you have in your home is the value of the home less the outstanding mortgage balance. In the example in Figure 8.10,

FIGURE 8.10   Building Up Equity

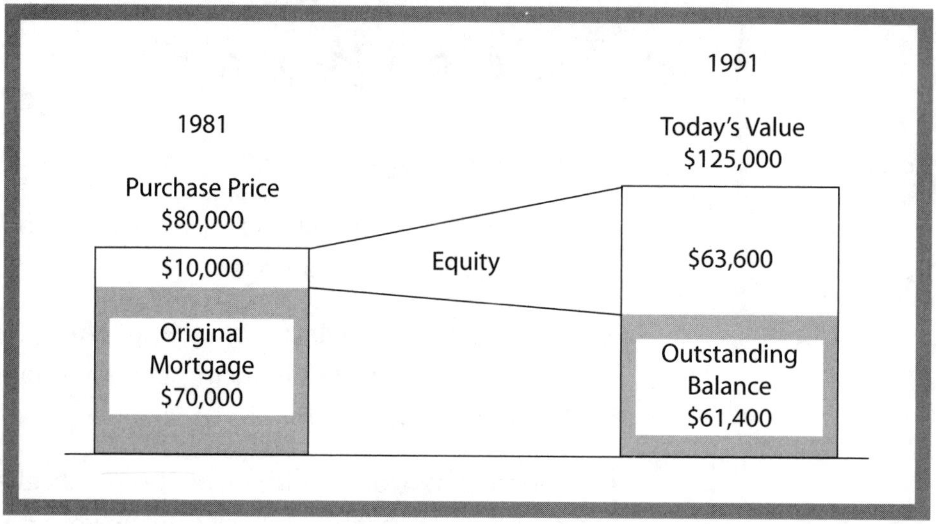

you would have had $10,000 equity (your down payment) in 1981. Today, your equity would have grown to $63,600.

How to Borrow against Your Home Equity

You can borrow more money using your equity as collateral in one of two ways:

1. Replace your old mortgage with a larger new one.
2. Get a second mortgage, leaving your first mortgage in place.

There is no formula or rule of thumb to tell you which method is best. The choice must be based on what you plan to do with the extra money, how much you need, and how quickly you plan to pay it off. You are borrowing more money, not saving money. Your new monthly payments probably will be higher, and your interest rates also may be higher.

If you need a lot of money over a long period, you could refinance your first mortgage, replacing it with a larger one, or you could get a long-term, fixed-rate second mortgage. Either choice serves the same purpose. To choose one method over the other, compare the refinancing costs and interest rates of each. (See Figure 8.11.)

FIGURE 8.11   Ways to Tap Equity

Term	Loan Size	
	Large $	Small $
Long-Term Loan	New first mortgage or long-term second mortgage	Long-term, fixed rate second mortgage
Short-Term Loan	Short-term second mortgage	Personal loan or short-term second mortgage

Choosing an Equity Loan

Carrying through with the example of the home purchased in 1981, assume that you have a $61,400 mortgage balance on a home that now is worth $125,000. Suppose that you want to borrow $35,000 to add some new rooms to your home. Your choice is between a new 30-year fixed-rate mortgage at 8.5 percent plus three points and $1,000 in settlement costs or a 15-year fixed-rate second mortgage at 10 percent plus one point and $500 in settlement costs. (See Figure 8.12.)

Option 1: Get New First Mortgage

- Loan Amount: $100,400
- Monthly Payment: $771.99
- Refinancing Costs: $3,500.00
- Interest Rate: 8.5%

Option 2: Get Second Mortgage; Retain Old First Mortgage

- Loan Amount: $35,850 (2nd) + $61,400 (1st) = $97,250
- Monthly Payments: $385.25 + $513.64 = $898.89
- Refinancing Costs: $850.00
- Interest Rate (Blended): ($35,850 × 10% + $61,400 × 7%) ÷ $97,250 = 8.1%

FIGURE 8.12   Choosing an Equity Loan: First Mortgage versus Second Mortgage

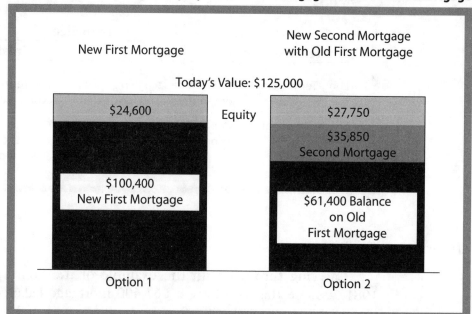

If you evaluate these two options, you can see that in this example, the second mortgage is a better choice than a new first mortgage. The monthly payments would be slightly higher ($898.99 versus $771.99), but the overall interest rate would be lower, the total loan amount would be lower, and the two mortgages would be paid off in 20 years versus 30 years for the new first mortgage.

If you need a large amount of money, but only for a few years, a second mortgage is cheaper than a new first mortgage because of the high cost of refinancing a first mortgage.

For the same reason, a second mortgage is usually better for borrowing a small amount for a long time. If you need a small amount of money for a short time, consider an unsecured personal loan. It may be less expensive than a second mortgage.

Line-of-Credit Loans

If you need additional funds, but not all at once (e.g., for college tuition payments over four years), inquire at your bank or savings-and-loan association about a line of credit secured by the equity in your home. A line of credit allows you to borrow what you need, as you need it, up to an agreed amount. You are charged interest on the outstanding balance.

Restrictions on Cash-Out Refinancing Transactions

When you refinance a first mortgage, increasing the loan amount to borrow more money, it is called a *cash-out transaction*. Maximum

---

M O R T G A G E   T I P

Borrowing More Money

- The equity that you have built up in your home can be used as collateral to borrow more money.

- For large loans, compare the costs of a new first mortgage versus a second mortgage. (Usually, a second mortgage will be cheaper.)

- For smaller loans, compare second mortgages and unsecured personal loans. Also consider line-of-credit mortgages.

$125,000

| $10,000 | Equity | $63,600 |

| Original Mortgage $70,000 | | Outstanding Balance $61,400 |

allowed LTV ratios are lower for cash-out refinancing transactions than mortgages for home purchase or refinancing transactions in which the loan is increased only enough to cover refinancing costs.

First Mortgages	Maximum LTV Ratio
Conventional mortgages (Fannie Mae, Freddie Mac):	75%
FHA mortgages:	85%
VA mortgages:	90%

Second Mortgages	
Fannie Mae standards:	70% combined LTV ratio
Most savings-and-loan associations:	80% combined LTV ratio
Mortgage companies:	up to 125% LTV (varies widely)

Restructuring

The final reason to refinance a mortgage is to restructure the financing that you have now.

Over the past 20 years, the prevailing rate for 30-year fixed-rate conforming conventional mortgages has ranged from a high of 17 percent to a low of $6\frac{1}{2}$ percent. Because mortgage rates rise and fall, and because family incomes rise and fall, many people find themselves with mortgage financing that does not match their current needs. The decisions that they made a few years ago in order to qualify for a loan may not give them the right financing package for their situation today.

They might have a first or second balloon mortgage that is coming due in the near future, or they might have an ARM with a current rate that is near the prevailing fixed-rate loans. Either of these situations would lead to restructuring.

Refinancing to replace an ARM with a fixed-rate mortgage is a difficult decision. If current rates on ARMs are lower than fixed-rate mortgages, refinancing to a fixed-rate loan will not only cost a few thousand dollars but also increase your interest rate and monthly payment.

Some ARMs have few or no consumer protection features such as rate caps and payment caps. If you have a "bad" ARM or you are simply uncomfortable with an ARM and if rates are down, then now is the time to refinance.

Some ARMs have a convertibility feature that allows you to convert your ARM to a fixed-rate mortgage by paying a small fee (typically a point). This is a lot cheaper than refinancing. Check your mortgage note to see if it has a convertibility feature and what the rate on the new mortgage would be.

M O R T G A G E   T I P

Restructuring

- When replacing a maturing second mortgage, compare the costs of a new second mortgage with the costs of replacing both old mortgages with a new first mortgage.

- Replacing an ARM with a fixed-rate mortgage will cost money up-front and may raise your monthly payments, but the security of a fixed rate could be worth the costs.

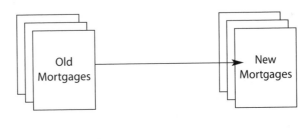

Getting Started on Your Mortgage

Throughout this book, we have attempted to describe in simple terms what can be a complicated and stressful process. There is often a feeling of not being in control during the process as well as the suspense of waiting to get an "answer" on your loan application. Just remember that, when you are buying a house and getting a mortgage to finance your purchase, *everyone is on your side.* The real estate agent doesn't get paid if the home purchase is not consummated. The loan officer usually gets paid on commission, so he or she doesn't get paid unless your loan is approved and closed. The mortgage company makes money, not by turning loans down or by arbitrarily making you jump through hoops, but by originating loans that can either be sold at a profit or by collecting interest on the loan over the years. So consider that, although some of the requirements may seem unintelligible, there are valid reasons for lenders requesting the types of information that they do. We hope that this book is helpful to you in that process and that some of the terminology will be more familiar to you after reading this book.

Appendixes
Worksheets, Forms, and Tables

A

PITI Form

Calculating Your Monthly Mortgage Payment

The PITI form following these instructions will help you calculate your total monthly mortgage payment. It is the sum of five items:

Principal and Interest Payment

Multiply your loan amount by the appropriate mortgage payment factor for your loan. If you do not know what your loan amount will be, you can estimate it using the Mortgage Data Form in Appendix D. Your mortgage payment factor depends on the interest rate and term of your mortgage. You can look it up in the Mortgage Payment Factor Table at the end of Appendix A, which covers interest rates from 2.000 percent to 17.875 percent for 30-year and 15-year loans. For example, the payment factor of a 10.750 percent, 30-year loan is 9.3348. (If the term of your loan is other than 15 or 30 years, use Appendix I.)

Real Estate Taxes

Enter your annual real estate tax assessment divided by 12. Real estate taxes on a home can vary widely depending on the state and local jurisdiction and the assessed value of the property. If you do not know what the real estate taxes are on the home that you are buying, ask your real estate agent. Generally, annual real estate taxes range from 0.75 percent to 2.0 percent of a home's value.

Homeowners Insurance

Enter your annual homeowners insurance premium divided by 12. The cost of homeowners insurance also varies widely depending on "fire districts" and the type and amount of coverage that you select. You can save as much as 50 percent on homeowners insurance by shopping around. Annual premiums range from $200 to $500 per $100,000 of coverage.

Mortgage Insurance (Conventional Loans)

Enter your loan amount multiplied by the annual premium rate divided by 12. Premium rates vary somewhat and depend on your LTV ratio and the type of loan you choose (ARM or fixed). For current premiums, you should consult a loan officer, but the following table can serve as a guideline.

Private Mortgage Insurance Premium Rates

LTV Ratio	Fixed-Rate/ Payment Loan Types	ARMs, GEMs, GPMs, Buydowns
90.0% to 95.0%	0.50%	0.54%
85.0% to 89.9%	0.34%	0.44%
80.1% to 84.9%	0.29%	0.34%

For example, a $100,000 conventional loan with an 85-percent LTV ratio requires mortgage insurance. The annual premium rate would be 0.3 percent ($300 per year or $25 per month).

Condominium/Homeowners Association Dues

If you are buying a condominium or a home that is subject to home-owners association dues, enter the annual assessment divided by 12. (Not all lenders require you to include this in your mortgage payment.)

PITI Form

Loan Amount: $ _____ (A)
Interest Rate: _____ %
Term of Loan: _____ years

Principal and Interest Payment

$ _____ × _____ ÷ 1000 = $ _____
   (A)   Payment Factor

Real Estate Taxes

$ _____ ÷ 12 =   + _____

Homeowners Insurance Premium

$ _____ ÷ 12 =   + _____

Mortgage Insurance (if required)

$ _____ × _____ ÷ 12 =   + _____
   (A)   Premium rate

Condominium/Homeowners Association Dues

$ _____ ÷ 12 =   + _____
Annual Assessment   ――――――――

Total Monthly Mortgage Payment: $ _____

Mortgage Payment Factor Table

	Payment Factor			Payment Factor			Payment Factor			Payment Factor	
Interest Rate	30-Year Term	15-Year Term	Interest Rate	30-Year Term	15-Year Term	Interest Rate	30-Year Term	15-Year Term	Interest Rate	30-Year Term	15-Year Term
2.000%	3.6962	6.4351	6.000%	5.9955	8.4386	10.000%	8.7757	10.7461	14.000%	11.8487	13.3174
2.125%	3.7590	6.4928	6.125%	6.0761	8.5062	10.125%	8.8682	10.8227	14.125%	11.9477	13.4015
2.250%	3.8225	6.5508	6.250%	6.1572	8.5742	10.250%	8.9610	10.8995	14.250%	12.0469	13.4858
2.375%	3.8865	6.6092	6.375%	6.2387	8.6425	10.375%	9.0541	10.9766	14.375%	12.1461	13.5703
2.500%	3.9512	6.6679	6.500%	6.3207	8.7111	10.500%	9.1474	11.0540	14.500%	12.2456	13.6550
2.625%	4.0165	6.7269	6.625%	6.4031	8.7799	10.625%	9.2410	11.1316	14.625%	12.3451	13.7399
2.750%	4.0824	6.7862	6.750%	6.4860	8.8491	10.750%	9.3348	11.2095	14.750%	12.4448	13.8250
2.875%	4.1489	6.8459	6.875%	6.5693	8.9185	10.875%	9.4289	11.2876	14.875%	12.5445	13.9104
3.000%	4.2160	6.9058	7.000%	6.6530	8.9883	11.000%	9.5232	11.3660	15.000%	12.6444	13.9959
3.125%	4.2838	6.9661	7.125%	6.7372	9.0583	11.125%	9.6178	11.4446	15.125%	12.7445	14.0816
3.250%	4.3521	7.0267	7.250%	6.8218	9.1286	11.250%	9.7126	11.5234	15.250%	12.8446	14.1675
3.375%	4.4210	7.0876	7.375%	6.9068	9.1992	11.375%	9.8077	11.6026	15.375%	12.9448	14.2536
3.500%	4.4904	7.1488	7.500%	6.9921	9.2701	11.500%	9.9029	11.6819	15.500%	13.0452	14.3399
3.625%	4.5605	7.2104	7.625%	7.0779	9.3413	11.625%	9.9984	11.7615	15.625%	13.1456	14.4264
3.750%	4.6312	7.2722	7.750%	7.1641	9.4128	11.750%	10.0941	11.8413	15.750%	13.2462	14.5131
3.875%	4.7024	7.3344	7.875%	7.2507	9.4845	11.875%	10.1900	11.9214	15.875%	13.3468	14.5999
4.000%	4.7742	7.3969	8.000%	7.3376	9.5565	12.000%	10.2861	12.0017	16.000%	13.4476	14.6870
4.125%	4.8465	7.4597	8.125%	7.4250	9.6288	12.125%	10.3824	12.0822	16.125%	13.5484	14.7743
4.250%	4.9194	7.5228	8.250%	7.5127	9.7014	12.250%	10.4790	12.1630	16.250%	13.6493	14.8617
4.375%	4.9929	7.5862	8.375%	7.6007	9.7743	12.375%	10.5757	12.2440	16.375%	13.7504	14.9493
4.500%	5.0669	7.6499	8.500%	7.6891	9.8474	12.500%	10.6726	12.3252	16.500%	13.8515	15.0371
4.625%	5.1414	7.7140	8.625%	7.7779	9.9208	12.625%	10.7697	12.4067	16.625%	13.9527	15.1251
4.750%	5.2165	7.7783	8.750%	7.8670	9.9945	12.750%	10.8669	12.4884	16.750%	14.0540	15.2132
4.875%	5.2921	7.8430	8.875%	7.9564	10.0684	12.875%	10.9644	12.5703	16.875%	14.1553	15.3015
5.000%	5.3682	7.9079	9.000%	8.0462	10.1427	13.000%	11.0620	12.6524	17.000%	14.2568	15.3900
5.125%	5.4449	7.9732	9.125%	8.1363	10.2172	13.125%	11.1598	12.7348	17.125%	14.3583	15.4787
5.250%	5.5220	8.0388	9.250%	8.2268	10.2919	13.250%	11.2577	12.8174	17.250%	14.4599	15.5676
5.375%	5.5997	8.1047	9.375%	8.3175	10.3670	13.375%	11.3558	12.9002	17.375%	14.5615	15.6566
5.500%	5.6779	8.1708	9.500%	8.4085	10.4422	13.500%	11.4541	12.9832	17.500%	14.6633	15.7458
5.625%	5.7566	8.2373	9.625%	8.4999	10.5178	13.625%	11.5525	13.0664	17.625%	14.7651	15.8351
5.750%	5.8357	8.3041	9.750%	8.5915	10.5936	13.750%	11.6511	13.1499	17.750%	14.8669	15.9247
5.875%	5.9154	8.3712	9.875%	8.6835	10.6697	13.875%	11.7498	13.2335	17.875%	14.9689	16.0144

B

Sample Mortgage Application

The Numbers Below Correspond to the Numbers on the Sample Application

1. Enter the type, amount, approximate interest rate, and number of monthly installments.
2. Address including property, city, county, state, ZIP code, and number of units.
3. Legal description or, if not available, a shortened lot and block number can be used. These should be obtained from the agent and/or from the seller.
4. Leave blank.
5. Complete this line only if you are refinancing your existing home.
6. Enter names exactly as they are to appear on the legal documents. Title may be in a single person, husband and wife, husband, wife, and child (children), or even nonrelated persons.
7. Leave blank.
8. The source of the down payment, such as sale of present home, gift letter, or savings.
9. List name and address (including ZIP codes) of employers. Please use addresses for locations of personnel departments, supervisors, etc.

10. If either the borrower or coborrower have worked at their present place of employment for less than two years or if currently employed in more than one position, this section must be completed. List address of previous employer, length of employment, and job title, for a minimum of two years of history for both the borrower and coborrower.

11. The information here must match with the information to be provided during the interview on the Verification of Employment Form. If you are self-employed, you must attach copies of your federal tax returns (1040) for the past two years, and your year-to-date profit-and-loss statement, or other verification and documentation of your gross income.

12. List the amount of any other income you want considered in your loan application. The other income listed here must be described in section 14, "Describe Other Income."

13. Leave blank.

14. Describe the type and amount of income listed above in the other column of "Gross Monthly Income." Addresses should be included along with the payer. It is necessary to bring in divorce decrees, 1099 forms, or other evidence of income declared.

15. It is important to complete the name of the financial institution, type of account, balance, and the account numbers of each account. Use an additional sheet if necessary. Bring addresses to the interview (including ZIP codes).

16. List the name, number of shares held, and market value of all stocks and bonds held. Attach a separate sheet if necessary. If applicant uses one or two investment brokers and all the securities are shown on their statements, bring the statements to the interview.

17. Complete the "Schedule of Real Estate Owned" listed below first. Show all real estate presently owned, including any that is income-producing, on the schedule. Include home presently owned even if it is pending sale. Use an additional sheet if necessary. Enter the Present Market Value total here.

18. Enter the value of vested rights set aside by an employer for retirement owned by the borrower for each applicant. Documentation will be needed to substantiate amounts.

Uniform Residential Loan Application

Uniform Residential Loan Application

This application is designed to be completed by the applicant(s) with the lender's assistance. Applicants should complete this form as ''Borrower'' or ''Co-Borrower'', as applicable. Co-Borrower information must also be provided (and the appropriate box checked) when ☒ the income or assets of a person other than the ''Borrower'' (including the Borrower's spouse) will be used as a basis for loan qualification or ☐ the income or assets of the Borrower's spouse will not be used as a basis for loan qualification, but his or her liabilities must be considered because the Borrower resides in a community property state, the security property is located in a community property state, or the Borrower is relying on other property located in a community property state as a basis for repayment of the loan.

I. TYPE OF MORTGAGE AND TERMS OF LOAN

Mortgage Applied for:	☐ VA ☒ Conventional ☐ Other: ☐ FHA ☐ FmHA	Agency Case Number	Lender Case No.

(1)
Amount $ 90,500	Interest Rate 8.5 %	No. of Months 360	Amortization Type:	☐ Fixed Rate ☐ GPM	☐ Other (explain): ☐ ARM (type):

II. PROPERTY INFORMATION AND PURPOSE OF LOAN

Subject Property Address (street, city, state, & ZIP): 9503 Kingsburg Drive   Fairfax, VA 22031   (2)   No. of Units: 1

Legal Description of Subject Property (attach description if necessary): Tract #11292 Lot 52   (3)   Year Built 1978

Purpose of Loan ☒ Purchase ☐ Construction ☐ Other (explain): ☐ Refinance ☐ Construction-Permanent	Property will be: ☒ Primary Residence ☐ Secondary Residence ☐ Investment

Complete this line if construction or construction-permanent loan.

Year Lot Acquired	Original Cost $	Amount Existing Liens (4) $	(a) Present Value of Lot $	(b) Cost of Improvements $	Total (a + b) $

Complete this line if this is a refinance loan. (5)

Year Acquired	Original Cost $	Amount Existing Liens $	Purpose of Refinance	Describe Improvements ☐ made ☐ to be made Cost: $

Title will be held in what Name(s): (6) John Peter Smith and Sara Marie Smith   Manner in which Title will be held (7)   Estate will be held in: ☒ Fee Simple   ☐ Leasehold (show expiration date)

Source of Down Payment, Settlement Charges and/or Subordinate Financing (explain): Sale of Present Home (8)

III. BORROWER INFORMATION

Borrower	Co-Borrower
Borrower's Name (include Jr. or Sr. if applicable): John Peter Smith	Co-Borrower's Name (include Jr. or Sr. if applicable): Sara Marie Smith
Social Security Number 289-75-8298 Home Phone (incl. area code) 703-571-1124 Age 36 Yrs. School 16	Social Security Number 267-69-9558 Home Phone (incl. area code) Same Age 35 Yrs. School 16
☒ Married ☐ Unmarried (include single, divorced, widowed) ☐ Separated Dependents (not listed by Co-Borrower) no. 2 ages 5, 3 years	☒ Married ☐ Unmarried (include single, divorced, widowed) ☐ Separated Dependents (not listed by Borrower) no. ages
Present Address (street, city, state, ZIP) ☒ Own ☐ Rent 2 No. Yrs. 193 Goose Lake Road Burke, VA 22390	Present Address (street, city, state, ZIP) ☐ Own ☐ Rent No. Yrs. Same

If residing at present address for less than two years, complete the following:

Former Address (street, city, state, ZIP) ☐ Own ☐ Rent ____ No. Yrs.	Former Address (street, city, state, ZIP) ☐ Own ☐ Rent ____ No. Yrs
Former Address (street, city, state, ZIP) ☐ Own ☐ Rent ____ No. Yrs.	Former Address (street, city, state, ZIP) ☐ Own ☐ Rent ____ No. Yrs

Uniform Residential Loan Application (Continued)

IV. EMPLOYMENT INFORMATION		
Borrower		**Co-Borrower**
Name & Address of Employer [ ] Self Employed	Yrs. on this job 2 1/2	Name & Address of Employer [ ] Self Employed	Yrs. on this job 6
Data Communications, Inc. 9100 Goldbridge Lane McLean, VA 22390 Attn: Personnel Dept. ⑨	Yrs. employed in this line of work/profession 13	Baldwin, Cohen, and Lesher 18th and K Sts. N.W. Washington, D.C. 25901	Yrs. employed in this line of work/profession 11
Position/Title/Type of Business Computer Analyst/Time Sharing	Business Phone (incl. area code) 703-349-0900	Position/Title/Type of Business Administrative Asst.	Business Phone (incl. area code) 202-795-3100

If employed in current position for less than two years or if currently employed in more than one position, complete the following:

Name & Address of Employer [ ] Self Employed	Dates (from - to)	Name & Address of Employer [ ] Self Employed	Dates (from - to) 5/91 - Present
⑩	Monthly Income $	Sprangles Dept. Store 1200 Clark Road McLean, VA 22313	Monthly Income $ 250
Position/Title/Type of Business	Business Phone (incl. area code)	Position/Title/Type of Business Sales Clerk	Business Phone (incl. area code)
Name & Address of Employer [ ] Self Employed	Dates (from - to)	Name & Address of Employer [ ] Self Employed	Dates (from - to)
	Monthly Income $		Monthly Income $
Position/Title/Type of Business	Business Phone (incl. area code)	Position/Title/Type of Business	Business Phone (incl. area code)

Freddie Mac Form 65 10/92 — Page 1 of 4 — Fannie Mae Form 1003 10/9:

V. MONTHLY INCOME AND COMBINED HOUSING EXPENSE INFORMATION						
Gross Monthly Income	Borrower	Co-Borrower	Total	Combined Monthly Housing Expense	Present	Proposed
Base Empl. Income*	$ 2,917	$ 1,500	$ 4,417	Rent	$	
Overtime			⑪	First Mortgage (P&I)	527	$
Bonuses				Other Financing (P&I)	90	
Commissions				Hazard Insurance	30	
Dividends/Interest	50		50	Real Estate Taxes	75	⑬
Net Rental Income				Mortgage Insurance		
Other before completing, see the notice in "describe other income," below)	⑫	250	250	Homeowner Assn. Dues		
				Other: Utilities	85	
Total	$ 2,967	$ 1,750	$ 4,717	Total	$ 807	$

* Self Employed Borrower(s) may be required to provide additional documentation such as tax returns and financial statements.

Describe Other Income *Notice:* Alimony, child support, or separate maintenance income need not be revealed if the Borrower (B) or Co-Borrower (C) does not choose to have it considered for repaying this loan.

B/C		Monthly Amount
C	Sprangles Dept. Store, 1200 Clark Road McLean, VA 22313 Employed 3 yrs - Part Time - Sales Clerk ⑭	$ 250

19. The verifiable value of any business that the borrower(s) owns is shown in this space. It could consist of shares of a family-owned business or a second business of the borrower. Audited copies of the financial statements should be brought to the interview.

20. List assets that are separated from normal personal property (e.g., automobiles, jewelry, airplanes, boats, valuable collections of money, stamps, or other objects). Bring verification such as an insurance policy or policies to the interview.

21. List all major credit cards including account numbers. The payment is the minimum amount due on the balance. The number of months is the balance divided by the minimum payment amount. Complete this section for all real estate mortgages, deeds of trust, or secondary real estate financing currently borrowed. Be sure to include names of institutions, account numbers, monthly installments, remaining life of the loan, and the unpaid balance. Attach a separate sheet if necessary. Bring addresses (including ZIP codes) to the interview.

22. Leave blank. Be prepared to give the name, address, and account number of the person or place where payments are made and the amount of the payment during the interview.

23. "Schedule of Real Estate Owned"—The type of property can be as follows:

Type	Unit Code
Single-Family Detached	SFD
Single-Family Attached	SFA
2-Unit	2
3-Unit	3
4-Unit	4
Apartment	Multi
Commercial	Com

24. Show the exact purchase price. Bring copy of Purchase Agreement to the interview.

25. Leave blank.

26. All questions must be answered by both the borrower and co-borrower. Any "yes" answers must have a complete explanation on a continuation sheet. Provide dates, courts, names of persons, and/or relevant data.

27. If any part of the down payment is borrowed, list the details such as if you intend to have a second loan, state its rate, number of months, and monthly payment.

28. Each applicant must sign in ink.

Uniform Residential Loan Application (Continued)

VI. ASSETS AND LIABILITIES

This Statement and any applicable supporting schedules may be completed jointly by both married and unmarried Co-Borrowers if their assets and liabilities are sufficiently joined so that the Statement can be meaningfully and fairly presented on a combined basis; otherwise separate Statements and Schedules are required. If the Co-Borrower section was completed about a spouse, this Statement and supporting schedules must be completed about that spouse also.

Completed ☒ Jointly ☐ Not Jointly

ASSETS Description	Cash or Market Value	Liabilities and Pledged Assets.	Monthly Payt. & Mos. Left to Pay	Unpaid Balance
Cash deposit toward purchase held by: ABC Realty	$ 5,000 (15)	Name and address of Company Master Charge (21)	$ Payt./Mos. 50/10	$ 500
List checking and savings accounts below		Acct. no. 393-750-131627		
Name and address of Bank, S&L, or Credit Union First Federal S/L Checking Acct. no. 1100-44	$ 300	Name and address of Company Visa	$ Payt./Mos. 25/16	$ 400
Name and address of Bank, S&L, or Credit Union First Federal S/L		Acct. no. 573299-835-1179		
Savings Acct. no. ✓1100-45	$ 8,000	Name and address of Company Sears	$ Payt./Mos. 0	$ 0
Name and address of Bank, S&L, or Credit Union		Acct. no. 54-7022-156335		
		Name and address of Company American Express	$ Payt./Mos. 0	$ 0
		Acct. no. 73-4592881-00		
Acct. no.	$	Name and address of Company Student Loan Marketing (CO)	$ Payt./Mos. 35/11	$ 385
Stocks & Bonds (Company name/number & description) (16)	$	Acct. no. 5773418		
		Name and address of Company Fairfax First Bank #7920	$ Payt./Mos. 921	$ 81,000
Life insurance net cash value Face amount: $ 60,000	$ 3,000	Government City Bank #199-44-76	90	3,000
Subtotal Liquid Assets	$ 11,300	Name and address of Company McLean Federal S/L #447607	$ Payt./Mos. 170/25	$ 4,250
Real estate owned (enter market value from schedule of real estate owned) (17)	$ 89,000	First Federal S/L #00199730	120/15	1,800
Vested interest in retirement fund (18)	$	Acct. no.		
Net worth of business(es) owned (attach financial statement) (19)	$	Alimony/Child Support/Separate Maintenance Payments Owed to: (22)	$	
Automobiles owned (make and year) 1991 Honda Accord 1989 VW Rabbit	6,500 3,200	Job Related Expense (child care, union dues, etc.)	$	
Other Assets (itemize) (20) Furniture and Personal Property	15,000	Total Monthly Payments	$ 1,321	
Total Assets a.	$ 122,000	$ 30,665	Total Liabilities b.	$ 91,385

Freddie Mac Form 65 10/92   Page 2 of 4   Fannie Mae Form 1003 10/92

Uniform Residential Loan Application (Continued)

VI. ASSETS AND LIABILITIES (cont.)

Schedule of Real Estate Owned (If additional properties are owned, use continuation sheet.) (23)

Property Address (enter S if sold, PS if pending sale or R if rental being held for income)	Type of Property	Present Market Value	Amount of Mortgages & Liens	Gross Rental Income	Mortgage Payments	Insurance, Maintenance, Taxes & Misc.	Net Rental Income
193 Goose Lake Road PS	SFD	89,000	81,000	N/A	921	1,200/yr	N/A
			3,000	N/A	90	N/A	N/A
Totals		89,000	84,000	N/A	1,011	1,200/yr	N/A

List any additional names under which credit has previously been received and indicate appropriate creditor name(s) and account number(s):

Alternate Name	Creditor Name	Account Number

VII. DETAILS OF TRANSACTION

a. Purchase price (24)	$ 105,200
b. Alterations, improvements, repairs	
c. Land (if acquired separately)	
d. Refinance (incl. debts to be paid off)	
e. Estimated prepaid items (25)	
f. Estimated closing costs	
g. PMI, MIP, Funding Fee	
h. Discount (if Borrower will pay)	
i. Total costs (add items a through h)	
j. Subordinate financing	
k. Borrower's closing costs paid by Seller	
l. Other Credits (explain)	
m. Loan amount (exclude PMI, MIP, Funding Fee financed)	
n. PMI, MIP, Funding Fee financed	
o. Loan amount (add m & n)	
p. Cash from/to Borrower (subtract j, k, l & o from i)	

VIII. DECLARATIONS

If you answer "yes" to any questions a through i, please use continuation sheet for explanation.

	Borrower Yes	Borrower No	Co-Borrower Yes	Co-Borrower No
a. Are there any outstanding judgments against you? (26)	☐	☒	☐	☒
b. Have you been declared bankrupt within the past 7 years?	☐	☒	☐	☒
c. Have you had property foreclosed upon or given title or deed in lieu thereof in the last 7 years?	☐	☒	☐	☒
d. Are you a party to a lawsuit?	☐	☒	☐	☒
e. Have you directly or indirectly been obligated on any loan which resulted in foreclosure, transfer of title in lieu of foreclosure, or judgment? (This would include such loans as home mortgage loans, SBA loans, home improvement loans, educational loans, manufactured (mobile) home loans, any mortgage, financial obligation, bond, or loan guarantee. If "Yes," provide details, including date, name and address of Lender, FHA or VA case number, if any, and reasons for the action.)	☐	☒	☐	☒
f. Are you presently delinquent or in default on any Federal debt or any other loan, mortgage, financial obligation, bond, or loan guarantee? If "Yes," give details as described in the preceding question.	☐	☒	☐	☒
g. Are you obligated to pay alimony, child support, or separate maintenance?	☐	☒	☐	☒
h. Is any part of the down payment borrowed? (27)	☐	☒	☐	☒
i. Are you a co-maker or endorser on a note?	☐	☒	☐	☒
j. Are you a U.S. citizen?	☒	☐	☒	☐
k. Are you a permanent resident alien?	☐	☒	☐	☒
l. Do you intend to occupy the property as your primary residence? If "Yes," complete question m below.	☒	☐	☒	☐
m. Have you had an ownership interest in a property in the last three years?	☒	☐	☒	☐
(1) What type of property did you own—principal residence (PR), second home (SH), or investment property (IP)?	PR		PR	
(2) How did you hold title to the home—solely by yourself (S), jointly with your spouse (SP), or jointly with another person (O)?	SP		SP	

Uniform Residential Loan Application (Continued)

IX. ACKNOWLEDGMENT AND AGREEMENT

The undersigned specifically acknowledge(s) and agree(s) that: (1) the loan requested by this application will be secured by a first mortgage or deed of trust on the property described herein; (2) the property will not be used for any illegal or prohibited purpose or use; (3) all statements made in this application are made for the purpose of obtaining the loan indicated herein; (4) occupation of the property will be as indicated above; (5) verification or reverification of any information contained in the application may be made at any time by the Lender, its agents, successors and assigns, either directly or through a credit reporting agency, from any source named in this application, and the original copy of this application will be retained by the Lender, even if the loan is not approved; (6) the Lender, its agents, successors and assigns will rely on the information contained in the application and I/we have a continuing obligation to amend and/or supplement the information provided in this application if any of the material facts which I/we have represented herein should change prior to closing; (7) in the event my/our payments on the loan indicated in this application become delinquent, the Lender, its agents, successors and assigns, may, in addition to all their other rights and remedies, report my/our name(s) and account information to a credit reporting agency; (8) ownership of the loan may be transferred to successor or assign of the Lender without notice to me and/or the administration of the loan account may be transferred to an agent, successor or assign of the Lender with prior notice to me; (9) the Lender, its agents, successors and assigns make no representations or warranties, express or implied, to the Borrower(s) regarding the property, the condition of the property, or the value of the property.

Certification: I/We certify that the information provided in this application is true and correct as of the date set forth opposite my/our signature(s) on this application and acknowledge my/our understanding that any intentional or negligent misrepresentation(s) of the information contained in this application may result in civil liability and/or criminal penalties including, but not limited to, fine or imprisonment or both under the provisions of Title 18, United States Code, Section 1001, et seq. and liability for monetary damages to the Lender, its agents, successors and assigns, insurers and any other person who may suffer any loss due to reliance upon any misrepresentation which I/we have made on this application.

Borrower's Signature	Date	Co-Borrower's Signature	Date
x *John P. Smith* (28)	05/05/94	x *Sara Marie Smith*	05/05/94

X. INFORMATION FOR GOVERNMENT MONITORING PURPOSES

The following information is requested by the Federal Government for certain types of loans related to a dwelling, in order to monitor the Lender's compliance with equal credit opportunity, fair housing and home mortgage disclosure laws. You are not required to furnish this information, but are encouraged to do so. The law provides that a Lender may neither discriminate on the basis of this information, nor on whether you choose to furnish it. However, if you choose not to furnish it, under Federal regulations this Lender is required to note race and sex on the basis of visual observation or surname. If you do not wish to furnish the above information, please check the box below. (Lender must review the above material to assure that the disclosures satisfy all requirements to which the Lender is subject under applicable state law for the particular type of loan applied for.)

BORROWER

Race/National Origin:
[ ] I do not wish to furnish this information
[ ] American Indian or Alaskan Native
[ ] Asian or Pacific Islander
[X] White, not of Hispanic Origin
[ ] Black, not of Hispanic origin
[ ] Hispanic
[ ] Other (specify) _____

Sex: [ ] Female [X] Male

CO-BORROWER

Race/National Origin:
[ ] I do not wish to furnish this information
[ ] American Indian or Alaskan Native
[ ] Asian or Pacific Islander
[X] White, not of Hispanic Origin
[ ] Black, not of Hispanic origin
[ ] Hispanic
[ ] Other (specify) _____

Sex: [X] Female [ ] Male

To be Completed by Interviewer	Interviewer's Name (print or type)		Name and Address of Interviewer's Employer
This application was taken by:			
[ ] face-to-face interview			
[ ] by mail	Interviewer's Signature	Date	
[ ] by telephone	Interviewer's Phone Number (incl. area code)		

Freddie Mac Form 65   10/92   Page 3 of 4   Fannie Mae Form 1003   10/92

Uniform Residental Loan Application (Continued)

Continuation Sheet/Residential Loan Application

Use this continuation sheet if you need more space to complete the Residential Loan Application. Mark B for Borrower or C for Co-Borrower.	Borrower:	Agency Case Number:
	Co-Borrower:	Lender Case Number:

I/We fully understand that it is a Federal crime punishable by fine or imprisonment, or both, to knowingly make any false statements concerning any of the above facts as applicable under the provisions of Title 18, United States Code, Section 1001, et seq.

Borrower's Signature:	Date	Co-Borrower's Signature:	Date
X		X	

Freddie Mac Form 65   10/92   Page 4 of 4   Fannie Mae Form 1003   10/9:

C

Do-It-Yourself Prequalification Worksheet

Calculating Housing and Debt Ratios for Conventional Loans

This worksheet will help you determine whether your income qualifies you for the loan amount that you want. Use this worksheet in conjunction with Chapter 2, "Qualifying for a Mortgage Loan."

Purchase Price (A)

Enter the price of the home that you are buying (or approximate value if you are refinancing).

Desired Mortgage Amount (B)

Enter the mortgage amount that you want.

Term of Mortgage

Enter the term of the mortgage (15 or 30 years).

Mortgage Rate

Enter the mortgage interest rate (for ARMs, GPMs, or buydowns, enter the starting payment rate). If you are unsure of what rates are available, call a lender and ask. Be sure to tell him or her your mortgage amount.

Loan-to-Value Ratio (C)

Divide the mortgage amount (B) by the purchase price (A) and enter as a percentage.

Gross Monthly Income (D)

Enter the sum of all sources of income—salaries, bonuses, commissions, dividends, interest, and other income. If you totaled your income on an annual basis, divide by 12. It may be helpful to use the past year's income tax return.

Mortgage Principal and Interest Payment

See Appendix A.

Real Estate Taxes

See Appendix A.

Homeowners Insurance Premium

See Appendix A.

Mortgage Insurance

See Appendix A.

Condominium/Homeowners Association Dues

See Appendix A.

Monthly Housing Expense (E)

Enter the sum of the five previous items (PITI).

Do-It-Yourself Prequalification Worksheet for Conventional Loans

Purchase Price	\$ _____	(A)
Desired Mortgage Amount	\$ _____	(B)
Term of Mortgage	_____ years	
Mortgage Rate	_____ %	
Loan-to-Value Ratio: (B) ÷ (A)	_____ % (C)	
GROSS MONTHLY INCOME	\$ _____	(D)
Mortgage Principal and Interest Payment (Payment Factor: _____) × (B) ÷ 1,000 =	\$ _____	
Annual Real Estate Taxes ÷ 12 =	+ _____	
Homeowner's Insurance Premium ÷ 12 =	+ _____	
Mortgage Insurance: (B) × .00025 =	+ _____	
Condominium/Homeowners' Association Dues	+ _____	
MONTHLY HOUSING EXPENSE	\$ _____	(E)
Car Payments	+ _____	
Alimony/Child Support Payments	+ _____	
Credit Card/Charge Account Payments	+ _____	
Other Loan Payments	+ _____	
FIXED MONTHLY OBLIGATIONS	\$ _____	(F)

HOUSING RATIO (E) ÷ (D) = _____ %

DEBT RATIO   (F) ÷ (D) = _____ %

Car Payments

Enter monthly car payments if you have ten or more payments due on your loan(s).

Alimony/Child Support

Enter required monthly payments.

Credit Card/Charge Account Payments

Enter the total of the minimum payments for all accounts.

Other Loan Payments

Enter the total of your monthly payments for all other loans—personal loans, student loans, and other mortgages with more than ten payments remaining (six months for FHA or VA loans).

Fixed Monthly Obligations

Enter the sum of the previous five items (monthly housing expense + car payments + alimony/child support + credit card/charge account payments + other loan payments).

Housing Ratio

Divide the monthly housing expense (E) by gross monthly income (D).

Debt Ratio

Divide your fixed monthly obligations (F) by gross monthly income (D).

Generally, your housing ratio and debt ratio should not exceed the following percentages:

Loan-to-Value Ratio	Housing Ratio	Debt Ratio
Conventional Loans	28% to 33%	36% to 38%
FHA Loans	29% to 31%	41% to 43%
VA Loans	n/a	41%

Some lenders are lenient; others are strict. Although the above standards are generally accepted, check with your lender for its guidelines.

D

Mortgage Data Form

Estimate your mortgage amount and select a mortgage type. Fill out the following Mortgage Data Form before you begin shopping for a loan.

Contract Purchase Price or Estimated Value (A)

If you are buying a home, enter the purchase price. If you are refinancing and bought your home less than two years ago, enter the purchase price. If you are refinancing and bought your home more than two years ago, enter a conservative estimate of your home's current value.

Estimated Closing Costs (B)

If you are purchasing a home, multiply 0.06 by your contract purchase price (A). If you are refinancing, multiply 0.04 by your estimated value (A). (This is a very gross estimate. Your closing costs will depend largely on the number of points charged by your lender.)

Estimated Total Funds Required (C)

Enter the sum of purchase price (A) and closing costs (B).

Mortgage Data Form

Contract Purchase Price (Home Purchase)
  or Estimated Value (Refinance) $ _____ (A)
Estimated Closing Costs: 6% × (A) for
  Purchase or 4% × (A) for Refinance   + _____ (B)
Estimated Total Funds Required: (A) + (B) $ _____ (C)
Cash Available (Home Purchase)
  or Equity (Refinance):
  (A)—Old Mortgage Balance   − _____ (D)
Estimated Mortgage Amount: (C) − (D) $ _____ (E)
Estimated Loan-to-Value Ratio: (E) ÷ (A)   _____ % (F)

TYPE OF LOAN   ### TERM

☐ FHA or   ☐ 30 Years
☐ VA or   ☐ 15 Years
☐ Conventional:
  (☐ Conforming or ☐ Jumbo)

                                                             ### OCCUPANCY

☐ Fixed Rate (Traditional)   ☐ Primary
☐ Graduated Payment (GPM):   Residence
  (☐ 5% or ☐ 7.5% Payment Increase) ☐ Vacation
☐ Adjustable-Rate Mortgage (ARM)   (Second) Home
☐ Growing Equity Mortgage (GEM)   ☐ Investor Property
☐ Balloon _____ Years
☐ Buydown _____ (Type)

Cash Available/Equity (D)

If you are buying a home, enter the amount of cash that you have available for a down payment and closing costs. If the seller is taking back a second mortgage, add the amount of that mortgage to your available cash. If you are refinancing, subtract the remaining principal balance on your old mortgage from your home's estimated value (A), and enter the difference (your equity). Call your current mortgage lender to get the remaining principal balance on your old mortgage, or estimate it using the table in Appendix H.

Estimated Mortgage Amount (E)

Subtract your cash available/equity (D) from the estimated total funds required (C) and enter the difference.

Estimated Loan-to-Value Ratio (F)

Divide the estimated mortgage amount (E) by the purchase price/ estimated value (A) and enter the ratio as a percentage.

Type of Loan

Check FHA, VA, or conventional. If you choose a conventional loan, check conforming if your estimated mortgage amount is $203,150 or less. Check jumbo if the estimated amount is greater than $203,150.

Check fixed rate, graduated payment (GPM), ARM, or GEM. If you pick a GPM, select an annual payment increase of 5 or 7.5 percent.

Term

Check 30 years or 15 years. Most GPMs and ARMs are available only with 30-year terms.

Occupancy

Check primary residence, vacation home, or investment property.

Fixed-Rate Loan Shopping List

Canvass Lenders and Record Available Rates

After you have selected a product type and filled out the Mortgage Data Form, use the following shopping list to help find a low rate.

✔ Lender

Note the lender's name and telephone number.

✔ Contact Person

Write down the name of the person at the lender's office who gives you the rate quote.

✔ Rate

Make sure that the quote you get is for the loan type, amount, and loan-to-value (LTV) ratio that you want.

✔ Points

Make sure that the points include the origination fee. If you are re-financing, ask for a quote with the fewest points available.

✔ Fees

Ask for all fees—appraisal, credit report, inspection fee, document preparation/review fee, and any others that the lender charges.

✔ Lock-In

Ask for the rate and point lock-in period. Ask if there is a cost for lock-ins. Ask how long it has been taking to process and close loans.

Some lenders may give you more than one quote, different combinations of rate and points. Copy them all down. One may have a lower effective rate than the others.

Fixed-Rate Loan Shopping List

Lender	Contact Person	Rate (%)	Points (%)	Fees ($)	Lock-In Days

F

ARM Shopping List

Canvass Lenders and Record Available Rates and ARM Features

After you have selected a product type (e.g., a one-year ARM) and filled out the Mortgage Data Form, use the following ARM shopping list to help you find the adjustable-rate mortgage that you want.

✔ Lender

Note the lender's name and telephone number.

✔ Contact Person

Write down the name of the person at the lender's office who gives you the rate quote.

✔ Starting Rate

Ask if the initial interest rate is also the rate that the lender uses for calculating the qualification ratios.

✔ Margin

Note the margin, but also confirm what index the lender uses.

✔ Points

Make sure that the points include the origination fee. If you are refinancing, ask for a quote with the fewest points available.

✔ Fees

Ask for all fees—appraisal, credit report, inspection fee, document
preparation/review fee, and any others that the lender charges.

✔ Life Interest Rate Cap

Ask for the maximum rate.

✔ Periodic Cap

Ask if the lender offers a periodic interest rate cap or a monthly
payment cap.

✔ Lock-In

Ask for the rate and point lock-in period. Ask if there is a cost for
lock-ins. Ask how long it has been taking to process and close loans.

Some lenders may give you more than one quote, different combinations of rate and points. Copy them all down. One may better meet
your needs than another.

ARM Shopping List

Lender	Contact Person	Starting Rate (%)	Margin (%)	Points (%)	Fees ($)	Life Cap (%)	Periodic Cap (%)	Lock-In (Days)

G

Fannie Mae/Freddie Mac Application Forms

Forms for Fannie Mae (Federal National Mortgage Association) and Freddie Mac (Federal Home Loan Mortgage Corporation) include the following:

Income property:

- Operating Income Statement
- Single-Family Comparable Rent Schedule
- Small Residential Income Property Appraisal Report

Owner-occupied property:

- Uniform Residential Appraisal Report
- Uniform Residential Loan Application. (See Appendix B for a sample filled-in form.)

Income Property: Operating Income Statement
(Fannie Mae Form 216/Freddie Mac Form 998)

Instructions

This form is prepared either by the loan applicant or the appraiser. If the applicant prepares the form, the appraiser also must include his or her comments about the reasonableness of the projected operating income of the property. The lender should retain the original of the completed form, and the appraiser should retain the copy. The lender's underwriter uses the second page of the form to calculate monthly operating income and net cash flow for the property, and to explain any adjustments he or she made to the applicant's figures.

Rent Schedule

The applicant (or appraiser) should complete this schedule by entering the current rents in effect, as well as market rents. Rental figures should be based on the rent for an unfurnished unit. The applicant should indicate which utility expenses he or she will provide as part of the rent and which must be paid separately by the tenants.

Income and Expense Projections

The applicant (or appraiser) should complete all items that apply to the subject property, and should provide actual year-end operating statements for the past two years.

If the applicant prepares the Operating Income Statement (Form 216), the lender should send the form and any previous actual operating and expense reports the applicant provides to the appraiser for review and comment. If the appraiser completes the form, the lender should make sure that the appraiser has the operating statements; any expense statements related to mortgage insurance premiums, owners association dues, leasehold payments, or subordinate financing payments; and any other pertinent information related to the property.

The lender's underwriter should carefully review the applicant's (or the appraiser's) projections (and if the applicant prepared the form, the appraiser's comments concerning those projections). Based on the appraiser's comments, the lender should make any necessary final adjustments for inconsistencies or missing data.

When the applicant will occupy one of the units of a two- to four-family property as a principal residence, income should not be calculated for the owner-occupied unit. Other specific instructions for completing the projections for *effective gross income* follow:

- *Annual rental at 100 percent occupancy.* Multiply the total monthly rental shown in the rent schedule by 12. If the lender disagrees with the applicant's figures, the reasons for the disagreement should be documented in writing.
- *Positive adjustments.* Any additional income should be added to the rental income. The source of that income—such as parking, laundry, etc.—also should be shown.
- *Negative adjustments.* The income should be reduced by the annual dollar amount of rent loss that can be expected as the result of anticipated vacancies or uncollectible rent from occupied units.

Specific instructions for completing the projections of *operating expenses* follow. Any operating expenses that relate to an owner-occupied unit in a two- to four-family property should not be included.

- *Heating, cooking, hot water.* If any of these items are provided by the applicant as part of the rent for a unit, the projected cost and type of fuel used should be included. When the costs for heating relate to public areas only, an appropriate notation should be made.
- *Electricity.* This should include only those projected expenses that will be incurred by the applicant over and above any similar expense for heating, cooking, or hot water already accounted for. If the expense relates to the cost of electricity for public areas only, an appropriate notation should be made.
- *Water/sewer.* These projected expenses should not be included when they are part of the real estate tax bill or when the units are serviced by an on-site private system.
- *Casual labor.* This includes the costs for public area cleaning, snow removal, etc., even though the applicant may not elect to contract for such services.
- *Interior paint/decorating.* This includes the costs of contract labor and materials that are required to maintain the interiors of the living units.
- *General repairs/maintenance.* This includes the costs of contract labor and materials that are required to maintain the public corridors, stairways, roofs, mechanical systems, grounds, etc.

- *Management expenses.* These are the customary expenses that a professional management company would charge to manage the property.
- *Supplies.* This includes the costs of items like light bulbs and janitorial supplies.
- *Total replacement reserves.* This represents the total average yearly reserves computed in the "Replacement Reserve Schedule" portion of the form. Generally, all equipment that has a remaining life of more than one year—such as refrigerators, stoves, clothes washers/dryers, trash compactors—should be expensed on a replacement cost basis, even if actual reserves are not provided for in the operating statement or are not customary in the local market.

Operating Income Reconciliation

The first formula in this section is used to determine the monthly operating income for a two- to four-family property when one unit is occupied by the applicant as a principal residence. The monthly operating income should be applied either as income or debt in accordance with the instructions on the form.

Both formulas must be used to determine the net cash flow for a single-family investment property or for a two- to four-family property that the applicant will not occupy. The net cash flow should be applied as either income or debt in accordance with the instructions on the form.

Single-Family Comparable Rent Schedule (Fannie Mae Form 1007/Freddie Mac Form 1000)

Instructions

The appraiser prepares this form as an attachment to the appraisal for a single-family investment property. The lender should retain the original of the form and the appraiser, the copy.

The form presents the information needed to determine the market rent for single-family properties. It calls for information on the physical structure, location and lease terms.

Small Residential Income Property Appraisal Report (Fannie Mae Form 1025/Freddie Mac Form 72)

Instructions

The lender should complete the top portion of the form before giving it to the appraiser, who should fill in any information the lender did not provide. The lender should retain the original of the completed form, and the appraiser should retain the copy.

The appraiser should provide a description and analysis of the neighborhood, site, and improvements. The valuation should include both rental and sales comparables; however, the same properties do not have to be used as both a rental and a sales comparable. In addition, the appraiser must attach the standard required exhibits—see Part VII, Section 204—to support each appraisal report.

Units of Comparison

If the comparable properties are not very similar to the subject property, the appraiser must reconcile the indicators of value—the value per unit, the value per room, the value per square foot of gross building area, and the value per the gross rent multiplier—to develop a valid unit comparison that can be used in the valuation process. The appraiser should indicate in a market data analysis (or in an addendum to the appraisal report form) the adjustments that were made, explain the reasons for each adjustment, and note which indicators were given the most weight.

Rent Forecasts

The appraiser must comment on how well the rent comparables compare to the subject property. He or she also should note and explain any adjustments that were made to arrive at the gross monthly forecasted rent (unfurnished) for the subject property. When estimating stabilized or forecasted rents, the appraiser must base the estimate on the level of rents currently obtainable on the effective date of the appraisal and must not use the projection of future rent values.

Operating Income Statement
One- to Four-Family Investment Property and Two- to Four-Family Owner-Occupied Property

Property Address

Street	City	State	Zip Code

General Instructions: This form is to be prepared jointly by the loan applicant, the appraiser, and the lender's underwriter. The applicant must complete the following schedule indicating each unit's rental status, lease expiration date, current rent, market rent, and the responsibility for utility expenses. Rental figures must be based on the rent for an "unfurnished" unit.

	Currently Rented	Expiration Date	Current Rent Per Month	Market Rent Per Month	Utility Expense	Paid By Owner	Paid By Tenant
Unit No. 1	Yes ___ No ___	_____	$_____	$_____	Electricity..........	☐	☐
Unit No. 2	Yes ___ No ___	_____	$_____	$_____	Gas.................	☐	☐
Unit No. 3	Yes ___ No ___	_____	$_____	$_____	Fuel Oil	☐	☐
Unit No. 4	Yes ___ No ___	_____	$_____	$_____	Fuel (Other)	☐	☐
Total			$_____	$_____	Water/Sewer	☐	☐
					Trash Removal	☐	☐

The applicant should complete all of the income and expense projections and for existing properties provide actual year-end operating statements for the past two years (for new properties the applicant's projected income and expenses must be provided). This Operating Income Statement and any previous operating statements the applicant provides must then be sent to the appraiser for review, comment, and/or adjustments next to the applicant's figures (e.g., Applicant/Appraiser 288/300). If the appraiser is retained to complete the form instead of the applicant, the lender must provide to the appraiser the aforementioned operating statements, mortgage insurance premium, HOA dues, leasehold payments, subordinate financing, and/or any other relevant information as to the income and expenses of the subject property received from the applicant to substantiate the projections. The underwriter should carefully review the applicant's/appraiser's projections and the appraiser's comments concerning those projections. The underwriter should make any final adjustments that are necessary to more accurately reflect any income or expense items that appear unreasonable for the market. (Real estate taxes and insurance on these types of properties are included in PITI and not calculated as an annual expense item.) Income should be based on current rents, but should not exceed market rents. When there are no current rents because the property is proposed, new, or currently vacant, market rents should be used.

Annual Income and Expense Projection for Next 12 months

Income (Do not include income for owner-occupied units)	By Applicant/Appraiser	Adjustments by Lender's Underwriter
Gross Annual Rental (from unit(s) to be rented)	$_____	$_____
Other Income (include sources)	+_____	+_____
Total	$_____	$_____
Less Vacancy/Rent Loss	-_____ (%)	-_____ (%)
Effective Gross Income	$_____	$_____

Expenses (Do not include expenses for owner-occupied units)

Electricity	_____	_____
Gas	_____	_____
Fuel Oil	_____	_____
Fuel ....(Type - _____)	_____	_____
Water/Sewer	_____	_____
Trash Removal	_____	_____
Pest Control	_____	_____
Other Taxes or Licenses	_____	_____
Casual Labor	_____	_____
This includes the costs for public area cleaning, snow removal, etc., even though the applicant may not elect to contract for such services.		
Interior Paint/Decorating	_____	_____
This includes the costs of contract labor and materials that are required to maintain the interiors of the living units.		
General Repairs/Maintenance	_____	_____
This includes the costs of contract labor and materials that are required to maintain the public corridors, stairways, roofs, mechanical systems, grounds, etc.		
Management Expenses	_____	_____
These are the customary expenses that a professional management company would charge to manage the property.		
Supplies	_____	_____
This includes the costs of items like light bulbs, janitorial supplies, etc.		
Total Replacement Reserves - See Schedule on Pg. 2	_____	_____
Miscellaneous	_____	_____
	_____	_____
	_____	_____
	_____	_____
	_____	_____
	_____	_____
	_____	_____
Total Operating Expenses	$_____	$_____

Replacement Reserve Schedule

Adequate replacement reserves must be calculated regardless of whether actual reserves are provided for on the owner's operating statements or are customary in the local market. This represents the total average yearly reserves. Generally, all equipment and components that have a remaining life of more than one year—such as refrigerators, stoves, clothes washers/dryers, trash compactors, furnaces, roofs, and carpeting, etc.—should be expensed on a replacement cost basis.

Equipment	Replacement Cost	Remaining Life		By Applicant/ Appraiser	Lender Adjustments
Stoves/Ranges	@ $_____ ea.	÷ ____ Yrs. x	_____ Units = $	$_____	$_____
Refrigerators	@ $_____ ea.	÷ ____ Yrs. x	_____ Units = $	$_____	$_____
Dishwashers	@ $_____ ea.	÷ ____ Yrs. x	_____ Units = $	$_____	$_____
A/C Units	@ $_____ ea.	÷ ____ Yrs. x	_____ Units = $	$_____	$_____
C. Washer/Dryers	@ $_____ ea.	÷ ____ Yrs. x	_____ Units = $	$_____	$_____
HW Heaters	@ $_____ ea.	÷ ____ Yrs. x	_____ Units = $	$_____	$_____
Furnace(s)	@ $_____ ea.	÷ ____ Yrs. x	_____ Units = $	$_____	$_____
(Other)	@ $_____ ea.	÷ ____ Yrs. x	_____ Units = $	$_____	$_____
Roof	@ $_____	÷ ____ Yrs. x One Bldg. =		$_____	$_____

Carpeting (Wall to Wall)   Remaining Life

(Units) ____ Total Sq. Yds. @ $____ Per Sq. Yd. ÷ ____Yrs. = $_____ $_____

(Public Areas) ____ Total Sq. Yds. @ $____ Per Sq. Yd. ÷ ____Yrs. = $_____ $_____

Total Replacement Reserves. (Enter on Pg. 1) $_____ $_____

Operating Income Reconciliation

$_____ − $_____ = $_____ ÷ 12 = $_____
Effective Gross Income — Total Operating Expenses — Operating Income — Monthly Operating Income

$_____ − $_____ = $_____
Monthly Operating Income — Monthly Housing Expense — Net Cash Flow

(Note: Monthly Housing Expense includes principal and interest on the mortgage, hazard insurance premiums, real estate taxes, mortgage insurance premiums, HOA dues, leasehold payments, and subordinate financing payments.)

Underwriter's instructions for 2-4 Family Owner-Occupied Properties

- If Monthly Operating Income is a positive number, enter as "Net Rental Income" in the "Gross Monthly Income" section of Freddie Mac Form 65/Fannie Mae Form 1003. If Monthly Operating Income is a negative number, it must be included as a liability for qualification purposes.

- The borrower's monthly housing expense-to-income ratio must be calculated by comparing the total Monthly Housing Expense for the subject property to the borrower's stable monthly income.

Underwriter's instructions for 1-4 Family Investment Properties

- If Net Cash Flow is a positive number, enter as "Net Rental Income" in the "Gross Monthly Income" section of Freddie Mac Form 65/Fannie Mae Form 1003. If Net Cash Flow is a negative number, it must be included as a liability for qualification purposes.

- The borrower's monthly housing expense-to-income ratio must be calculated by comparing the total monthly housing expense for the borrower's primary residence to the borrower's stable monthly income.

Appraiser's Comments (Including sources for data and rationale for the projections)

Appraiser Name _____ Appraiser Signature _____ Date _____

Underwriter's Comments and Rationale for Adjustments

Underwriter Name _____ Underwriter Signature _____ Date _____

Freddie Mac
Form 998 Aug 88   Page 2 of 2   Fannie Mae Form 216 Aug 88

SINGLE FAMILY COMPARABLE RENT SCHEDULE

This form is intended to provide the appraiser with a familiar format to estimate the market rent of the subject property. Adjustments should be made only for items of significant difference between the comparables and the subject property.

ITEM	SUBJECT	COMPARABLE NO. 1		COMPARABLE NO. 2		COMPARABLE NO. 3	
Address							
Proximity to Subject							
Date Lease Begins Date Lease Expires							
Monthly Rental	If Currently Rented: $	$		$		$	
Less: Utilities Furniture	$	$		$		$	
Adjusted Monthly Rent	$	$		$		$	
Data Source							
RENT ADJUSTMENTS	DESCRIPTION	DESCRIPTION	+(−) $ Adjustment	DESCRIPTION	+(−) $ Adjustment	DESCRIPTION	+(−) $ Adjustment
Rent Concessions							
Location/View							
Design and Appeal							
Age/Condition							
Above Grade Room Count	Total Bdrms Baths	Total Bdrms Baths		Total Bdrms Baths		Total Bdrms Baths	
Gross Living Area	Sq. Ft.	Sq. Ft.		Sq. Ft.		Sq. Ft.	
Other (e.g., basement, etc.)							
Other:							
Net Adj. (total)		+ − $		+ − $		+ − $	
Indicated Monthly Market Rent		$		$		$	

Comments on market data, including the range of rents for single family properties, an estimate of vacancy for single family rental properties, the general trend of rents and vacancy, and support for the above adjustments. (Rent concessions should be adjusted to the market, not to the subject property.)

Final Reconciliation of Market Rent:

I (WE) ESTIMATE THE MONTHLY MARKET RENT OF THE SUBJECT AS OF _____ 19____ TO BE $_____

Appraiser(s) SIGNATURE _____

NAME _____

Review Appraiser SIGNATURE _____
(If applicable)

NAME _____

This form must be reproduced by the Seller.

Freddie Mac Form 1000 (8/88)

Fannie Mae Form 1007 (8/88)

X X

SMALL RESIDENTIAL INCOME PROPERTY APPRAISAL REPORT   File No.

Property Address		City		State	Zip Code

Legal Description			County	

Assessor's Parcel No.	Tax Year	R.E. Taxes $	Special Assessments $

Neighborhood or Project Name	Map Reference	Census Tract

Borrower	Current Owner	Occupant	☐ Owner	☐ Tenant	☐ Vacant

Property rights appraised	☐ Fee Simple	☐ Leasehold	Project Type	☐ PUD	☐ Condominium	HOA$	/Mo.

Sales Price $	Date of Sale	Description and $ amount of loan charges/concessions to be paid by seller

Lender/Client	Address

Appraiser	Address

Location	☐ Urban	☐ Suburban	☐ Rural	Predominant Single Family Occupancy	Single family housing PRICE $ (000) / AGE (yrs)	Predominant 2-4 Family Occupancy	2-4 family housing PRICE $ (000) / AGE (yrs)
Built up	☐ Over 75%	☐ 25-75%	☐ Under 25%	☐ Owner	Low	☐ Owner	Low
Growth rate	☐ Rapid	☐ Stable	☐ Slow	☐ Tenant	High	☐ Tenant	High
Property values	☐ Increasing	☐ Stable	☐ Declining	☐ Vacant (0-5%)	Predominant	☐ Vacant (0-5%)	Predominant
Demand/supply	☐ Shortage	☐ In balance	☐ Over supply	☐ Vacant (over 5%)		☐ Vacant (over 5%)	
Marketing time	☐ Under 3 mos.	☐ 3-6 mos.	☐ Over 6 mos.				

Typical 2-4 family bldg. Type _____ No. stories _____ No. units _____ Age _____ yrs.

Typical rents $ _____ to $ _____ ☐ increasing ☐ Stable ☐ Declining

Est. neighborhood apt. vacancy _____ % ☐ increasing ☐ Stable ☐ Declining

Rent controls ☐ Yes ☐ No ☐ Likely If yes or likely, describe _____

Present land use %		Land use change	
One family	_____	☐ Not likely	☐ Likely
2-4 family	_____	☐ In process to:	
Multi-family	_____		
Commercial	_____		
( )			

Note: Race and the racial composition of the neighborhood are not appraisal factors.

Neighborhood boundaries and characteristics: _____

Factors that affect the marketability of the properties in the neighborhood (proximity to employment and amenities, employment stability, appeal to market, etc.): _____

The following available listings represent the most current, similar, and proximate competitive properties to the subject property in the subject neighborhood. This analysis is intended to evaluate the inventory currently on the market competing with the subject property in the subject neighborhood and recent price and marketing time trends affecting the subject property. (Listings outside the subject neighborhood are not considered applicable). The listing comparables can be the rental or sale comparables if they are currently for sale.

ITEM	SUBJECT	COMPARABLE LISTING NO. 1	COMPARABLE LISTING NO. 2	COMPARABLE LISTING NO. 3
Address				
Proximity to subject				
Listing price	$	☐ Unf. ☐ Furn. $	☐ Unf. ☐ Furn. $	☐ Unf. ☐ Furn. $
Approximate GBA				
Data source				
# Units/Tot. rms./BR/BA				
Approximate year built				
Approx. days on market				

Comparison of listings to subject property: _____

Market conditions that affect 2-4 family properties in the subject neighborhood (including the above neighborhood indicators of growth rate, property values, demand/supply, and marketing time) and the prevalence and impact in the subject market area regarding loan discounts, interest buydowns and concessions, and identification of trends in listing prices, average days on market and any change over past year, etc.: _____

Dimensions _____

Site area _____ Corner lot ☐ No ☐ Yes

Specific zoning classification and description _____

Zoning compliance ☐ Legal ☐ Legal nonconforming (Grandfathered use) ☐ Illegal ☐ No zoning

Highest & best use as improved: ☐ Present use ☐ Other use (explain) _____

Topography	_____
Size	_____
Shape	_____
Drainage	_____
View	_____
Landscaping	_____
Driveway	_____
Apparent easements	_____

Utilities	Public	Other	Off-site improvements	Type	Public	Private
Electricity			Street			
Gas			Curb/gutter			
Water			Sidewalk			
Sanitary sewer			Street lights			
Storm sewer			Alley			

FEMA Special Flood Hazard Area ☐ Yes ☐ No

FEMA Zone _____ Map Date _____

FEMA Map No. _____

Comments (apparent adverse easements, encroachments, special assessments, slide areas, illegal or legal nonconforming zoning, use, etc.): _____

SMALL RESIDENTIAL INCOME PROPERTY APPRAISAL REPORT

General description	Exterior description (Materials/condition)	Foundation	Insulation (R-value if known)
Units/bldgs. ___ /	Foundation ___	Slab ___	☐ Roof
Stories ___	Exterior walls ___	Crawl space ___	☐ Ceiling
Type (det./att.) ___	Roof surface ___	Sump Pump ___	☐ Walls
Design (style) ___	Gutters & dwnspts. ___	Dampness ___	☐ Floor
Existing/proposed ___	Window type ___	Settlement ___	☐ None
Under construction ___	Storm sash/Screens ___	Infestation ___	Adequacy ___
Year Built ___	Manufactured housing* ☐ Yes ☐ No	Basement ___ % of 1st floor area	Energy efficient items: ___
Effective age(yrs.) ___	*(Complies with the HUD Manufactured Housing Construction and Safety Standards.)	Basement finish ___	

Units	Level(s)	Foyer	Living	Dining	Kitchen	Den	Family rm.	Bedrooms	# Baths	Laundry	Other	Sq. ft./unit	Total ☑

Improvements contain: ___ Rooms; ___ Bedroom(s); ___ Bath(s); ___ Square feet of GROSS BUILDING AREA

GROSS BUILDING AREA (GBA) IS DEFINED AS THE TOTAL FINISHED AREA (INCLUDING COMMON AREAS) OF THE IMPROVEMENTS BASED UPON EXTERIOR MEASUREMENTS.

Surfaces	(Materials/condition)	Heating		Kitchen equip.	(# / unit- cond.)	Attic		Car Storage	No. Cars
Floors ___		Type ___		Refrigerator ___		☐ None		Garage	☐
Walls ___		Fuel ___		Range/oven ___		☐ Stairs		Carport	☐
Trim/finish ___		Condition ___		Disposal ___		☐ Drop stair		Attached	☐
Bath floor ___				Dishwasher ___		☐ Scuttle		Detached	☐
Bath wainscot ___		Cooling ___		Fan/hood ___		☐ Floor		Adequate	☐
Doors ___		Central ___		Compactor ___		☐ Heated		Inadequate	☐
		Other ___		Washer/dryer ___		☐ Finished		Offstreet	☐
		Condition ___		Microwave ___		☐ Unfinished		None	☐
Fireplace(s) # ___				Intercom ___					

Condition of the improvements, repairs needed, quality of construction, additional features, modernization, etc.: ___

Depreciation (physical, functional, and external inadequacies, etc.): ___

Adverse environmental conditions (such as, but not limited to, hazardous wastes, toxic substances, etc.) present in the improvements, on the site, or in the immediate vicinity of the subject property: ___

ESTIMATED SITE VALUE . . . . = $ ___
ESTIMATED REPRODUCTION COST—NEW OF IMPROVEMENTS:

___ Sq. Ft. @ $ ___	= $ ___	
___ Sq. Ft. @ $ ___	= $ ___	
___ Sq. Ft. @ $ ___	= $ ___	
___ Sq. Ft. @ $ ___	= $ ___	
___ Sq. Ft. @ $ ___	= $ ___	
	= $ ___	
	= $ ___	
	= $ ___	
	= $ ___	

Comments on Cost Approach (such as, source of cost estimate, site value, square foot calculation and, for HUD and VA, the estimated remaining economic life of the property): ___

Special Energy Efficient Items ___ = $ ___
Porches, Patios, etc. ___ = $ ___
Total Estimated Cost New . . . . = $ ___

	Physical	Functional	External
Less Depreciation			= $ ___

Depreciated Value of Improvements . . . . = $ ___
"As is" Value of Site Improvements . . . . = $ ___
INDICATED VALUE BY COST APPROACH . . . . . . = $ ___

SMALL RESIDENTIAL INCOME PROPERTY APPRAISAL REPORT

At least three rental comparables should be reported and analyzed in this section. The rental comparables should represent the most current rental information on properties as similar and proximate to the subject property as possible. (This comparison is based on current rental data, therefore, the rental comparables typically are not the same comparables used in the sales comparison analysis.) The appraisal report should assure the reader that the units and properties selected as comparables are comparable to the subject property (both the units and the overall property) and accurately represent the rental market for the subject property (unless otherwise stated within the report).

ITEM	SUBJECT	COMPARABLE RENTAL NO. 1	COMPARABLE RENTAL NO. 2	COMPARABLE RENTAL NO. 3
Address				
Proximity to subject				
Lease dates (if available)				
Rent survey date				
Data source				
Rent concessions				
Description of property—units, design, appeal, age, vacancies, and conditions	No. Units / No. Vac. / Yr. Blt.:	No. Units / No. Vac. / Yr. Blt.:	No. Units / No. Vac. / Yr. Blt.:	No. Units / No. Vac. / Yr. Blt.:

Individual unit breakdown	Rm. Count (Tot/Br/Ba)	Size Sq. Ft.		Rm. Count (Tot/Br/Ba)	Size Sq. Ft.	Total Monthly Rent	Rm. Count (Tot/Br/Ba)	Size Sq. Ft.	Total Monthly Rent	Rm. Count (Tot/Br/Ba)	Size Sq. Ft.	Total Monthly Rent

Utilities, furniture, and amenities included in rent				
Functional utility, basement, heating/cooling, project amenities, etc.				

Analysis of rental data and support for estimated market rents for the individual subject units (including the adjustments used, the adequacy of comparables, rental concessions, etc.)

Subject's rent schedule   The rent schedule reconciles the applicable indicated monthly market rents to the appropriate subject unit, and provides the estimated rents for the subject property. The appraiser must review the rent characteristics of the comparable sales to determine whether estimated rents should reflect actual or market rents. For example, if actual rents were available on the sales comparables and used to derive the gross rent multiplier (GRM), actual rents for the subject should be used. If market rents were used to construct the comparables' rents and derive the GRM, market rents should be used. The total gross estimated rent is not adjusted for vacancy. The total gross estimated rent must represent rent characteristics consistent with the sales comparable data used to derive the GRM.

Unit	LEASES		No. Units Vacant	ACTUAL RENTS			ESTIMATED RENTS		
	Lease Date Begin	End		Per Unit Unfurnished	Furnished	Total Rents	Per Unit Unfurnished	Furnished	Total Rents
				$		$	$		$
						$			$

Other monthly income (itemize) _____ $ _____
Vacancy: Actual last year _____ % Previous year _____ % Estimated: _____ % $ _____ Annually Total gross estimated rent $ _____
Utilities included in estimated rents: ☐ Electric ☐ Water ☐ Sewer ☐ Gas ☐ Oil ☐ Trash collection

Comments on the rent schedule, actual rents, estimated rents (especially regarding differences between actual and estimated rents), utilities, etc.: _____

SMALL RESIDENTIAL INCOME PROPERTY APPRAISAL REPORT

The undersigned has recited three recent sales of properties most similar and proximate to the subject property and has described and analyzed these in this analysis. If there is a significant variation between the subject and comparable properties, the analysis includes a dollar adjustment reflecting the market reaction to those items or an explanation supported by the market data. If a significant item in the comparable property is superior to, or more favorable than, the subject property, a minus (–) adjustment is made, thus reducing the adjusted sales price of the comparable property; if a significant item in the comparable property is inferior to, or less favorable than, the subject property, a plus (+) adjustment is made, thus increasing the adjusted sales price of the comparable property. [(1) Sales Price ÷ Gross Monthly Rent]

ITEM	SUBJECT	COMPARABLE SALE NO. 1		COMPARABLE SALE NO. 2		COMPARABLE SALE NO. 3	
Address							
Proximity to subject							
Sales price	$	Unf. ☐ Furn. $		Unf. ☐ Furn. $		Unf. ☐ Furn. $	
Sales price per GBA	$	$		$		$	
Gross monthly rent	$	$		$		$	
Gross mo. rent mult. (1)							
Sales price per unit	$	$		$		$	
Sales price per room	$	$		$		$	
Data and/or Verification Sources							
ADJUSTMENTS	DESCRIPTION	DESCRIPTION	+ (–) $ Adjustment	DESCRIPTION	+ (–) $ Adjustment	DESCRIPTION	+ (–) $ Adjustment
Sales or financing concessions							
Date of sale/time							
Location							
Leasehold/Fee Simple							
Site							
View							
Design and appeal							
Quality of construction							
Age							
Condition							
Gross Building Area	Sq. ft.	Sq. ft.		Sq. ft.		Sq. ft.	
Unit breakdown	No. of units / Rm. count Tot Br Ba / No. Vac.	No. of units / Rm. count Tot Br Ba / No. Vac.		No. of units / Rm. count Tot Br Ba / No. Vac.		No. of units / Rm. count Tot Br Ba / No. Vac.	
Basement description							
Functional utility							
Heating/cooling							
Parking on/off site							
Project amenities and fee (if applicable)							
Net Adj. (total)		+ ☐ – $		+ ☐ – $		+ ☐ – $	
Adjusted sales price of comparable		$		$		$	

Comments on sales comparison (including reconciliation of all indicators of value as to consistency and relative strength and evaluation of the typical investor's/purchaser's motivation in that market): _____

ITEM	SUBJECT	COMPARABLE NO. 1	COMPARABLE NO. 2	COMPARABLE NO. 3
Date, Price and Data Source for prior sales within year of appraisal				

Analysis of any current agreement of sale, option, or listing of the subject property and analysis of any prior sales of subject and comparables within one year of the date of appraisal: _____

Total gross monthly estimated rent $ _____ x gross rent multiplier (GRM) _____ = $ _____ INDICATED VALUE BY INCOME APPROACH
Comments on income approach (including expense ratios, if available, and reconciliation of the GRM) _____

INDICATED VALUE BY SALES COMPARISON APPROACH . . . . $ _____
INDICATED VALUE BY INCOME APPROACH . . . . $ _____
INDICATED VALUE BY COST APPROACH . . . . $ _____
This appraisal is made ☐ "as is" ☐ subject to the repairs, alterations, inspections, or conditions listed below ☐ subject to completion per plans and specifications.
Comments and conditions of appraisal: _____

Final reconciliation: _____

The purpose of this appraisal is to estimate the market value of the real property that is the subject of this report, based on the above conditions and the certification, contingent and limiting conditions, and market value definition that are stated in the attached Freddie Mac Form 439/Fannie Mae Form 1004B (Revised _____).
I (WE) ESTIMATE THE MARKET VALUE, AS DEFINED, OF THE REAL PROPERTY THAT IS THE SUBJECT OF THIS REPORT, AS OF _____
(WHICH IS THE DATE OF INSPECTION AND THE EFFECTIVE DATE OF THIS REPORT) TO BE $ _____

APPRAISER:	SUPERVISORY APPRAISER (ONLY IF REQUIRED):	
Signature	Signature	☐ Did ☐ Did Not
Name	Name	Inspect Property
Date Report Signed	Date Report Signed	
State Certification # _____ State	State Certification # _____ State	
Or State License # _____ State	Or State License # _____ State	

Freddie Mac Form 72 10-94   10 CH.   PAGE 4 OF 4   Fannie Mae Form 1025 10-94

XX

Property Description

UNIFORM RESIDENTIAL APPRAISAL REPORT File No. ___

Property Address	City	State	Zip Code
Legal Description		County	
Assessor's Parcel No.	Tax Year	R.E. Taxes $	Special Assessments $
Borrower	Current Owner	Occupant	Owner ☐ Tenant ☐ Vacant ☐
Property rights appraised ☐ Fee Simple ☐ Leasehold	Project Type ☐ PUD ☐ Condominium (HUD/VA only)	HOA $	/Mo.
Neighborhood or Project Name	Map Reference	Census Tract	
Sales Price $	Date of Sale	Description and $ amount of loan charges/concessions to be paid by seller	
Lender/Client	Address		
Appraiser	Address		

SUBJECT

NEIGHBORHOOD

Location	Urban ☐	Suburban ☐	Rural ☐	Predominant occupancy	Single family housing		Present land use %	Land use change
					PRICE $ (000)	AGE (yrs)		
Built up	Over 75% ☐	25-75% ☐	Under 25% ☐	Owner ☐			One family	Not likely ☐ Likely ☐
Growth rate	Rapid ☐	Stable ☐	Slow ☐	Tenant ☐	Low		2-4 family	In process ☐
Property values	Increasing ☐	Stable ☐	Declining ☐	Vacant (0-5%) ☐	High		Multi-family	To:
Demand/supply	Shortage ☐	In balance ☐	Over supply ☐	Vacant (over 5%) ☐	Predominant		Commercial	
Marketing time	Under 3 mos. ☐	3-6 mos. ☐	Over 6 mos. ☐				( )	

Note: Race and the racial composition of the neighborhood are not appraisal factors.

Neighborhood boundaries and characteristics: ___

Factors that affect the marketability of the properties in the neighborhood (proximity to employment and amenities, employment stability, appeal to market, etc.): ___

Market conditions in the subject neighborhood (including support for the above conclusions related to the trend of property values, demand/supply, and marketing time -- such as data on competitive properties for sale in the neighborhood, description of the prevalence of sales and financing concessions, etc.): ___

PUD

Project Information for PUDs (if applicable) - - Is the developer/builder in control of the Home Owners' Association (HOA)?   Yes ☐   No ☐

Approximate total number of units in the subject project ___ . Approximate total number of units for sale in the subject project ___ .

Describe common elements and recreational facilities: ___

SITE

Dimensions ___	Topography ___	
Site area ___	Corner Lot Yes ☐ No ☐	Size ___
Specific zoning classification and description ___	Shape ___	
Zoning compliance ☐ Legal ☐ Legal nonconforming (Grandfathered use) ☐ Illegal ☐ No zoning	Drainage ___	
Highest & best use as improved ☐ Present use ☐ Other use (explain)	View ___	

Utilities	Public	Other	Off-site Improvements	Type	Public	Private	
Electricity	☐		Street		☐	☐	Landscaping ___
Gas	☐		Curb/gutter		☐	☐	Driveway Surface ___
Water	☐		Sidewalk		☐	☐	Apparent easements ___
Sanitary sewer	☐		Street lights		☐	☐	FEMA Special Flood Hazard Area Yes ☐ No ☐
Storm sewer	☐		Alley		☐	☐	FEMA Zone ___ Map Date ___
							FEMA Map No. ___

Comments (apparent adverse easements, encroachments, special assessments, slide areas, illegal or legal nonconforming zoning use, etc.): ___

DESCRIPTION OF IMPROVEMENTS

GENERAL DESCRIPTION	EXTERIOR DESCRIPTION	FOUNDATION	BASEMENT	INSULATION
No. of Units	Foundation	Slab	Area Sq. Ft.	Roof
No. of Stories	Exterior Walls	Crawl Space	% Finished	Ceiling ☐
Type (Det./Att.)	Roof Surface	Basement	Ceiling	Walls ☐
Design (Style)	Gutters & Dwnspts.	Sump Pump	Walls	Floor ☐
Existing/Proposed	Window Type	Dampness	Floor	None ☐
Age (Yrs.)	Storm/Screens	Settlement	Outside Entry	Unknown ☐
Effective Age (Yrs.)	Manufactured House	Infestation		

ROOMS	Foyer	Living	Dining	Kitchen	Den	Family Rm.	Rec. Rm.	Bedrooms	# Baths	Laundry	Other	Area Sq. Ft.
Basement												
Level 1												
Level 2												

Finished area above grade contains: Rooms;   Bedroom(s);   Bath(s);   Square Feet of Gross Living Area

INTERIOR	Materials/Condition	HEATING		KITCHEN EQUIP.		ATTIC		AMENITIES		CAR STORAGE	
Floors		Type		Refrigerator	☐	None	☐	Fireplace(s) #		None	☐
Walls		Fuel		Range/Oven	☐	Stairs	☐	Patio		Garage	# of cars
Trim/Finish		Condition		Disposal	☐	Drop Stair	☐	Deck		Attached	
Bath Floor		COOLING		Dishwasher	☐	Scuttle	☐	Porch		Detached	
Bath Wainscot		Central		Fan/Hood	☐	Floor	☐	Fence		Built-In	
Doors		Other		Microwave	☐	Heated	☐	Pool		Carport	
		Condition		Washer/Dryer	☐	Finished	☐			Driveway	

Additional features (special energy efficient items, etc.): ___

COMMENTS

Condition of the improvements, depreciation (physical, functional, and external), repairs needed, quality of construction, remodeling/additions, etc.: ___

Adverse environmental conditions (such as, but not limited to, hazardous wastes, toxic substances, etc.) present in the improvements, on the site, or in the immediate vicinity of the subject property: ___

Valuation Section

UNIFORM RESIDENTIAL APPRAISAL REPORT

File No.

COST APPROACH

ESTIMATED SITE VALUE . . . . = $ ________

ESTIMATED REPRODUCTION COST-NEW OF IMPROVEMENTS:

Dwelling ________ Sq. Ft @ $ ________ = $ ________

________ Sq. Ft @ $ ________ = ________

________ = ________

________ = ________

Garage/Carport ________ Sq. Ft @ $ ________ = ________

Total Estimated Cost-New . . . . = $ ________

Less	Physical	Functional	External
Depreciation			= $

Depreciated Value of Improvements . . . . = $ ________

"As-is" Value of Site Improvements . . . . = $ ________

INDICATED VALUE BY COST APPROACH . . . . = $ ________

Comments on Cost Approach (such as, source of cost estimate, site value, square foot calculation and, for HUD, VA and FmHA, the estimated remaining economic life of the property): ________

SALES COMPARISON ANALYSIS

ITEM	SUBJECT	COMPARABLE NO. 1		COMPARABLE NO. 2		COMPARABLE NO. 3	
Address							
Proximity to Subject							
Sales Price	$		$		$		$
Price/Gross Liv. Area	$ ☐	$ ☐		$ ☐		$ ☐	
Data and/or Verification Sources							
VALUE ADJUSTMENTS	DESCRIPTION	DESCRIPTION	+ (-) $ Adjustment	DESCRIPTION	+ (-) $ Adjustment	DESCRIPTION	+ (-) $ Adjustment
Sales or Financing Concessions							
Date of Sale/Time							
Location							
Leasehold/Fee Simple							
Site							
View							
Design and Appeal							
Quality of Construction							
Age							
Condition							
Above Grade Room Count	Total Bdrms Baths	Total Bdrms Baths		Total Bdrms Baths		Total Bdrms Baths	
Gross Living Area	Sq. Ft.	Sq. Ft.		Sq. Ft.		Sq. Ft.	
Basement & Finished Rooms Below Grade							
Functional Utility							
Heating/Cooling							
Energy Efficient Items							
Garage/Carport							
Porch, Patio, Deck, Fireplace(s), etc.							
Fence, Pool, etc.							
Net Adj. (total)		☐ + ☐ -	$	☐ + ☐ -	$	☐ + ☐ -	$
Adjusted Sales Price of Comparable			$		$		$

Comments on Sales Comparison (including the subject property's compatibility to the neighborhood, etc.): ________

ITEM	SUBJECT	COMPARABLE NO. 1	COMPARABLE NO. 2	COMPARABLE NO. 3
Date, Price and Data Source for prior sales within year of appraisal				

Analysis of any current agreement of sale, option, or listing of the subject property and analysis of any prior sales of subject and comparables within one year of the date of appraisal:

INDICATED VALUE BY SALES COMPARISON APPROACH . . . . $ ________

INDICATED VALUE BY INCOME APPROACH (If Applicable) Estimated Market Rent $ ________ /Mo. x Gross Rent Multiplier ________ = $ ________

RECONCILIATION

This appraisal is made ☐ "as is" ☐ subject to the repairs, alterations, inspections, or conditions listed below ☐ subject to completion per plans and specifications.

Conditions of Appraisal: ________

Final Reconciliation: ________

The purpose of this appraisal is to estimate the market value of the real property that is the subject of this report, based on the above conditions and the certification, contingent and limiting conditions, and market value definition that are stated in the attached Freddie Mac Form 439/Fannie Mae Form 1004B (Revised ________).

I (WE) ESTIMATE THE MARKET VALUE, AS DEFINED, OF THE REAL PROPERTY THAT IS THE SUBJECT OF THIS REPORT, AS OF ________

(WHICH IS THE DATE OF INSPECTION AND THE EFFECTIVE DATE OF THIS REPORT) TO BE $ ________.

APPRAISER:		SUPERVISORY APPRAISER (ONLY IF REQUIRED):	
Signature		Signature	☐ Did ☐ Did Not
Name		Name	Inspect Property
Date Report Signed		Date Report Signed	
State Certification #	State	State Certification #	State
Or State License #	State	Or State License #	State

Freddie Mac Form 70 6-93 10 CH. PAGE 2 OF 2 Fannie Mae Form 1004 6-93

Do-It-Yourself Refinance Worksheet

Should you refinance? Refinancing can save you a lot of money, but it costs a lot to refinance. Estimate your interest savings and pay-back period. The following worksheet helps you decide whether the savings justify the costs.

Old Mortgage

Initial Mortgage Amount (A)

Enter the original amount of your old mortgage.

Age of Mortgage (B)

Enter the number of years that you have had your old mortgage.

Old Interest Rate (C)

Enter the interest rate of your old mortgage. If your old loan-to-value (LTV) ratio is greater than 80 percent, you probably are paying a mortgage insurance premium. If so, and you have a conventional mortgage, add 0.25 percent to your old interest rate and enter the sum. If you have an FHA loan, add 0.50 percent to your old interest rate and enter the sum. If you have a VA loan, simply enter the old interest rate.

Remaining Principal Balance (D)

Call your current lender for an approximate balance on your old mortgage, or you can estimate your remaining principal balance by multiplying your initial mortgage amount (A) times the appropriate factor from the table in Appendix J. If your loan has a 30-year term and is less than six years old, you can use the following abbreviated table.

Remaining Principal Balance Factors (for 30-Year Loans)

Interest Rate	Age of Mortgage (Years)				
	1	2	3	4	5
15%	0.998	0.996	0.993	0.991	0.987
14	0.998	0.995	0.992	0.988	0.984
13	0.997	0.994	0.990	0.986	0.981
12	0.996	0.992	0.988	0.982	0.977
11	0.995	0.990	0.985	0.979	0.972
10	0.994	0.988	0.982	0.974	0.966
9	0.993	0.986	0.978	0.969	0.959
8	0.992	0.983	0.973	0.962	0.951

New Mortgage

Estimated Refinancing Costs

The following is a gross estimate. When you apply for a loan, your lender will give you a much more accurate "good faith estimate" of your closing (refinancing) costs. For purposes of this worksheet, this estimate should be close enough for you to decide whether to refinance.

Points

Enter the number of points quoted by your lender. Multiply the points (percentage) by the remaining principal balance (D) of your old mortgage and enter the dollar amount.

Do-It-Yourself Refinance Worksheet

OLD MORTGAGE

Initial Mortgage Amount $ _____ (A)

Age of Mortgage _____ Years (B)

Old Interest Rate ___._____ % (C)

Remaining Principal Balance

   Factor from Table ___._____ × (A) = $ _____ (D)

NEW MORTGAGE

Estimated Refinancing Costs

   Points ___._____ % × (D) = $ _____

   Fees + 700.00

   Other Costs 0.6% (or 1.1%) × (D) = + _____

      Total Estimated Costs $ _____ (E)

Estimated New Mortgage Amount (E) + (D) = $ _____ (F)

New Interest Rate ___._____ % (G)

SAVINGS AND PAYBACK PERIOD

Interest (Old Loan) (C) × (D) = $ _____

Interest (New Loan) (G) × (F) = – _____

Estimated First-Year Savings $ _____ (H)

PAYBACK PERIOD 12 × (E) ÷ (H) = _____ Months

Fees

The sum of the lender's other fees plus other professional services will amount to about $700.

Other Costs

Other costs will include title insurance, recording fees, and mortgage insurance. Multiply 0.6 percent (1.1 percent if your LTV ratio is greater than 80 percent and you are getting a conventional loan) by the remaining principal balance (D) of your old mortgage and enter the dollar amount.

Total Estimated Costs (E)

Enter the sum of the points, fees, and other costs.

Estimated New Mortgage Amount (F)

Enter the sum of total estimated costs (E) and remaining principal balance (D).

New Interest Rate (G)

Enter the current mortgage interest rate quoted by your lender. If your new loan-to-value ratio is greater than 80 percent and you are getting a conventional loan, add 0.30 percent to the new interest rate and enter the sum. If you are getting an FHA loan, add 0.50 percent to the new interest rate and enter the sum. If you are getting a VA loan, simply enter the new mortgage rate.

Savings and Payback Period

Calculating actual savings and payback period requires a computer for the complex mathematical formulas, but the following estimates are close enough for you to decide whether to refinance.

Interest (Old Loan)

Multiply old interest rate (C) by the remaining principal balance (D) and enter the dollar amount.

Interest (New Loan)

Multiply new interest rate (G) by the estimated new mortgage amount (F) and enter the dollar amount.

Estimated First-Year Savings (H)

Subtract interest (new loan) from interest (old loan) and enter the difference.

Payback Period

Multiply 12 by the total estimated costs (E) and divide by estimated first-year savings (H). Enter the answer.

I

Mortgage Payment Factor Tables

Principal repayment and interest make up the largest portion of your monthly mortgage payment (see "Introduction" and Appendix A). Initially, most of your payment goes to pay interest. After several years, however, much more of your payment is used to reduce the principal balance of your loan. For fully amortizing loans, your payment is set just high enough to pay off your loan by the final monthly payment.

You can estimate your monthly payment by using the following tables for loans with a term from 1 to 30 years, 35 years, or 40 years, and with interest rates from 2 percent to 19 percent.

Instructions

- Locate the table that has the term and interest rate of your loan.
- Read down the column for the term of your loan to the row for your interest rate to locate your mortgage payment factor.
- Multiply the factor times your loan amount and divide by 1,000.

For example, if you have a $75,000 30-year mortgage at 9.5 percent interest, your monthly principal and interest payment would be:

8.4085 (payment factor) × $75,000 ÷ 1,000 = $630.64

MONTHLY PAYMENT TO AMORTIZE A LOAN OF $1,000

Term of Loan

Interest Rate	1 Year	2 Years	3 Years	4 Years	5 Years	6 Years	7 Years	8 Years
2.000%	84.2389	42.5403	28.6426	21.6951	17.5278	14.7504	12.7674	11.2809
2.125%	84.2956	42.5952	28.6972	21.7497	17.5825	14.8054	12.8226	11.3364
2.250%	84.3524	42.6502	28.7518	21.8044	17.6373	14.8605	12.8780	11.3920
2.375%	84.4093	42.7053	28.8066	21.8592	17.6923	14.9157	12.9335	11.4478
2.500%	84.4661	42.7604	28.8614	21.9140	17.7474	14.9710	12.9892	11.5038
2.625%	84.5230	42.8155	28.9162	21.9690	17.8025	15.0265	13.0450	11.5600
2.750%	84.5799	42.8707	28.9712	22.0240	17.8578	15.0821	13.1009	11.6164
2.875%	84.6368	42.9259	29.0262	22.0791	17.9132	15.1378	13.1570	11.6729
3.000%	84.6937	42.9812	29.0812	22.1343	17.9687	15.1937	13.2133	11.7296
3.125%	84.7506	43.0365	29.1363	22.1896	18.0243	15.2497	13.2697	11.7864
3.250%	84.8076	43.0919	29.1915	22.2450	18.0800	15.3058	13.3263	11.8435
3.375%	84.8646	43.1473	29.2468	22.3005	18.1358	15.3620	13.3830	11.9007
3.500%	84.9216	43.2027	29.3021	22.3560	18.1917	15.4184	13.4399	11.9581
3.625%	84.9787	43.2582	29.3575	22.4116	18.2478	15.4749	13.4969	12.0156
3.750%	85.0357	43.3137	29.4129	22.4674	18.3039	15.5315	13.5540	12.0733
3.875%	85.0928	43.3693	29.4684	22.5232	18.3602	15.5883	13.6113	12.1312
4.000%	85.1499	43.4249	29.5240	22.5791	18.4165	15.6452	13.6688	12.1893
4.125%	85.2070	43.4806	29.5796	22.6350	18.4730	15.7022	13.7264	12.2475
4.250%	85.2642	43.5363	29.6353	22.6911	18.5296	15.7593	13.7842	12.3059
4.375%	85.3213	43.5920	29.6911	22.7472	18.5862	15.8166	13.8421	12.3645
4.500%	85.3785	43.6478	29.7469	22.8035	18.6430	15.8740	13.9002	12.4232
4.625%	85.4357	43.7036	29.8028	22.8598	18.6999	15.9316	13.9584	12.4822
4.750%	85.4930	43.7595	29.8588	22.9162	18.7569	15.9892	14.0167	12.5412
4.875%	85.5502	43.8154	29.9148	22.9727	18.8140	16.0470	14.0752	12.6005
5.000%	85.6075	43.8714	29.9709	23.0293	18.8712	16.1049	14.1339	12.6599
5.125%	85.6648	43.9274	30.0271	23.0860	18.9286	16.1630	14.1927	12.7195
5.250%	85.7221	43.9834	30.0833	23.1427	18.9860	16.2212	14.2517	12.7793
5.375%	85.7794	44.0395	30.1396	23.1996	19.0435	16.2795	14.3108	12.8392
5.500%	85.8368	44.0957	30.1959	23.2565	19.1012	16.3379	14.3700	12.8993
5.625%	85.8942	44.1518	30.2523	23.3135	19.1589	16.3964	14.4294	12.9596
5.750%	85.9516	44.2080	30.3088	23.3706	19.2168	16.4551	14.4890	13.0200
5.875%	86.0090	44.2643	30.3653	23.4278	19.2747	16.5139	14.5487	13.0807
6.000%	86.0664	44.3206	30.4219	23.4850	19.3328	16.5729	14.6086	13.1414
6.125%	86.1239	44.3770	30.4786	23.5424	19.3910	16.6320	14.6686	13.2024
6.250%	86.1814	44.4333	30.5353	23.5998	19.4493	16.6912	14.7287	13.2635
6.375%	86.2389	44.4898	30.5921	23.6573	19.5077	16.7505	14.7890	13.3248
6.500%	86.2964	44.5463	30.6490	23.7150	19.5661	16.8099	14.8494	13.3862
6.625%	86.3540	44.6028	30.7059	23.7726	19.6248	16.8695	14.9100	13.4479
6.750%	86.4115	44.6593	30.7629	23.8304	19.6835	16.9292	14.9708	13.5096
6.875%	86.4691	44.7159	30.8200	23.8883	19.7423	16.9890	15.0316	13.5716

MONTHLY PAYMENT TO AMORTIZE A LOAN OF $1,000

Term of Loan

Interest Rate	9 Years	10 Years	11 Years	12 Years	13 Years	14 Years	15 Years	16 Years
2.000%	10.1253	9.2013	8.4459	7.8168	7.2850	6.8295	6.4351	6.0903
2.125%	10.1811	9.2574	8.5023	7.8736	7.3420	6.8869	6.4928	6.1484
2.250%	10.2370	9.3137	8.5590	7.9305	7.3994	6.9446	6.5508	6.2068
2.375%	10.2932	9.3703	8.6158	7.9878	7.4570	7.0025	6.6092	6.2655
2.500%	10.3496	9.4270	8.6729	8.0453	7.5149	7.0608	6.6679	6.3246
2.625%	10.4061	9.4839	8.7303	8.1031	7.5730	7.1194	6.7269	6.3840
2.750%	10.4629	9.5411	8.7879	8.1611	7.6315	7.1783	6.7862	6.4438
2.875%	10.5198	9.5985	8.8457	8.2193	7.6902	7.2375	6.8459	6.5039
3.000%	10.5769	9.6561	8.9038	8.2779	7.7492	7.2970	6.9058	6.5643
3.125%	10.6343	9.7139	8.9621	8.3367	7.8085	7.3567	6.9661	6.6251
3.250%	10.6918	9.7719	9.0206	8.3957	7.8680	7.4168	7.0267	6.6862
3.375%	10.7495	9.8301	9.0793	8.4550	7.9279	7.4772	7.0876	6.7477
3.500%	10.8074	9.8886	9.1383	8.5145	7.9880	7.5378	7.1488	6.8095
3.625%	10.8655	9.9472	9.1976	8.5743	8.0484	7.5988	7.2104	6.8716
3.750%	10.9238	10.0061	9.2570	8.6344	8.1090	7.6601	7.2722	6.9340
3.875%	10.9823	10.0652	9.3167	8.6947	8.1700	7.7216	7.3344	6.9968
4.000%	11.0410	10.1245	9.3767	8.7553	8.2312	7.7835	7.3969	7.0600
4.125%	11.0998	10.1840	9.4368	8.8161	8.2926	7.8456	7.4597	7.1234
4.250%	11.1589	10.2438	9.4972	8.8772	8.3544	7.9080	7.5228	7.1872
4.375%	11.2181	10.3037	9.5579	8.9385	8.4164	7.9707	7.5862	7.2513
4.500%	11.2776	10.3638	9.6187	9.0001	8.4787	8.0338	7.6499	7.3158
4.625%	11.3372	10.4242	9.6798	9.0619	8.5413	8.0971	7.7140	7.3805
4.750%	11.3971	10.4848	9.7411	9.1240	8.6041	8.1607	7.7783	7.4456
4.875%	11.4571	10.5456	9.8027	9.1863	8.6672	8.2245	7.8430	7.5111
5.000%	11.5173	10.6066	9.8645	9.2489	8.7306	8.2887	7.9079	7.5768
5.125%	11.5777	10.6678	9.9265	9.3117	8.7942	8.3532	7.9732	7.6429
5.250%	11.6383	10.7292	9.9888	9.3748	8.8582	8.4179	8.0388	7.7093
5.375%	11.6990	10.7908	10.0512	9.4381	8.9223	8.4829	8.1047	7.7760
5.500%	11.7600	10.8526	10.1139	9.5017	8.9868	8.5483	8.1708	7.8430
5.625%	11.8212	10.9147	10.1769	9.5655	9.0515	8.6139	8.2373	7.9104
5.750%	11.8825	10.9769	10.2400	9.6296	9.1165	8.6797	8.3041	7.9781
5.875%	11.9440	11.0394	10.3034	9.6939	9.1817	8.7459	8.3712	8.0461
6.000%	12.0057	11.1021	10.3670	9.7585	9.2472	8.8124	8.4386	8.1144
6.125%	12.0677	11.1649	10.4309	9.8233	9.3130	8.8791	8.5062	8.1830
6.250%	12.1298	11.2280	10.4949	9.8884	9.3790	8.9461	8.5742	8.2519
6.375%	12.1920	11.2913	10.5592	9.9537	9.4453	9.0134	8.6425	8.3212
6.500%	12.2545	11.3548	10.6238	10.0192	9.5119	9.0810	8.7111	8.3908
6.625%	12.3172	11.4185	10.6885	10.0850	9.5787	9.1488	8.7799	8.4606
6.750%	12.3800	11.4824	10.7535	10.1510	9.6458	9.2169	8.8491	8.5308
6.875%	12.4431	11.5465	10.8187	10.2173	9.7131	9.2853	8.9185	8.6013

MONTHLY PAYMENT TO AMORTIZE A LOAN OF $1,000

Term of Loan

Interest Rate	17 Years	18 Years	19 Years	20 Years	21 Years	22 Years	23 Years	24 Years
2.000%	5.7865	5.5167	5.2756	5.0588	4.8630	4.6852	4.5232	4.3748
2.125%	5.8449	5.5754	5.3346	5.1182	4.9228	4.7453	4.5836	4.4356
2.250%	5.9036	5.6345	5.3941	5.1781	4.9830	4.8059	4.6445	4.4969
2.375%	5.9627	5.6940	5.4540	5.2383	5.0436	4.8669	4.7059	4.5587
2.500%	6.0222	5.7539	5.5143	5.2990	5.1047	4.9284	4.7678	4.6209
2.625%	6.0821	5.8142	5.5750	5.3601	5.1662	4.9904	4.8302	4.6837
2.750%	6.1423	5.8748	5.6360	5.4217	5.2282	5.0528	4.8930	4.7470
2.875%	6.2028	5.9358	5.6975	5.4836	5.2906	5.1156	4.9564	4.8108
3.000%	6.2637	5.9972	5.7594	5.5460	5.3534	5.1790	5.0202	4.8751
3.125%	6.3250	6.0590	5.8217	5.6088	5.4167	5.2427	5.0844	4.9399
3.250%	6.3867	6.1212	5.8844	5.6720	5.4804	5.3070	5.1492	5.0051
3.375%	6.4487	6.1837	5.9474	5.7356	5.5446	5.3717	5.2144	5.0709
3.500%	6.5110	6.2466	6.0109	5.7996	5.6092	5.4368	5.2801	5.1371
3.625%	6.5737	6.3099	6.0748	5.8640	5.6742	5.5024	5.3463	5.2039
3.750%	6.6368	6.3736	6.1390	5.9289	5.7396	5.5684	5.4129	5.2711
3.875%	6.7002	6.4376	6.2037	5.9941	5.8055	5.6349	5.4800	5.3387
4.000%	6.7639	6.5020	6.2687	6.0598	5.8718	5.7018	5.5475	5.4069
4.125%	6.8280	6.5667	6.3341	6.1259	5.9385	5.7692	5.6155	5.4755
4.250%	6.8925	6.6319	6.3999	6.1923	6.0056	5.8370	5.6840	5.5446
4.375%	6.9573	6.6974	6.4661	6.2592	6.0732	5.9052	5.7529	5.6142
4.500%	7.0225	6.7632	6.5327	6.3265	6.1412	5.9739	5.8222	5.6842
4.625%	7.0880	6.8295	6.5996	6.3942	6.2096	6.0430	5.8920	5.7547
4.750%	7.1538	6.8961	6.6670	6.4622	6.2784	6.1125	5.9623	5.8257
4.875%	7.2200	6.9630	6.7347	6.5307	6.3476	6.1824	6.0329	5.8971
5.000%	7.2866	7.0303	6.8028	6.5996	6.4172	6.2528	6.1041	5.9690
5.125%	7.3534	7.0980	6.8712	6.6688	6.4872	6.3236	6.1756	6.0413
5.250%	7.4206	7.1660	6.9401	6.7384	6.5576	6.3948	6.2476	6.1140
5.375%	7.4882	7.2344	7.0093	6.8085	6.6285	6.4664	6.3200	6.1872
5.500%	7.5561	7.3032	7.0789	6.8789	6.6997	6.5385	6.3929	6.2609
5.625%	7.6243	7.3723	7.1488	6.9497	6.7713	6.6109	6.4661	6.3350
5.750%	7.6929	7.4417	7.2191	7.0208	6.8434	6.6838	6.5398	6.4095
5.875%	7.7618	7.5115	7.2898	7.0924	6.9158	6.7571	6.6139	6.4844
6.000%	7.8310	7.5816	7.3608	7.1643	6.9886	6.8307	6.6885	6.5598
6.125%	7.9006	7.6521	7.4322	7.2366	7.0618	6.9048	6.7634	6.6356
6.250%	7.9705	7.7229	7.5040	7.3093	7.1353	6.9793	6.8387	6.7118
6.375%	8.0407	7.7941	7.5761	7.3823	7.2093	7.0541	6.9145	6.7884
6.500%	8.1112	7.8656	7.6486	7.4557	7.2836	7.1294	6.9906	6.8654
6.625%	8.1821	7.9375	7.7214	7.5295	7.3583	7.2050	7.0672	6.9429
6.750%	8.2533	8.0096	7.7945	7.6036	7.4334	7.2811	7.1441	7.0207
6.875%	8.3248	8.0822	7.8681	7.6781	7.5089	7.3575	7.2215	7.0990

MONTHLY PAYMENT TO AMORTIZE A LOAN OF $1,000

Term of Loan

Interest Rate	25 Years	26 Years	27 Years	28 Years	29 Years	30 Years	35 Years	40 Years
2.000%	4.2385	4.1130	3.9969	3.8893	3.7893	3.6962	3.3126	3.0283
2.125%	4.2997	4.1744	4.0587	3.9515	3.8518	3.7590	3.3771	3.0944
2.250%	4.3613	4.2364	4.1211	4.0142	3.9149	3.8225	3.4424	3.1614
2.375%	4.4235	4.2990	4.1840	4.0775	3.9786	3.8865	3.5083	3.2292
2.500%	4.4862	4.3621	4.2475	4.1414	4.0429	3.9512	3.5750	3.2978
2.625%	4.5494	4.4257	4.3115	4.2058	4.1078	4.0165	3.6423	3.3671
2.750%	4.6131	4.4899	4.3761	4.2709	4.1732	4.0824	3.7103	3.4373
2.875%	4.6774	4.5546	4.4413	4.3365	4.2393	4.1489	3.7791	3.5082
3.000%	4.7421	4.6198	4.5070	4.4027	4.3059	4.2160	3.8485	3.5798
3.125%	4.8074	4.6856	4.5733	4.4694	4.3732	4.2838	3.9186	3.6523
3.250%	4.8732	4.7519	4.6401	4.5367	4.4410	4.3521	3.9894	3.7254
3.375%	4.9394	4.8187	4.7074	4.6046	4.5094	4.4210	4.0608	3.7993
3.500%	5.0062	4.8860	4.7753	4.6730	4.5783	4.4904	4.1329	3.8739
3.625%	5.0735	4.9539	4.8437	4.7420	4.6478	4.5605	4.2057	3.9492
3.750%	5.1413	5.0222	4.9126	4.8115	4.7179	4.6312	4.2791	4.0253
3.875%	5.2096	5.0911	4.9821	4.8815	4.7885	4.7024	4.3531	4.1020
4.000%	5.2784	5.1605	5.0521	4.9521	4.8597	4.7742	4.4277	4.1794
4.125%	5.3476	5.2304	5.1226	5.0233	4.9315	4.8465	4.5030	4.2575
4.250%	5.4174	5.3008	5.1936	5.0949	5.0038	4.9194	4.5789	4.3362
4.375%	5.4876	5.3717	5.2652	5.1671	5.0766	4.9929	4.6555	4.4156
4.500%	5.5583	5.4430	5.3372	5.2398	5.1499	5.0669	4.7326	4.4956
4.625%	5.6295	5.5149	5.4098	5.3130	5.2238	5.1414	4.8103	4.5763
4.750%	5.7012	5.5873	5.4828	5.3868	5.2982	5.2165	4.8886	4.6576
4.875%	5.7733	5.6601	5.5564	5.4610	5.3732	5.2921	4.9674	4.7395
5.000%	5.8459	5.7334	5.6304	5.5357	5.4486	5.3682	5.0469	4.8220
5.125%	5.9190	5.8072	5.7049	5.6110	5.5246	5.4449	5.1269	4.9050
5.250%	5.9925	5.8815	5.7799	5.6867	5.6010	5.5220	5.2074	4.9887
5.375%	6.0665	5.9562	5.8554	5.7629	5.6780	5.5997	5.2885	5.0729
5.500%	6.1409	6.0314	5.9314	5.8397	5.7554	5.6779	5.3702	5.1577
5.625%	6.2157	6.1071	6.0078	5.9168	5.8334	5.7566	5.4523	5.2430
5.750%	6.2911	6.1832	6.0847	5.9945	5.9118	5.8357	5.5350	5.3289
5.875%	6.3668	6.2598	6.1620	6.0726	5.9907	5.9154	5.6182	5.4153
6.000%	6.4430	6.3368	6.2399	6.1512	6.0700	5.9955	5.7019	5.5021
6.125%	6.5196	6.4142	6.3181	6.2303	6.1499	6.0761	5.7861	5.5895
6.250%	6.5967	6.4921	6.3968	6.3098	6.2302	6.1572	5.8708	5.6774
6.375%	6.6742	6.5704	6.4760	6.3898	6.3109	6.2387	5.9559	5.7657
6.500%	6.7521	6.6492	6.5555	6.4702	6.3921	6.3207	6.0415	5.8546
6.625%	6.8304	6.7284	6.6356	6.5510	6.4738	6.4031	6.1276	5.9438
6.750%	6.9091	6.8079	6.7160	6.6323	6.5558	6.4860	6.2142	6.0336
6.875%	6.9883	6.8880	6.7969	6.7140	6.6384	6.5693	6.3011	6.1237

MONTHLY PAYMENT TO AMORTIZE A LOAN OF $1,000

Term of Loan

Interest Rate	1 Year	2 Years	3 Years	4 Years	5 Years	6 Years	7 Years	8 Years
7.000%	86.5267	44.7726	30.8771	23.9462	19.8012	17.0490	15.0927	13.6337
7.125%	86.5844	44.8293	30.9343	24.0043	19.8602	17.1091	15.1539	13.6960
7.250%	86.6420	44.8860	30.9915	24.0624	19.9194	17.1693	15.2152	13.7585
7.375%	86.6997	44.9428	31.0488	24.1206	19.9786	17.2296	15.2767	13.8211
7.500%	86.7574	44.9996	31.1062	24.1789	20.0379	17.2901	15.3383	13.8839
7.625%	86.8151	45.0565	31.1637	24.2373	20.0974	17.3507	15.4000	13.9468
7.750%	86.8729	45.1134	31.2212	24.2957	20.1570	17.4114	15.4620	14.0099
7.875%	86.9306	45.1703	31.2787	24.3543	20.2166	17.4723	15.5240	14.0732
8.000%	86.9884	45.2273	31.3364	24.4129	20.2764	17.5332	15.5862	14.1367
8.125%	87.0462	45.2843	31.3941	24.4716	20.3363	17.5943	15.6486	14.2003
8.250%	87.1041	45.3414	31.4518	24.5304	20.3963	17.6556	15.7111	14.2641
8.375%	87.1619	45.3985	31.5096	24.5893	20.4563	17.7169	15.7737	14.3280
8.500%	87.2198	45.4557	31.5675	24.6483	20.5165	17.7784	15.8365	14.3921
8.625%	87.2777	45.5129	31.6255	24.7074	20.5768	17.8400	15.8994	14.4564
8.750%	87.3356	45.5701	31.6835	24.7665	20.6372	17.9017	15.9625	14.5208
8.875%	87.3935	45.6274	31.7416	24.8257	20.6977	17.9636	16.0257	14.5854
9.000%	87.4515	45.6847	31.7997	24.8850	20.7584	18.0255	16.0891	14.6502
9.125%	87.5095	45.7421	31.8579	24.9444	20.8191	18.0876	16.1526	14.7151
9.250%	87.5675	45.7995	31.9162	25.0039	20.8799	18.1499	16.2162	14.7802
9.375%	87.6255	45.8570	31.9745	25.0635	20.9408	18.2122	16.2800	14.8455
9.500%	87.6835	45.9145	32.0329	25.1231	21.0019	18.2747	16.3440	14.9109
9.625%	87.7416	45.9720	32.0914	25.1829	21.0630	18.3373	16.4081	14.9765
9.750%	87.7997	46.0296	32.1499	25.2427	21.1242	18.4000	16.4723	15.0422
9.875%	87.8578	46.0873	32.2085	25.3026	21.1856	18.4629	16.5367	15.1081
10.000%	87.9159	46.1449	32.2672	25.3626	21.2470	18.5258	16.6012	15.1742
10.125%	87.9740	46.2026	32.3259	25.4227	21.3086	18.5889	16.6658	15.2404
10.250%	88.0322	46.2604	32.3847	25.4828	21.3703	18.6522	16.7306	15.3068
10.375%	88.0904	46.3182	32.4435	25.5431	21.4320	18.7155	16.7956	15.3733
10.500%	88.1486	46.3760	32.5024	25.6034	21.4939	18.7790	16.8607	15.4400
10.625%	88.2068	46.4339	32.5614	25.6638	21.5559	18.8426	16.9259	15.5069
10.750%	88.2651	46.4919	32.6205	25.7243	21.6180	18.9063	16.9913	15.5739
10.875%	88.3234	46.5498	32.6796	25.7849	21.6801	18.9701	17.0568	15.6411
11.000%	88.3817	46.6078	32.7387	25.8455	21.7424	19.0341	17.1224	15.7084
11.125%	88.4400	46.6659	32.7979	25.9063	21.8048	19.0982	17.1882	15.7759
11.250%	88.4983	46.7240	32.8572	25.9671	21.8673	19.1624	17.2542	15.8436
11.375%	88.5567	46.7821	32.9166	26.0280	21.9299	19.2267	17.3202	15.9114
11.500%	88.6151	46.8403	32.9760	26.0890	21.9926	19.2912	17.3865	15.9794
11.625%	88.6735	46.8985	33.0355	26.1501	22.0554	19.3557	17.4528	16.0475
11.750%	88.7319	46.9568	33.0950	26.2113	22.1183	19.4204	17.5193	16.1158
11.875%	88.7903	47.0151	33.1546	26.2725	22.1813	19.4853	17.5860	16.1842

MONTHLY PAYMENT TO AMORTIZE A LOAN OF $1,000

Term of Loan

Interest Rate	9 Years	10 Years	11 Years	12 Years	13 Years	14 Years	15 Years	16 Years
7.000%	12.5063	11.6108	10.8841	10.2838	9.7807	9.3540	8.9883	8.6721
7.125%	12.5697	11.6754	10.9497	10.3506	9.8486	9.4230	9.0583	8.7432
7.250%	12.6333	11.7401	11.0156	10.4176	9.9167	9.4922	9.1286	8.8146
7.375%	12.6971	11.8050	11.0817	10.4848	9.9851	9.5617	9.1992	8.8863
7.500%	12.7610	11.8702	11.1480	10.5523	10.0537	9.6314	9.2701	8.9583
7.625%	12.8252	11.9355	11.2145	10.6200	10.1226	9.7015	9.3413	9.0306
7.750%	12.8895	12.0011	11.2813	10.6879	10.1917	9.7718	9.4128	9.1032
7.875%	12.9540	12.0668	11.3483	10.7561	10.2611	9.8423	9.4845	9.1761
8.000%	13.0187	12.1328	11.4154	10.8245	10.3307	9.9132	9.5565	9.2493
8.125%	13.0836	12.1989	11.4829	10.8932	10.4006	9.9843	9.6288	9.3227
8.250%	13.1487	12.2653	11.5505	10.9621	10.4708	10.0557	9.7014	9.3965
8.375%	13.2139	12.3318	11.6183	11.0312	10.5412	10.1273	9.7743	9.4706
8.500%	13.2794	12.3986	11.6864	11.1006	10.6118	10.1992	9.8474	9.5449
8.625%	13.3450	12.4655	11.7547	11.1701	10.6827	10.2713	9.9208	9.6195
8.750%	13.4108	12.5327	11.8232	11.2400	10.7538	10.3438	9.9945	9.6945
8.875%	13.4767	12.6000	11.8919	11.3100	10.8252	10.4164	10.0684	9.7697
9.000%	13.5429	12.6676	11.9608	11.3803	10.8968	10.4894	10.1427	9.8452
9.125%	13.6093	12.7353	12.0299	11.4508	10.9687	10.5626	10.2172	9.9209
9.250%	13.6758	12.8033	12.0993	11.5216	11.0408	10.6360	10.2919	9.9970
9.375%	13.7425	12.8714	12.1689	11.5925	11.1131	10.7097	10.3670	10.0733
9.500%	13.8094	12.9398	12.2386	11.6637	11.1857	10.7837	10.4422	10.1499
9.625%	13.8764	13.0083	12.3086	11.7352	11.2586	10.8579	10.5178	10.2268
9.750%	13.9437	13.0770	12.3788	11.8068	11.3316	10.9324	10.5936	10.3039
9.875%	14.0111	13.1460	12.4493	11.8787	11.4049	11.0071	10.6697	10.3813
10.000%	14.0787	13.2151	12.5199	11.9508	11.4785	11.0820	10.7461	10.4590
10.125%	14.1465	13.2844	12.5907	12.0231	11.5523	11.1572	10.8227	10.5370
10.250%	14.2144	13.3539	12.6618	12.0957	11.6263	11.2327	10.8995	10.6152
10.375%	14.2826	13.4236	12.7330	12.1684	11.7005	11.3084	10.9766	10.6937
10.500%	14.3509	13.4935	12.8045	12.2414	11.7750	11.3843	11.0540	10.7724
10.625%	14.4193	13.5636	12.8761	12.3146	11.8497	11.4605	11.1316	10.8514
10.750%	14.4880	13.6339	12.9480	12.3880	11.9247	11.5370	11.2095	10.9307
10.875%	14.5568	13.7043	13.0201	12.4617	11.9999	11.6136	11.2876	11.0102
11.000%	14.6259	13.7750	13.0923	12.5356	12.0753	11.6905	11.3660	11.0900
11.125%	14.6950	13.8459	13.1648	12.6096	12.1509	11.7677	11.4446	11.1700
11.250%	14.7644	13.9169	13.2375	12.6839	12.2268	11.8451	11.5234	11.2503
11.375%	14.8339	13.9881	13.3104	12.7584	12.3029	11.9227	11.6026	11.3309
11.500%	14.9037	14.0595	13.3835	12.8332	12.3792	12.0006	11.6819	11.4116
11.625%	14.9735	14.1312	13.4568	12.9081	12.4557	12.0786	11.7615	11.4927
11.750%	15.0436	14.2029	13.5303	12.9833	12.5325	12.1570	11.8413	11.5740
11.875%	15.1138	14.2749	13.6040	13.0586	12.6095	12.2355	11.9214	11.6555

MONTHLY PAYMENT TO AMORTIZE A LOAN OF $1,000

Term of Loan

Interest Rate	17 Years	18 Years	19 Years	20 Years	21 Years	22 Years	23 Years	24 Years
7.000%	8.3966	8.1550	7.9419	7.7530	7.5847	7.4342	7.2992	7.1776
7.125%	8.4688	8.2282	8.0161	7.8282	7.6609	7.5114	7.3773	7.2566
7.250%	8.5412	8.3017	8.0907	7.9038	7.7375	7.5889	7.4558	7.3361
7.375%	8.6140	8.3756	8.1656	7.9797	7.8144	7.6668	7.5347	7.4159
7.500%	8.6871	8.4497	8.2408	8.0559	7.8917	7.7451	7.6139	7.4960
7.625%	8.7605	8.5242	8.3163	8.1325	7.9693	7.8237	7.6935	7.5766
7.750%	8.8342	8.5990	8.3922	8.2095	8.0473	7.9027	7.7735	7.6576
7.875%	8.9082	8.6742	8.4685	8.2868	8.1256	7.9821	7.8538	7.7389
8.000%	8.9826	8.7496	8.5450	8.3644	8.2043	8.0618	7.9345	7.8205
8.125%	9.0572	8.8254	8.6219	8.4424	8.2833	8.1418	8.0156	7.9026
8.250%	9.1321	8.9015	8.6991	8.5207	8.3627	8.2222	8.0970	7.9850
8.375%	9.2074	8.9779	8.7766	8.5993	8.4424	8.3030	8.1788	8.0677
8.500%	9.2829	9.0546	8.8545	8.6782	8.5224	8.3841	8.2609	8.1508
8.625%	9.3588	9.1316	8.9326	8.7575	8.6028	8.4655	8.3433	8.2343
8.750%	9.4349	9.2089	9.0111	8.8371	8.6834	8.5472	8.4261	8.3181
8.875%	9.5113	9.2865	9.0899	8.9170	8.7645	8.6293	8.5092	8.4022
9.000%	9.5880	9.3644	9.1690	8.9973	8.8458	8.7117	8.5927	8.4866
9.125%	9.6650	9.4427	9.2484	9.0778	8.9275	8.7945	8.6765	8.5714
9.250%	9.7423	9.5212	9.3281	9.1587	9.0094	8.8775	8.7606	8.6566
9.375%	9.8199	9.6000	9.4081	9.2398	9.0917	8.9609	8.8450	8.7420
9.500%	9.8978	9.6791	9.4884	9.3213	9.1743	9.0446	8.9297	8.8277
9.625%	9.9760	9.7585	9.5690	9.4031	9.2573	9.1286	9.0148	8.9138
9.750%	10.0544	9.8382	9.6499	9.4852	9.3405	9.2129	9.1002	9.0002
9.875%	10.1331	9.9182	9.7311	9.5675	9.4240	9.2975	9.1858	9.0869
10.000%	10.2121	9.9984	9.8126	9.6502	9.5078	9.3825	9.2718	9.1739
10.125%	10.2914	10.0790	9.8944	9.7332	9.5919	9.4677	9.3581	9.2612
10.250%	10.3709	10.1598	9.9764	9.8164	9.6763	9.5532	9.4447	9.3488
10.375%	10.4507	10.2409	10.0588	9.9000	9.7610	9.6390	9.5315	9.4366
10.500%	10.5308	10.3223	10.1414	9.9838	9.8460	9.7251	9.6187	9.5248
10.625%	10.6112	10.4039	10.2243	10.0679	9.9312	9.8114	9.7061	9.6133
10.750%	10.6918	10.4858	10.3075	10.1523	10.0168	9.8981	9.7938	9.7020
10.875%	10.7727	10.5680	10.3909	10.2370	10.1026	9.9850	9.8818	9.7910
11.000%	10.8538	10.6505	10.4746	10.3219	10.1887	10.0722	9.9701	9.8803
11.125%	10.9352	10.7332	10.5586	10.4071	10.2751	10.1597	10.0586	9.9698
11.250%	11.0169	10.8162	10.6429	10.4926	10.3617	10.2475	10.1474	10.0596
11.375%	11.0988	10.8994	10.7274	10.5783	10.4486	10.3355	10.2365	10.1497
11.500%	11.1810	10.9830	10.8122	10.6643	10.5358	10.4237	10.3258	10.2400
11.625%	11.2634	11.0667	10.8972	10.7506	10.6232	10.5123	10.4154	10.3306
11.750%	11.3461	11.1507	10.9825	10.8371	10.7109	10.6011	10.5052	10.4214
11.875%	11.4290	11.2350	11.0681	10.9238	10.7988	10.6901	10.5953	10.5125

MONTHLY PAYMENT TO AMORTIZE A LOAN OF $1,000

Term of Loan

Interest Rate	25 Years	26 Years	27 Years	28 Years	29 Years	30 Years	35 Years	40 Years
7.000%	7.0678	6.9684	6.8781	6.7961	6.7213	6.6530	6.3886	6.2143
7.125%	7.1477	7.0492	6.9598	6.8786	6.8047	6.7372	6.4764	6.3053
7.250%	7.2281	7.1304	7.0419	6.9616	6.8884	6.8218	6.5647	6.3967
7.375%	7.3088	7.2121	7.1244	7.0449	6.9726	6.9068	6.6533	6.4885
7.500%	7.3899	7.2941	7.2073	7.1287	7.0572	6.9921	6.7424	6.5807
7.625%	7.4714	7.3765	7.2906	7.2128	7.1422	7.0779	6.8319	6.6733
7.750%	7.5533	7.4593	7.3743	7.2974	7.2276	7.1641	6.9218	6.7662
7.875%	7.6355	7.5424	7.4584	7.3823	7.3133	7.2507	7.0120	6.8595
8.000%	7.7182	7.6260	7.5428	7.4676	7.3995	7.3376	7.1026	6.9531
8.125%	7.8012	7.7099	7.6276	7.5533	7.4860	7.4250	7.1936	7.0471
8.250%	7.8845	7.7942	7.7128	7.6393	7.5729	7.5127	7.2849	7.1414
8.375%	7.9682	7.8788	7.7983	7.7257	7.6601	7.6007	7.3766	7.2360
8.500%	8.0523	7.9638	7.8842	7.8125	7.7477	7.6891	7.4686	7.3309
8.625%	8.1367	8.0491	7.9705	7.8996	7.8357	7.7779	7.5610	7.4262
8.750%	8.2214	8.1348	8.0570	7.9871	7.9240	7.8670	7.6536	7.5217
8.875%	8.3065	8.2209	8.1440	8.0749	8.0126	7.9564	7.7466	7.6175
9.000%	8.3920	8.3072	8.2313	8.1630	8.1016	8.0462	7.8399	7.7136
9.125%	8.4777	8.3939	8.3189	8.2515	8.1909	8.1363	7.9335	7.8100
9.250%	8.5638	8.4810	8.4068	8.3403	8.2805	8.2268	8.0274	7.9066
9.375%	8.6502	8.5683	8.4950	8.4294	8.3705	8.3175	8.1216	8.0035
9.500%	8.7370	8.6560	8.5836	8.5188	8.4607	8.4085	8.2161	8.1006
9.625%	8.8240	8.7440	8.6725	8.6086	8.5513	8.4999	8.3109	8.1980
9.750%	8.9114	8.8323	8.7617	8.6986	8.6421	8.5915	8.4059	8.2956
9.875%	8.9990	8.9209	8.8512	8.7890	8.7333	8.6835	8.5012	8.3934
10.000%	9.0870	9.0098	8.9410	8.8796	8.8248	8.7757	8.5967	8.4915
10.125%	9.1753	9.0990	9.0311	8.9705	8.9165	8.8682	8.6925	8.5897
10.250%	9.2638	9.1885	9.1214	9.0618	9.0085	8.9610	8.7886	8.6882
10.375%	9.3527	9.2782	9.2121	9.1533	9.1008	9.0541	8.8848	8.7868
10.500%	9.4418	9.3683	9.3030	9.2450	9.1934	9.1474	8.9813	8.8857
10.625%	9.5312	9.4586	9.3943	9.3371	9.2862	9.2410	9.0781	8.9847
10.750%	9.6209	9.5492	9.4857	9.4294	9.3793	9.3348	9.1750	9.0840
10.875%	9.7109	9.6401	9.5775	9.5220	9.4727	9.4289	9.2722	9.1834
11.000%	9.8011	9.7313	9.6695	9.6148	9.5663	9.5232	9.3696	9.2829
11.125%	9.8916	9.8227	9.7618	9.7079	9.6601	9.6178	9.4672	9.3827
11.250%	9.9824	9.9143	9.8543	9.8012	9.7542	9.7126	9.5649	9.4826
11.375%	10.0734	10.0063	9.9471	9.8948	9.8486	9.8077	9.6629	9.5826
11.500%	10.1647	10.0984	10.0401	9.9886	9.9431	9.9029	9.7611	9.6828
11.625%	10.2562	10.1909	10.1333	10.0826	10.0379	9.9984	9.8594	9.7832
11.750%	10.3480	10.2835	10.2268	10.1769	10.1329	10.0941	9.9579	9.8836
11.875%	10.4400	10.3764	10.3205	10.2714	10.2281	10.1900	10.0566	9.9843

MONTHLY PAYMENT TO AMORTIZE A LOAN OF $1,000

Term of Loan

Interest Rate	1 Year	2 Years	3 Years	4 Years	5 Years	6 Years	7 Years	8 Years
12.000%	88.8488	47.0735	33.2143	26.3338	22.2444	19.5502	17.6527	16.2528
12.125%	88.9073	47.1319	33.2740	26.3953	22.3077	19.6153	17.7197	16.3216
12.250%	88.9658	47.1903	33.3338	26.4568	22.3710	19.6804	17.7867	16.3905
12.375%	89.0243	47.2488	33.3937	26.5183	22.4344	19.7457	17.8539	16.4596
12.500%	89.0829	47.3073	33.4536	26.5800	22.4979	19.8112	17.9212	16.5288
12.625%	89.1414	47.3659	33.5136	26.6417	22.5616	19.8767	17.9887	16.5982
12.750%	89.2000	47.4245	33.5737	26.7036	22.6253	19.9424	18.0563	16.6677
12.875%	89.2586	47.4831	33.6338	26.7655	22.6891	20.0082	18.1241	16.7374
13.000%	89.3173	47.5418	33.6940	26.8275	22.7531	20.0741	18.1920	16.8073
13.125%	89.3759	47.6006	33.7542	26.8896	22.8171	20.1401	18.2600	16.8773
13.250%	89.4346	47.6593	33.8145	26.9517	22.8813	20.2063	18.3282	16.9474
13.375%	89.4933	47.7182	33.8749	27.0140	22.9455	20.2726	18.3965	17.0177
13.500%	89.5520	47.7770	33.9353	27.0763	23.0098	20.3390	18.4649	17.0882
13.625%	89.6108	47.8359	33.9958	27.1387	23.0743	20.4055	18.5335	17.1588
13.750%	89.6695	47.8949	34.0563	27.2012	23.1388	20.4721	18.6022	17.2295
13.875%	89.7283	47.9539	34.1169	27.2638	23.2035	20.5389	18.6710	17.3004
14.000%	89.7871	48.0129	34.1776	27.3265	23.2683	20.6057	18.7400	17.3715
14.125%	89.8459	48.0720	34.2384	27.3892	23.3331	20.6727	18.8091	17.4427
14.250%	89.9048	48.1311	34.2992	27.4520	23.3981	20.7398	18.8784	17.5141
14.375%	89.9637	48.1902	34.3600	27.5150	23.4631	20.8071	18.9478	17.5856
14.500%	90.0225	48.2494	34.4210	27.5780	23.5283	20.8744	19.0173	17.6573
14.625%	90.0815	48.3087	34.4820	27.6410	23.5935	20.9419	19.0870	17.7291
14.750%	90.1404	48.3680	34.5430	27.7042	23.6589	21.0095	19.1568	17.8010
14.875%	90.1993	48.4273	34.6041	27.7674	23.7244	21.0772	19.2267	17.8731
15.000%	90.2583	48.4866	34.6653	27.8307	23.7899	21.1450	19.2968	17.9454
15.125%	90.3173	48.5461	34.7266	27.8942	23.8556	21.2130	19.3670	18.0178
15.250%	90.3763	48.6055	34.7879	27.9576	23.9214	21.2810	19.4373	18.0904
15.375%	90.4354	48.6650	34.8492	28.0212	23.9872	21.3492	19.5077	18.1631
15.500%	90.4944	48.7245	34.9107	28.0849	24.0532	21.4175	19.5783	18.2359
15.625%	90.5535	48.7841	34.9722	28.1486	24.1193	21.4859	19.6491	18.3089
15.750%	90.6126	48.8437	35.0337	28.2124	24.1854	21.5544	19.7199	18.3821
15.875%	90.6717	48.9034	35.0954	28.2763	24.2517	21.6231	19.7909	18.4554
16.000%	90.7309	48.9631	35.1570	28.3403	24.3181	21.6918	19.8621	18.5288
16.125%	90.7900	49.0229	35.2188	28.4043	24.3845	21.7607	19.9333	18.6024
16.250%	90.8492	49.0826	35.2806	28.4685	24.4511	21.8297	20.0047	18.6761
16.375%	90.9084	49.1425	35.3425	28.5327	24.5178	21.8988	20.0762	18.7500
16.500%	90.9676	49.2024	35.4044	28.5970	24.5845	21.9681	20.1479	18.8240
16.625%	91.0269	49.2623	35.4664	28.6614	24.6514	22.0374	20.2197	18.8981
16.750%	91.0862	49.3222	35.5284	28.7259	24.7184	22.1069	20.2916	18.9724
16.875%	91.1454	49.3822	35.5909	28.7904	24.7854	22.1764	20.3636	19.0469

MONTHLY PAYMENT TO AMORTIZE A LOAN OF $1,000

Term of Loan

Interest Rate	9 Years	10 Years	11 Years	12 Years	13 Years	14 Years	15 Years	16 Years
12.000%	15.1842	14.3471	13.6779	13.1342	12.6867	12.3143	12.0017	11.7373
12.125%	15.2548	14.4194	13.7520	13.2100	12.7641	12.3933	12.0822	11.8193
12.250%	15.3256	14.4920	13.8263	13.2860	12.8417	12.4725	12.1630	11.9015
12.375%	15.3965	14.5647	13.9007	13.3622	12.9196	12.5520	12.2440	11.9840
12.500%	15.4676	14.6376	13.9754	13.4386	12.9977	12.6317	12.3252	12.0667
12.625%	15.5388	14.7107	14.0503	13.5152	13.0760	12.7116	12.4067	12.1496
12.750%	15.6102	14.7840	14.1254	13.5920	13.1545	12.7917	12.4884	12.2328
12.875%	15.6818	14.8574	14.2006	13.6690	13.2332	12.8721	12.5703	12.3162
13.000%	15.7536	14.9311	14.2761	13.7463	13.3121	12.9526	12.6524	12.3999
13.125%	15.8255	15.0049	14.3518	13.8237	13.3912	13.0334	12.7348	12.4837
13.250%	15.8976	15.0789	14.4276	13.9013	13.4706	13.1144	12.8174	12.5678
13.375%	15.9699	15.1531	14.5036	13.9791	13.5502	13.1956	12.9002	12.6521
13.500%	16.0423	15.2274	14.5799	14.0572	13.6299	13.2771	12.9832	12.7367
13.625%	16.1149	15.3020	14.6563	14.1354	13.7099	13.3587	13.0664	12.8214
13.750%	16.1877	15.3767	14.7329	14.2138	13.7901	13.4406	13.1499	12.9064
13.875%	16.2606	15.4516	14.8097	14.2925	13.8704	13.5226	13.2335	12.9916
14.000%	16.3337	15.5266	14.8867	14.3713	13.9510	13.6049	13.3174	13.0770
14.125%	16.4070	15.6019	14.9638	14.4503	14.0318	13.6874	13.4015	13.1626
14.250%	16.4804	15.6773	15.0412	14.5295	14.1128	13.7701	13.4858	13.2484
14.375%	16.5540	15.7529	15.1187	14.6089	14.1940	13.8529	13.5703	13.3345
14.500%	16.6277	15.8287	15.1964	14.6885	14.2754	13.9360	13.6550	13.4207
14.625%	16.7016	15.9046	15.2743	14.7683	14.3570	14.0193	13.7399	13.5071
14.750%	16.7757	15.9807	15.3524	14.8483	14.4387	14.1028	13.8250	13.5938
14.875%	16.8499	16.0570	15.4307	14.9284	14.5207	14.1865	13.9104	13.6806
15.000%	16.9243	16.1335	15.5091	15.0088	14.6029	14.2704	13.9959	13.7677
15.125%	16.9989	16.2101	15.5878	15.0893	14.6852	14.3545	14.0816	13.8549
15.250%	17.0736	16.2869	15.6666	15.1700	14.7678	14.4388	14.1675	13.9424
15.375%	17.1485	16.3639	15.7456	15.2509	14.8505	14.5232	14.2536	14.0300
15.500%	17.2235	16.4411	15.8247	15.3320	14.9335	14.6079	14.3399	14.1179
15.625%	17.2987	16.5184	15.9041	15.4133	15.0166	14.6928	14.4264	14.2059
15.750%	17.3741	16.5958	15.9836	15.4948	15.0999	14.7778	14.5131	14.2941
15.875%	17.4496	16.6735	16.0633	15.5764	15.1834	14.8630	14.5999	14.3825
16.000%	17.5253	16.7513	16.1432	15.6583	15.2670	14.9485	14.6870	14.4711
16.125%	17.6011	16.8293	16.2232	15.7403	15.3509	15.0341	14.7743	14.5599
16.250%	17.6771	16.9074	16.3034	15.8224	15.4349	15.1199	14.8617	14.6488
16.375%	17.7532	16.9858	16.3838	15.9048	15.5192	15.2058	14.9493	14.7380
16.500%	17.8295	17.0642	16.4644	15.9873	15.6036	15.2920	15.0371	14.8273
16.625%	17.9059	17.1429	16.5451	16.0700	15.6881	15.3783	15.1251	14.9168
16.750%	17.9825	17.2217	16.6260	16.1529	15.7729	15.4648	15.2132	15.0065
16.875%	18.0593	17.3006	16.7071	16.2360	15.8578	15.5515	15.3015	15.0963

MONTHLY PAYMENT TO AMORTIZE A LOAN OF $1,000

Term of Loan

Interest Rate	17 Years	18 Years	19 Years	20 Years	21 Years	22 Years	23 Years	24 Years
12.000%	11.5122	11.3195	11.1539	11.0109	10.8870	10.7794	10.6856	10.6038
12.125%	11.5956	11.4043	11.2399	11.0981	10.9754	10.8689	10.7762	10.6954
12.250%	11.6792	11.4893	11.3262	11.1856	11.0641	10.9587	10.8670	10.7872
12.375%	11.7631	11.5745	11.4127	11.2734	11.1530	11.0487	10.9581	10.8792
12.500%	11.8473	11.6600	11.4995	11.3614	11.2422	11.1390	11.0494	10.9714
12.625%	11.9316	11.7457	11.5865	11.4496	11.3316	11.2294	11.1409	11.0639
12.750%	12.0162	11.8317	11.6738	11.5381	11.4212	11.3202	11.2326	11.1566
12.875%	12.1011	11.9179	11.7613	11.6268	11.5111	11.4111	11.3246	11.2495
13.000%	12.1861	12.0043	11.8490	11.7158	11.6011	11.5023	11.4168	11.3427
13.125%	12.2714	12.0910	11.9369	11.8049	11.6915	11.5937	11.5092	11.4360
13.250%	12.3570	12.1779	12.0251	11.8943	11.7820	11.6853	11.6018	11.5296
13.375%	12.4427	12.2650	12.1135	11.9839	11.8727	11.7771	11.6946	11.6233
13.500%	12.5287	12.3523	12.2021	12.0737	11.9637	11.8691	11.7876	11.7173
13.625%	12.6149	12.4399	12.2910	12.1638	12.0549	11.9613	11.8808	11.8114
13.750%	12.7013	12.5276	12.3800	12.2541	12.1463	12.0538	11.9743	11.9058
13.875%	12.7879	12.6156	12.4693	12.3445	12.2379	12.1464	12.0679	12.0003
14.000%	12.8748	12.7038	12.5588	12.4352	12.3297	12.2393	12.1617	12.0950
14.125%	12.9618	12.7922	12.6485	12.5261	12.4217	12.3323	12.2557	12.1900
14.250%	13.0491	12.8809	12.7384	12.6172	12.5139	12.4256	12.3500	12.2851
14.375%	13.1366	12.9697	12.8285	12.7085	12.6063	12.5190	12.4443	12.3803
14.500%	13.2242	13.0587	12.9188	12.8000	12.6989	12.6126	12.5389	12.4758
14.625%	13.3121	13.1480	13.0093	12.8917	12.7917	12.7065	12.6337	12.5714
14.750%	13.4002	13.2374	13.1000	12.9836	12.8847	12.8004	12.7286	12.6672
14.875%	13.4885	13.3271	13.1909	13.0756	12.9778	12.8946	12.8237	12.7632
15.000%	13.5770	13.4169	13.2820	13.1679	13.0712	12.9890	12.9190	12.8593
15.125%	13.6657	13.5069	13.3733	13.2603	13.1647	13.0835	13.0144	12.9556
15.250%	13.7546	13.5972	13.4647	13.3530	13.2584	13.1782	13.1100	13.0520
15.375%	13.8437	13.6876	13.5564	13.4458	13.3523	13.2731	13.2058	13.1486
15.500%	13.9329	13.7782	13.6483	13.5388	13.4464	13.3681	13.3018	13.2454
15.625%	14.0224	13.8690	13.7403	13.6320	13.5406	13.4633	13.3979	13.3423
15.750%	14.1120	13.9600	13.8325	13.7253	13.6350	13.5587	13.4941	13.4394
15.875%	14.2019	14.0511	13.9249	13.8189	13.7296	13.6542	13.5905	13.5366
16.000%	14.2919	14.1425	14.0175	13.9126	13.8243	13.7499	13.6871	13.6339
16.125%	14.3821	14.2340	14.1102	14.0064	13.9192	13.8457	13.7838	13.7314
16.250%	14.4725	14.3257	14.2031	14.1005	14.0143	13.9417	13.8806	13.8290
16.375%	14.5630	14.4176	14.2962	14.1946	14.1095	14.0379	13.9776	13.9268
16.500%	14.6538	14.5096	14.3894	14.2890	14.2048	14.1342	14.0747	14.0247
16.625%	14.7447	14.6018	14.4829	14.3835	14.3004	14.2306	14.1720	14.1227
16.750%	14.8358	14.6942	14.5764	14.4782	14.3960	14.3272	14.2694	14.2208
16.875%	14.9270	14.7868	14.6702	14.5730	14.4919	14.4239	14.3669	14.3191

MONTHLY PAYMENT TO AMORTIZE A LOAN OF $1,000

Term of Loan

Interest Rate	25 Years	26 Years	27 Years	28 Years	29 Years	30 Years	35 Years	40 Years
12.000%	10.5322	10.4695	10.4145	10.3661	10.3236	10.2861	10.1555	10.0850
12.125%	10.6247	10.5629	10.5087	10.4611	10.4192	10.3824	10.2545	10.1859
12.250%	10.7174	10.6565	10.6030	10.5562	10.5151	10.4790	10.3537	10.2869
12.375%	10.8104	10.7503	10.6977	10.6516	10.6112	10.5757	10.4531	10.3880
12.500%	10.9035	10.8443	10.7925	10.7471	10.7074	10.6726	10.5525	10.4892
12.625%	10.9969	10.9385	10.8875	10.8429	10.8039	10.7697	10.6522	10.5905
12.750%	11.0905	11.0329	10.9827	10.9388	10.9005	10.8669	10.7520	10.6920
12.875%	11.1843	11.1276	11.0781	11.0350	10.9973	10.9644	10.8519	10.7935
13.000%	11.2784	11.2224	11.1738	11.1313	11.0943	11.0620	10.9519	10.8951
13.125%	11.3726	11.3175	11.2696	11.2279	11.1915	11.1598	11.0521	10.9969
13.250%	11.4670	11.4127	11.3656	11.3246	11.2888	11.2577	11.1524	11.0987
13.375%	11.5616	11.5082	11.4618	11.4214	11.3864	11.3558	11.2529	11.2006
13.500%	11.6564	11.6038	11.5581	11.5185	11.4841	11.4541	11.3534	11.3026
13.625%	11.7515	11.6996	11.6547	11.6157	11.5819	11.5525	11.4541	11.4047
13.750%	11.8467	11.7956	11.7514	11.7131	11.6799	11.6511	11.5549	11.5069
13.875%	11.9420	11.8917	11.8483	11.8107	11.7781	11.7498	11.6557	11.6091
14.000%	12.0376	11.9881	11.9453	11.9084	11.8764	11.8487	11.7567	11.7114
14.125%	12.1334	12.0846	12.0425	12.0062	11.9749	11.9477	11.8578	11.8138
14.250%	12.2293	12.1813	12.1399	12.1043	12.0735	12.0469	11.9590	11.9162
14.375%	12.3254	12.2781	12.2375	12.2024	12.1722	12.1461	12.0603	12.0187
14.500%	12.4216	12.3751	12.3351	12.3007	12.2711	12.2456	12.1617	12.1213
14.625%	12.5181	12.4723	12.4330	12.3992	12.3701	12.3451	12.2632	12.2240
14.750%	12.6146	12.5696	12.5310	12.4978	12.4693	12.4448	12.3647	12.3267
14.875%	12.7114	12.6671	12.6291	12.5965	12.5686	12.5445	12.4664	12.4294
15.000%	12.8083	12.7647	12.7274	12.6954	12.6680	12.6444	12.5681	12.5322
15.125%	12.9054	12.8625	12.8258	12.7944	12.7675	12.7445	12.6699	12.6351
15.250%	13.0026	12.9604	12.9243	12.8935	12.8672	12.8446	12.7718	12.7380
15.375%	13.0999	13.0584	13.0230	12.9928	12.9669	12.9448	12.8738	12.8410
15.500%	13.1975	13.1566	13.1218	13.0922	13.0668	13.0452	12.9758	12.9440
15.625%	13.2951	13.2550	13.2208	13.1916	13.1668	13.1456	13.0780	13.0471
15.750%	13.3929	13.3534	13.3198	13.2913	13.2669	13.2462	13.1801	13.1502
15.875%	13.4908	13.4520	13.4190	13.3910	13.3671	13.3468	13.2824	13.2533
16.000%	13.5889	13.5507	13.5183	13.4908	13.4674	13.4476	13.3847	13.3565
16.125%	13.6871	13.6496	13.6178	13.5908	13.5679	13.5484	13.4871	13.4597
16.250%	13.7854	13.7485	13.7173	13.6908	13.6684	13.6493	13.5895	13.5630
16.375%	13.8839	13.8476	13.8169	13.7910	13.7690	13.7504	13.6920	13.6663
16.500%	13.9824	13.9468	13.9167	13.8912	13.8697	13.8515	13.7945	13.7696
16.625%	14.0811	14.0461	14.0166	13.9916	13.9705	13.9527	13.8971	13.8730
16.750%	14.1800	14.1456	14.1165	14.0921	14.0714	14.0540	13.9998	13.9764
16.875%	14.2789	14.2451	14.2166	14.1926	14.1724	14.1553	14.1025	14.0798

MONTHLY PAYMENT TO AMORTIZE A LOAN OF $1,000

Term of Loan

Interest Rate	1 Year	2 Years	3 Years	4 Years	5 Years	6 Years	7 Years	8 Years
17.000%	91.2048	49.4423	35.6527	28.8550	24.8526	22.2461	20.4358	19.1215
17.125%	91.2641	49.5023	35.7150	28.9198	24.9198	22.3159	20.5081	19.1962
17.250%	91.3234	49.5625	35.7773	28.9845	24.9872	22.3859	20.5805	19.2710
17.375%	91.3828	49.6226	35.8396	29.0494	25.0547	22.4559	20.6531	19.3461
17.500%	91.4422	49.6828	35.9021	29.1144	25.1222	22.5260	20.7258	19.4212
17.625%	91.5016	49.7431	35.9646	29.1794	25.1899	22.5963	20.7986	19.4965
17.750%	91.5611	49.8034	36.0271	29.2445	25.2576	22.6667	20.8716	19.5719
17.875%	91.6205	49.8637	36.0897	29.3097	25.3255	22.7372	20.9446	19.6475
18.000%	91.6800	49.9241	36.1524	29.3750	25.3934	22.8078	21.0178	19.7232
18.125%	91.7395	49.9845	36.2151	29.4404	25.4615	22.8785	21.0912	19.7991
18.250%	91.7990	50.0450	36.2779	29.5058	25.5296	22.9493	21.1646	19.8751
18.375%	91.8586	50.1055	36.3408	29.5713	25.5979	23.0203	21.2382	19.9512
18.500%	91.9181	50.1660	36.4037	29.6369	25.6662	23.0914	21.3119	20.0274
18.625%	91.9777	50.2266	36.4667	29.7026	25.7346	23.1625	21.3858	20.1038
18.750%	92.0373	50.2872	36.5297	29.7684	25.8032	23.2338	21.4597	20.1804
18.875%	92.0969	50.3479	36.5929	29.8342	25.8718	23.3052	21.5338	20.2571
19.000%	92.1566	50.4086	36.6560	29.9001	25.9406	23.3767	21.6080	20.3339

MONTHLY PAYMENT TO AMORTIZE A LOAN OF $1,000

Term of Loan

Interest Rate	9 Years	10 Years	11 Years	12 Years	13 Years	14 Years	15 Years	16 Years
17.000%	18.1362	17.3798	16.7883	16.3192	15.9430	15.6384	15.3900	15.1863
17.125%	18.2132	17.4591	16.8697	16.4026	16.0282	15.7254	15.4787	15.2765
17.250%	18.2905	17.5385	16.9513	16.4862	16.1137	15.8126	15.5676	15.3669
17.375%	18.3678	17.6181	17.0330	16.5700	16.1993	15.9000	15.6566	15.4574
17.500%	18.4453	17.6979	17.1149	16.6539	16.2851	15.9876	15.7458	15.5481
17.625%	18.5230	17.7778	17.1970	16.7380	16.3711	16.0753	15.8351	15.6390
17.750%	18.6008	17.8579	17.2792	16.8222	16.4572	16.1632	15.9247	15.7300
17.875%	18.6788	17.9381	17.3616	16.9066	16.5435	16.2513	16.0144	15.8212
18.000%	18.7569	18.0185	17.4442	16.9912	16.6300	16.3395	16.1042	15.9126
18.125%	18.8351	18.0991	17.5269	17.0759	16.7166	16.4279	16.1942	16.0041
18.250%	18.9136	18.1798	17.6098	17.1608	16.8034	16.5165	16.2844	16.0957
18.375%	18.9921	18.2606	17.6928	17.2459	16.8904	16.6052	16.3747	16.1875
18.500%	19.0708	18.3417	17.7760	17.3311	16.9775	16.6941	16.4652	16.2795
18.625%	19.1497	18.4228	17.8593	17.4165	17.0648	16.7831	16.5559	16.3716
18.750%	19.2287	18.5041	17.9428	17.5021	17.1523	16.8723	16.6467	16.4639
18.875%	19.3078	18.5856	18.0265	17.5878	17.2399	16.9616	16.7376	16.5564
19.000%	19.3871	18.6672	18.1103	17.6736	17.3276	17.0511	16.8288	16.6489

MONTHLY PAYMENT TO AMORTIZE A LOAN OF $1,000

Term of Loan

Interest Rate	17 Years	18 Years	19 Years	20 Years	21 Years	22 Years	23 Years	24 Years
17.000%	15.0184	14.8795	14.7641	14.6680	14.5878	14.5208	14.4646	14.4175
17.125%	15.1100	14.9724	14.8581	14.7631	14.6839	14.6178	14.5624	14.5160
17.250%	15.2018	15.0654	14.9524	14.8584	14.7802	14.7149	14.6603	14.6147
17.375%	15.2937	15.1586	15.0467	14.9538	14.8766	14.8122	14.7584	14.7134
17.500%	15.3858	15.2519	15.1412	15.0494	14.9731	14.9095	14.8565	14.8123
17.625%	15.4780	15.3455	15.2359	15.1451	15.0698	15.0071	14.9548	14.9113
17.750%	15.5704	15.4391	15.3307	15.2410	15.1666	15.1047	15.0532	15.0104
17.875%	15.6630	15.5329	15.4257	15.3370	15.2635	15.2025	15.1518	15.1096
18.000%	15.7557	15.6269	15.5208	15.4331	15.3605	15.3004	15.2504	15.2089
18.125%	15.8486	15.7210	15.6160	15.5294	15.4577	15.3984	15.3492	15.3083
18.250%	15.9146	15.8153	15.7114	15.6258	15.5550	15.4965	15.4480	15.4078
18.375%	16.0348	15.9097	15.8069	15.7223	15.6525	15.5948	15.5470	15.5074
18.500%	16.1281	16.0042	15.9026	15.8190	15.7500	15.6931	15.6461	15.6071
18.625%	16.2216	16.0989	15.9984	15.9158	15.8477	15.7916	15.7452	15.7069
18.750%	16.3152	16.1938	16.0943	16.0127	15.9455	15.8902	15.8445	15.8068
18.875%	16.4090	16.2887	16.1904	16.1097	16.0434	15.9889	15.9429	15.9068
19.000%	16.5029	16.3838	16.2866	16.2068	16.1414	16.0876	16.0434	16.0069

MONTHLY PAYMENT TO AMORTIZE A LOAN OF $1,000

Term of Loan

Interest Rate	25 Years	26 Years	27 Years	28 Years	29 Years	30 Years	35 Years	40 Years
17.000%	14.3780	14.3447	14.3168	14.2933	14.2734	14.2568	14.2053	14.1832
17.125%	14.4771	14.4445	14.4171	14.3940	14.3746	14.3583	14.3081	14.2867
17.250%	14.5764	14.5443	14.5174	14.4948	14.4758	14.4599	14.4109	14.3902
17.375%	14.6758	14.6443	14.6179	14.5957	14.5771	14.5615	14.5138	14.4938
17.500%	14.7753	14.7443	14.7184	14.6967	14.6785	14.6633	14.6168	14.5973
17.625%	14.8749	14.8445	14.8191	14.7978	14.7800	14.7651	14.7197	14.7009
17.750%	14.9746	14.9447	14.9198	14.8989	14.8815	14.8669	14.8228	14.8045
17.875%	15.0744	15.0451	15.0206	15.0002	14.9831	14.9689	14.9258	14.9082
18.000%	15.1743	15.1455	15.1215	15.1015	15.0848	15.0709	15.0289	15.0118
18.125%	15.2743	15.2460	15.2225	15.2029	15.1865	15.1729	15.1321	15.1155
18.250%	15.3744	15.3466	15.3235	15.3043	15.2883	15.2750	15.2352	15.2192
18.375%	15.4746	15.4473	15.4247	15.4059	15.3902	15.3772	15.3384	15.3229
18.500%	15.5748	15.5481	15.5259	15.5075	15.4922	15.4794	15.4417	15.4266
18.625%	15.6752	15.6489	15.6272	15.6091	15.5942	15.5817	15.5449	15.5304
18.750%	15.7757	15.7499	15.7285	15.7109	15.6962	15.6841	15.6483	15.6342
18.875%	15.8762	15.8509	15.8300	15.8127	15.7983	15.7865	15.7516	15.7379
19.000%	15.9768	15.9520	15.9315	15.9145	15.9005	15.8889	15.8549	15.8417

Mortgage Amortization Tables

The rate at which your mortgage is paid off (amortized) depends on its interest rate and term. Loans with lower interest rates are amortized slightly more quickly than loans with higher rates (i.e., more of the principal is paid off per month). For example, a $100,000 30-year loan at 8 percent interest would have a remaining principal balance of about $87,700 after ten years. A 14-percent loan would have a higher remaining balance after ten years of about $95,300.

Loans with shorter terms (and higher monthly payments) are amortized much more quickly. More money goes to pay off your loan each month. For example, a $100,000 15-year loan at 8 percent would have a remaining balance after ten years of only $47,100 compared with the $87,700 balance of the 30-year loan.

The only practical way to get your exact loan balance is to ask your lender, but you can estimate your remaining balance by using the following tables.

Instructions

- Locate the table that most nearly equals your interest rate.
- Use the column on that table that matches the term of your loan.

- Read down the column until you find the remaining principal balance factor to the approximate age of your loan.
- Multiply the factor by your initial loan amount to get the estimated remaining principal balance.

For example, if nine years ago, you got a $75,000 30-year mortgage at 9.5 percent interest, your principal balance now would be approximately:

0.917 (remaining principal balance factor) × $75,000 = $68,775

Remaining Principal Balance Factors

For Mortgages with an Interest Rate of 2.00% and an Original Term of:

Age of Loan in Years	5 Years	6 Years	7 Years	8 Years	9 Years	10 Years	11 Years	12 Years	15 Years	20 Years	25 Years	30 Years	35 Years	40 Years
1	0.808	0.842	0.866	0.884	0.898	0.909	0.918	0.926	0.942	0.959	0.969	0.975	0.980	0.984
2	0.612	0.680	0.728	0.765	0.793	0.816	0.834	0.850	0.883	0.917	0.937	0.950	0.960	0.967
3	0.412	0.515	0.588	0.644	0.686	0.721	0.749	0.772	0.823	0.874	0.905	0.925	0.939	0.950
4	0.208	0.347	0.446	0.520	0.578	0.624	0.662	0.693	0.762	0.831	0.872	0.899	0.918	0.932
5	0.000	0.175	0.300	0.394	0.467	0.525	0.573	0.612	0.699	0.786	0.838	0.872	0.896	0.914
6		0.000	0.152	0.265	0.354	0.424	0.482	0.530	0.636	0.741	0.803	0.845	0.874	0.896
7			0.000	0.134	0.238	0.321	0.389	0.446	0.570	0.694	0.768	0.817	0.852	0.877
8				0.000	0.120	0.216	0.295	0.360	0.504	0.647	0.732	0.789	0.829	0.858
9					0.000	0.109	0.199	0.273	0.436	0.599	0.696	0.760	0.805	0.839
10						0.000	0.100	0.184	0.367	0.550	0.659	0.731	0.782	0.819
11							0.000	0.093	0.297	0.500	0.621	0.701	0.757	0.799
12								0.000	0.225	0.448	0.582	0.670	0.732	0.779
15									0.000	0.289	0.461	0.574	0.655	0.714
20										0.000	0.242	0.402	0.515	0.599
25											0.000	0.211	0.360	0.471
30												0.000	0.189	0.329
35													0.000	0.173
40														0.000

For Mortgages with an Interest Rate of 2.25% and an Original Term of:

Age of Loan in Years	5 Years	6 Years	7 Years	8 Years	9 Years	10 Years	11 Years	12 Years	15 Years	20 Years	25 Years	30 Years	35 Years	40 Years
1	0.809	0.843	0.867	0.885	0.899	0.910	0.919	0.927	0.943	0.960	0.970	0.976	0.981	0.984
2	0.613	0.682	0.730	0.767	0.795	0.818	0.836	0.851	0.885	0.919	0.939	0.952	0.962	0.968
3	0.414	0.517	0.591	0.646	0.689	0.723	0.751	0.775	0.826	0.877	0.907	0.928	0.942	0.952
4	0.209	0.348	0.448	0.522	0.580	0.627	0.665	0.696	0.765	0.834	0.875	0.902	0.921	0.935
5	0.000	0.176	0.302	0.396	0.469	0.528	0.576	0.616	0.703	0.790	0.842	0.876	0.901	0.918
6		0.000	0.153	0.267	0.356	0.427	0.485	0.534	0.640	0.746	0.809	0.850	0.879	0.901
7			0.000	0.135	0.240	0.324	0.393	0.450	0.575	0.700	0.774	0.823	0.858	0.883
8				0.000	0.121	0.218	0.298	0.364	0.509	0.653	0.739	0.795	0.835	0.865
9					0.000	0.110	0.201	0.276	0.441	0.605	0.703	0.767	0.813	0.846
10						0.000	0.101	0.186	0.371	0.556	0.666	0.738	0.789	0.827
11							0.000	0.094	0.300	0.506	0.628	0.709	0.766	0.808
12								0.000	0.228	0.455	0.589	0.678	0.741	0.788
15									0.000	0.294	0.468	0.584	0.665	0.725
20										0.000	0.247	0.410	0.524	0.615
25											0.000	0.217	0.370	0.483
30												0.000	0.195	0.339
35													0.000	0.179
40														0.000

Remaining Principal Balance Factors

For Mortgages with an Interest Rate of 2.50% and an Original Term of:

Age of Loan in Years	5 Years	6 Years	7 Years	8 Years	9 Years	10 Years	11 Years	12 Years	15 Years	20 Years	25 Years	30 Years	35 Years	40 Years
1	0.810	0.844	0.868	0.886	0.900	0.911	0.920	0.928	0.944	0.961	0.971	0.977	0.982	0.985
2	0.615	0.683	0.732	0.768	0.797	0.819	0.838	0.853	0.887	0.921	0.941	0.954	0.963	0.970
3	0.415	0.519	0.593	0.648	0.691	0.726	0.754	0.777	0.829	0.880	0.910	0.930	0.944	0.955
4	0.210	0.350	0.450	0.525	0.583	0.630	0.668	0.699	0.769	0.838	0.879	0.906	0.925	0.939
5	0.000	0.177	0.304	0.399	0.472	0.531	0.579	0.619	0.707	0.795	0.847	0.881	0.905	0.922
6		0.000	0.154	0.269	0.359	0.430	0.489	0.537	0.644	0.750	0.814	0.855	0.884	0.906
7			0.000	0.136	0.242	0.327	0.396	0.453	0.580	0.705	0.780	0.829	0.863	0.889
8				0.000	0.123	0.220	0.301	0.367	0.513	0.659	0.745	0.802	0.842	0.871
9					0.000	0.112	0.203	0.279	0.445	0.611	0.709	0.774	0.820	0.853
10						0.000	0.103	0.188	0.376	0.562	0.673	0.746	0.797	0.835
11							0.000	0.095	0.304	0.512	0.635	0.717	0.774	0.816
12								0.000	0.231	0.461	0.597	0.687	0.750	0.796
15									0.000	0.299	0.476	0.593	0.675	0.735
20										0.000	0.253	0.419	0.536	0.622
25											0.000	0.223	0.379	0.495
30												0.000	0.201	0.350
35													0.000	0.186
40														0.000

For Mortgages with an Interest Rate of 2.75% and an Original Term of:

Age of Loan in Years	5 Years	6 Years	7 Years	8 Years	9 Years	10 Years	11 Years	12 Years	15 Years	20 Years	25 Years	30 Years	35 Years	40 Years
1	0.811	0.845	0.869	0.887	0.901	0.912	0.921	0.929	0.945	0.962	0.972	0.978	0.983	0.986
2	0.616	0.685	0.734	0.770	0.799	0.821	0.840	0.855	0.889	0.923	0.943	0.956	0.965	0.972
3	0.417	0.521	0.595	0.650	0.694	0.728	0.757	0.780	0.832	0.883	0.913	0.933	0.947	0.957
4	0.211	0.352	0.452	0.527	0.586	0.633	0.671	0.703	0.772	0.841	0.882	0.909	0.928	0.942
5	0.000	0.178	0.306	0.401	0.475	0.534	0.583	0.623	0.711	0.799	0.851	0.885	0.909	0.926
6		0.000	0.155	0.271	0.361	0.433	0.492	0.541	0.649	0.755	0.819	0.860	0.889	0.910
7			0.000	0.137	0.244	0.329	0.399	0.457	0.584	0.710	0.785	0.834	0.869	0.894
8				0.000	0.124	0.223	0.303	0.371	0.518	0.664	0.751	0.808	0.848	0.877
9					0.000	0.113	0.205	0.282	0.450	0.617	0.716	0.781	0.826	0.860
10						0.000	0.104	0.190	0.380	0.568	0.680	0.753	0.804	0.842
11							0.000	0.096	0.308	0.518	0.643	0.724	0.782	0.824
12								0.000	0.234	0.467	0.604	0.695	0.758	0.805
15									0.000	0.304	0.483	0.602	0.684	0.745
20										0.000	0.258	0.428	0.547	0.634
25											0.000	0.229	0.389	0.507
30												0.000	0.208	0.360
35													0.000	0.192
40														0.000

Remaining Principal Balance Factors

For Mortgages with an Interest Rate of 3.00% and an Original Term of:

Age of Loan in Years	5 Years	6 Years	7 Years	8 Years	9 Years	10 Years	11 Years	12 Years	15 Years	20 Years	25 Years	30 Years	35 Years	40 Years
1	0.812	0.846	0.870	0.888	0.902	0.913	0.922	0.930	0.946	0.963	0.973	0.979	0.984	0.987
2	0.618	0.686	0.735	0.772	0.800	0.823	0.842	0.857	0.891	0.925	0.945	0.958	0.967	0.973
3	0.418	0.522	0.597	0.653	0.696	0.731	0.759	0.783	0.834	0.885	0.916	0.935	0.949	0.959
4	0.212	0.353	0.454	0.530	0.589	0.636	0.674	0.706	0.776	0.845	0.886	0.913	0.931	0.945
5	0.000	0.179	0.307	0.403	0.478	0.537	0.586	0.626	0.715	0.803	0.855	0.889	0.913	0.930
6		0.000	0.156	0.273	0.364	0.436	0.496	0.545	0.653	0.760	0.823	0.865	0.894	0.915
7			0.000	0.138	0.246	0.332	0.402	0.461	0.589	0.716	0.791	0.840	0.874	0.899
8				0.000	0.125	0.225	0.306	0.374	0.523	0.670	0.757	0.814	0.854	0.883
9					0.000	0.114	0.207	0.285	0.455	0.623	0.722	0.788	0.833	0.866
10						0.000	0.105	0.193	0.384	0.574	0.687	0.760	0.812	0.849
11							0.000	0.098	0.312	0.524	0.650	0.732	0.789	0.831
12								0.000	0.237	0.473	0.612	0.703	0.767	0.813
15									0.000	0.309	0.491	0.611	0.694	0.755
20										0.000	0.264	0.437	0.557	0.645
25											0.000	0.235	0.399	0.518
30												0.000	0.214	0.371
35													0.000	0.199
40														0.000

For Mortgages with an Interest Rate of 3.25% and an Original Term of:

Age of Loan in Years	5 Years	6 Years	7 Years	8 Years	9 Years	10 Years	11 Years	12 Years	15 Years	20 Years	25 Years	30 Years	35 Years	40 Years
1	0.813	0.847	0.871	0.889	0.903	0.914	0.923	0.931	0.947	0.964	0.974	0.980	0.984	0.988
2	0.619	0.688	0.737	0.774	0.802	0.825	0.844	0.859	0.893	0.927	0.946	0.959	0.968	0.975
3	0.420	0.524	0.599	0.655	0.699	0.733	0.762	0.785	0.837	0.888	0.918	0.938	0.952	0.962
4	0.213	0.355	0.457	0.532	0.591	0.638	0.677	0.709	0.779	0.848	0.889	0.916	0.934	0.948
5	0.000	0.180	0.309	0.406	0.481	0.540	0.589	0.630	0.719	0.807	0.859	0.893	0.917	0.934
6		0.000	0.157	0.275	0.366	0.439	0.499	0.549	0.657	0.765	0.828	0.870	0.898	0.919
7			0.000	0.140	0.248	0.335	0.406	0.464	0.593	0.721	0.796	0.845	0.879	0.904
8				0.000	0.126	0.227	0.309	0.377	0.527	0.676	0.763	0.820	0.860	0.889
9					0.000	0.115	0.209	0.288	0.459	0.629	0.729	0.794	0.840	0.873
10						0.000	0.106	0.195	0.389	0.580	0.694	0.767	0.819	0.856
11							0.000	0.099	0.316	0.530	0.657	0.740	0.797	0.839
12								0.000	0.241	0.479	0.619	0.711	0.775	0.821
15									0.000	0.314	0.499	0.619	0.703	0.764
20										0.000	0.270	0.445	0.568	0.657
25											0.000	0.241	0.408	0.530
30												0.000	0.221	0.381
35													0.000	0.206
40														0.000

Remaining Principal Balance Factors

For Mortgages with an Interest Rate of 3.50% and an Original Term of:

Age of Loan in Years	5 Years	6 Years	7 Years	8 Years	9 Years	10 Years	11 Years	12 Years	15 Years	20 Years	25 Years	30 Years	35 Years	40 Years
1	0.814	0.848	0.872	0.890	0.904	0.915	0.924	0.932	0.948	0.965	0.975	0.981	0.985	0.988
2	0.621	0.690	0.739	0.776	0.804	0.827	0.846	0.861	0.895	0.928	0.948	0.961	0.970	0.976
3	0.421	0.526	0.601	0.657	0.701	0.736	0.764	0.788	0.840	0.891	0.921	0.940	0.954	0.964
4	0.214	0.357	0.459	0.535	0.594	0.641	0.680	0.712	0.782	0.852	0.893	0.919	0.937	0.951
5	0.000	0.182	0.311	0.408	0.483	0.544	0.593	0.634	0.723	0.811	0.863	0.897	0.920	0.937
6		0.000	0.158	0.277	0.369	0.442	0.502	0.552	0.661	0.769	0.833	0.874	0.903	0.923
7			0.000	0.141	0.250	0.337	0.409	0.468	0.598	0.726	0.801	0.850	0.884	0.909
8				0.000	0.127	0.229	0.312	0.381	0.532	0.681	0.769	0.826	0.865	0.894
9					0.000	0.116	0.212	0.291	0.464	0.635	0.735	0.801	0.846	0.879
10						0.000	0.108	0.197	0.393	0.586	0.700	0.774	0.826	0.863
11							0.000	0.100	0.320	0.537	0.664	0.747	0.805	0.846
12								0.000	0.244	0.485	0.627	0.719	0.783	0.829
15									0.000	0.319	0.506	0.628	0.713	0.774
20										0.000	0.275	0.454	0.578	0.668
25											0.000	0.247	0.418	0.542
30												0.000	0.227	0.392
35													0.000	0.213
40														0.000

For Mortgages with an Interest Rate of 3.75% and an Original Term of:

Age of Loan in Years	5 Years	6 Years	7 Years	8 Years	9 Years	10 Years	11 Years	12 Years	15 Years	20 Years	25 Years	30 Years	35 Years	40 Years
1	0.815	0.849	0.873	0.891	0.905	0.916	0.925	0.933	0.949	0.966	0.975	0.982	0.986	0.989
2	0.622	0.691	0.740	0.777	0.806	0.829	0.847	0.863	0.897	0.930	0.950	0.963	0.971	0.978
3	0.423	0.528	0.603	0.660	0.703	0.738	0.767	0.790	0.842	0.893	0.923	0.943	0.956	0.966
4	0.215	0.359	0.461	0.537	0.597	0.644	0.683	0.715	0.786	0.855	0.896	0.922	0.940	0.953
5	0.000	0.183	0.313	0.410	0.486	0.547	0.596	0.637	0.727	0.815	0.867	0.901	0.924	0.941
6		0.000	0.159	0.279	0.371	0.445	0.506	0.556	0.666	0.774	0.837	0.879	0.907	0.927
7			0.000	0.142	0.252	0.340	0.412	0.472	0.602	0.731	0.807	0.856	0.889	0.914
8				0.000	0.128	0.231	0.315	0.384	0.537	0.687	0.775	0.832	0.871	0.899
9					0.000	0.118	0.214	0.294	0.468	0.640	0.741	0.807	0.852	0.885
10						0.000	0.109	0.199	0.397	0.593	0.707	0.781	0.832	0.869
11							0.000	0.102	0.324	0.543	0.671	0.754	0.812	0.853
12								0.000	0.247	0.491	0.634	0.727	0.791	0.837
15									0.000	0.324	0.514	0.637	0.722	0.783
20										0.000	0.281	0.463	0.588	0.679
25											0.000	0.253	0.428	0.554
30												0.000	0.234	0.402
35													0.000	0.220
40														0.000

Remaining Principal Balance Factors

For Mortgages with an Interest Rate of 4.00% and an Original Term of:

Age of Loan in Years	5 Years	6 Years	7 Years	8 Years	9 Years	10 Years	11 Years	12 Years	15 Years	20 Years	25 Years	30 Years	35 Years	40 Years
1	0.816	0.850	0.874	0.892	0.906	0.917	0.926	0.934	0.950	0.967	0.976	0.982	0.987	0.990
2	0.624	0.693	0.742	0.779	0.808	0.831	0.849	0.865	0.899	0.932	0.951	0.964	0.973	0.979
3	0.424	0.530	0.605	0.662	0.706	0.741	0.769	0.793	0.845	0.896	0.926	0.945	0.958	0.968
4	0.216	0.360	0.463	0.540	0.600	0.647	0.686	0.718	0.789	0.858	0.899	0.925	0.943	0.956
5	0.000	0.184	0.315	0.413	0.489	0.550	0.599	0.641	0.731	0.819	0.871	0.904	0.927	0.944
6		0.000	0.161	0.281	0.374	0.448	0.509	0.560	0.670	0.779	0.842	0.883	0.911	0.931
7			0.000	0.143	0.254	0.343	0.415	0.475	0.607	0.736	0.812	0.861	0.894	0.918
8				0.000	0.130	0.233	0.318	0.388	0.541	0.692	0.780	0.837	0.876	0.904
9					0.000	0.119	0.216	0.297	0.473	0.646	0.748	0.813	0.858	0.890
10						0.000	0.110	0.202	0.402	0.599	0.714	0.788	0.839	0.875
11							0.000	0.103	0.328	0.549	0.678	0.762	0.819	0.860
12								0.000	0.251	0.497	0.641	0.734	0.798	0.844
15									0.000	0.329	0.521	0.645	0.731	0.792
20										0.000	0.287	0.472	0.599	0.690
25											0.000	0.259	0.437	0.565
30												0.000	0.240	0.413
35													0.000	0.227
40														0.000

For Mortgages with an Interest Rate of 4.25% and an Original Term of:

Age of Loan in Years	5 Years	6 Years	7 Years	8 Years	9 Years	10 Years	11 Years	12 Years	15 Years	20 Years	25 Years	30 Years	35 Years	40 Years
1	0.817	0.850	0.875	0.893	0.907	0.918	0.927	0.935	0.951	0.968	0.977	0.983	0.987	0.990
2	0.625	0.695	0.744	0.781	0.810	0.832	0.851	0.867	0.900	0.934	0.953	0.966	0.974	0.980
3	0.426	0.532	0.607	0.664	0.708	0.743	0.772	0.796	0.847	0.898	0.928	0.947	0.960	0.970
4	0.217	0.362	0.465	0.542	0.602	0.650	0.689	0.721	0.792	0.862	0.902	0.928	0.946	0.959
5	0.000	0.185	0.317	0.415	0.492	0.553	0.603	0.644	0.734	0.823	0.875	0.908	0.931	0.947
6		0.000	0.162	0.283	0.377	0.451	0.513	0.563	0.674	0.783	0.846	0.887	0.915	0.935
7			0.000	0.144	0.256	0.346	0.419	0.479	0.611	0.741	0.817	0.865	0.899	0.922
8				0.000	0.131	0.235	0.320	0.391	0.546	0.698	0.786	0.843	0.882	0.909
9					0.000	0.120	0.218	0.300	0.477	0.652	0.754	0.819	0.864	0.896
10						0.000	0.111	0.204	0.406	0.604	0.720	0.794	0.845	0.881
11							0.000	0.104	0.332	0.555	0.685	0.769	0.826	0.867
12								0.000	0.254	0.503	0.648	0.742	0.806	0.851
15									0.000	0.334	0.529	0.654	0.739	0.800
20										0.000	0.292	0.480	0.609	0.700
25											0.000	0.265	0.447	0.576
30												0.000	0.247	0.423
35													0.000	0.234
40														0.000

Remaining Principal Balance Factors

For Mortgages with an Interest Rate of 4.50% and an Original Term of:

Age of Loan in Years	5 Years	6 Years	7 Years	8 Years	9 Years	10 Years	11 Years	12 Years	15 Years	20 Years	25 Years	30 Years	35 Years	40 Years
1	0.818	0.851	0.876	0.894	0.908	0.919	0.928	0.936	0.952	0.968	0.978	0.984	0.988	0.991
2	0.627	0.696	0.746	0.783	0.811	0.834	0.853	0.868	0.902	0.935	0.955	0.967	0.975	0.981
3	0.427	0.534	0.610	0.666	0.710	0.746	0.774	0.798	0.850	0.901	0.930	0.949	0.962	0.971
4	0.218	0.364	0.467	0.545	0.605	0.653	0.692	0.724	0.795	0.865	0.905	0.931	0.948	0.961
5	0.000	0.186	0.318	0.418	0.495	0.556	0.606	0.647	0.738	0.827	0.879	0.912	0.934	0.950
6		0.000	0.163	0.285	0.379	0.454	0.516	0.567	0.678	0.787	0.851	0.891	0.919	0.938
7			0.000	0.146	0.258	0.348	0.422	0.483	0.616	0.746	0.822	0.870	0.903	0.927
8				0.000	0.132	0.237	0.323	0.395	0.550	0.703	0.792	0.848	0.887	0.914
9					0.000	0.121	0.220	0.303	0.482	0.658	0.760	0.825	0.869	0.901
10						0.000	0.113	0.206	0.410	0.610	0.727	0.801	0.851	0.887
11							0.000	0.105	0.335	0.561	0.692	0.776	0.833	0.873
12								0.000	0.257	0.509	0.656	0.749	0.813	0.858
15									0.000	0.339	0.536	0.662	0.748	0.809
20										0.000	0.298	0.489	0.619	0.711
25											0.000	0.272	0.457	0.588
30												0.000	0.254	0.434
35													0.000	0.241
40														0.000

For Mortgages with an Interest Rate of 4.75% and an Original Term of:

Age of Loan in Years	5 Years	6 Years	7 Years	8 Years	9 Years	10 Years	11 Years	12 Years	15 Years	20 Years	25 Years	30 Years	35 Years	40 Years
1	0.818	0.852	0.877	0.895	0.909	0.920	0.929	0.937	0.953	0.969	0.979	0.985	0.989	0.991
2	0.628	0.698	0.747	0.784	0.813	0.836	0.855	0.870	0.904	0.937	0.956	0.968	0.977	0.982
3	0.429	0.535	0.612	0.669	0.713	0.748	0.777	0.801	0.853	0.903	0.933	0.951	0.964	0.973
4	0.219	0.365	0.469	0.547	0.608	0.656	0.695	0.728	0.799	0.868	0.908	0.934	0.951	0.963
5	0.000	0.187	0.320	0.420	0.497	0.559	0.609	0.651	0.742	0.831	0.882	0.915	0.937	0.953
6		0.000	0.164	0.287	0.382	0.458	0.519	0.571	0.682	0.792	0.855	0.895	0.923	0.942
7			0.000	0.147	0.260	0.351	0.425	0.486	0.620	0.751	0.827	0.875	0.908	0.930
8				0.000	0.133	0.240	0.326	0.398	0.555	0.708	0.797	0.853	0.892	0.919
9					0.000	0.123	0.223	0.306	0.486	0.663	0.766	0.831	0.875	0.906
10						0.000	0.114	0.209	0.415	0.616	0.733	0.807	0.857	0.893
11							0.000	0.107	0.339	0.567	0.699	0.782	0.839	0.879
12								0.000	0.261	0.515	0.663	0.756	0.820	0.865
15									0.000	0.345	0.544	0.671	0.756	0.817
20										0.000	0.304	0.498	0.628	0.721
25											0.000	0.278	0.466	0.599
30												0.000	0.261	0.444
35													0.000	0.248
40														0.000

Remaining Principal Balance Factors

For Mortgages with an Interest Rate of 5.00% and an Original Term of:

Age of Loan in Years	5 Years	6 Years	7 Years	8 Years	9 Years	10 Years	11 Years	12 Years	15 Years	20 Years	25 Years	30 Years	35 Years	40 Years
1	0.819	0.853	0.878	0.896	0.910	0.921	0.930	0.938	0.954	0.970	0.979	0.985	0.989	0.992
2	0.630	0.699	0.749	0.786	0.815	0.838	0.856	0.872	0.906	0.939	0.958	0.970	0.978	0.983
3	0.430	0.537	0.614	0.671	0.715	0.750	0.779	0.803	0.855	0.906	0.935	0.953	0.966	0.975
4	0.220	0.367	0.472	0.550	0.610	0.659	0.698	0.731	0.802	0.871	0.911	0.936	0.953	0.965
5	0.000	0.188	0.322	0.422	0.500	0.562	0.613	0.654	0.746	0.835	0.886	0.918	0.940	0.955
6		0.000	0.165	0.289	0.384	0.461	0.523	0.574	0.687	0.796	0.859	0.899	0.926	0.945
7			0.000	0.148	0.263	0.354	0.428	0.490	0.625	0.756	0.832	0.879	0.912	0.934
8				0.000	0.135	0.242	0.329	0.402	0.560	0.714	0.802	0.859	0.896	0.923
9					0.000	0.124	0.225	0.309	0.491	0.669	0.772	0.837	0.880	0.911
10						0.000	0.115	0.211	0.419	0.622	0.739	0.813	0.863	0.898
11							0.000	0.108	0.343	0.573	0.705	0.789	0.846	0.885
12								0.000	0.264	0.521	0.670	0.764	0.827	0.871
15									0.000	0.350	0.551	0.679	0.765	0.825
20										0.000	0.310	0.506	0.638	0.731
25											0.000	0.284	0.476	0.610
30												0.000	0.267	0.455
35													0.000	0.256
40														0.000

For Mortgages with an Interest Rate of 5.25% and an Original Term of:

Age of Loan in Years	5 Years	6 Years	7 Years	8 Years	9 Years	10 Years	11 Years	12 Years	15 Years	20 Years	25 Years	30 Years	35 Years	40 Years
1	0.820	0.854	0.879	0.897	0.911	0.922	0.931	0.939	0.955	0.971	0.980	0.986	0.990	0.992
2	0.631	0.701	0.751	0.788	0.817	0.840	0.858	0.874	0.908	0.940	0.959	0.971	0.979	0.985
3	0.432	0.539	0.616	0.673	0.717	0.753	0.782	0.806	0.857	0.908	0.937	0.955	0.968	0.976
4	0.221	0.369	0.474	0.552	0.613	0.661	0.701	0.734	0.805	0.874	0.914	0.939	0.956	0.967
5	0.000	0.189	0.324	0.425	0.503	0.565	0.616	0.658	0.749	0.838	0.889	0.921	0.943	0.958
6		0.000	0.166	0.291	0.387	0.464	0.526	0.578	0.691	0.800	0.863	0.903	0.930	0.948
7			0.000	0.149	0.265	0.357	0.432	0.494	0.629	0.761	0.836	0.884	0.916	0.938
8				0.000	0.136	0.244	0.332	0.405	0.564	0.719	0.808	0.864	0.901	0.927
9					0.000	0.125	0.227	0.312	0.496	0.675	0.777	0.842	0.885	0.916
10						0.000	0.117	0.213	0.423	0.628	0.745	0.819	0.869	0.903
11							0.000	0.109	0.347	0.579	0.712	0.796	0.852	0.891
12								0.000	0.267	0.527	0.676	0.771	0.834	0.877
15									0.000	0.355	0.559	0.687	0.773	0.832
20										0.000	0.316	0.515	0.648	0.740
25											0.000	0.291	0.485	0.621
30												0.000	0.274	0.465
35													0.000	0.263
40														0.000

Remaining Principal Balance Factor

Factors For Mortgages with an Interest Rate of 5.50% and an Original Term of:

Age of Loan in Years	5 Years	6 Years	7 Years	8 Years	9 Years	10 Years	11 Years	12 Years	15 Years	20 Years	25 Years	30 Years	35 Years	40 Years
1	0.821	0.855	0.880	0.898	0.912	0.923	0.932	0.939	0.956	0.972	0.981	0.987	0.990	0.993
2	0.633	0.703	0.752	0.790	0.818	0.841	0.860	0.876	0.909	0.942	0.961	0.972	0.980	0.985
3	0.433	0.541	0.618	0.675	0.720	0.755	0.784	0.808	0.860	0.910	0.939	0.957	0.969	0.978
4	0.223	0.371	0.476	0.555	0.616	0.664	0.704	0.737	0.808	0.877	0.917	0.941	0.958	0.969
5	0.000	0.190	0.326	0.427	0.506	0.568	0.619	0.661	0.753	0.842	0.893	0.925	0.946	0.960
6		0.000	0.167	0.293	0.389	0.467	0.529	0.582	0.695	0.805	0.867	0.907	0.933	0.951
7			0.000	0.150	0.267	0.359	0.435	0.497	0.633	0.765	0.841	0.888	0.920	0.941
8				0.000	0.137	0.246	0.335	0.409	0.569	0.724	0.813	0.868	0.905	0.931
9					0.000	0.126	0.229	0.315	0.500	0.680	0.783	0.847	0.890	0.920
10						0.000	0.118	0.215	0.428	0.634	0.752	0.825	0.874	0.908
11							0.000	0.111	0.351	0.585	0.718	0.802	0.858	0.896
12								0.000	0.271	0.533	0.683	0.777	0.840	0.883
15									0.000	0.360	0.566	0.695	0.781	0.840
20										0.000	0.321	0.523	0.657	0.750
25											0.000	0.297	0.495	0.631
30												0.000	0.281	0.475
35													0.000	0.270
40														0.000

For Mortgages with an Interest Rate of 5.75% and an Original Term of:

Age of Loan in Years	5 Years	6 Years	7 Years	8 Years	9 Years	10 Years	11 Years	12 Years	15 Years	20 Years	25 Years	30 Years	35 Years	40 Years
1	0.822	0.856	0.881	0.899	0.913	0.924	0.933	0.940	0.957	0.973	0.982	0.987	0.991	0.993
2	0.634	0.704	0.754	0.791	0.820	0.843	0.862	0.877	0.911	0.943	0.962	0.974	0.981	0.986
3	0.435	0.543	0.620	0.678	0.722	0.758	0.786	0.810	0.862	0.913	0.941	0.959	0.971	0.979
4	0.224	0.372	0.478	0.557	0.618	0.667	0.707	0.740	0.811	0.880	0.919	0.944	0.960	0.971
5	0.000	0.191	0.328	0.430	0.508	0.571	0.622	0.665	0.757	0.845	0.896	0.928	0.948	0.963
6		0.000	0.169	0.295	0.392	0.470	0.533	0.585	0.699	0.809	0.871	0.910	0.936	0.954
7			0.000	0.151	0.269	0.362	0.438	0.501	0.638	0.770	0.845	0.892	0.923	0.945
8				0.000	0.138	0.248	0.338	0.412	0.573	0.729	0.818	0.873	0.910	0.935
9					0.000	0.128	0.232	0.318	0.505	0.686	0.789	0.853	0.895	0.924
10						0.000	0.119	0.218	0.432	0.640	0.758	0.831	0.880	0.913
11							0.000	0.112	0.355	0.591	0.725	0.808	0.864	0.901
12								0.000	0.274	0.539	0.690	0.784	0.846	0.889
15									0.000	0.365	0.573	0.703	0.788	0.847
20										0.000	0.327	0.532	0.667	0.759
25											0.000	0.304	0.504	0.642
30												0.000	0.288	0.485
35													0.000	0.277
40														0.000

Remaining Principal Balance Factors

For Mortgages with an Interest Rate of 6.00% and an Original Term of:

Age of Loan in Years	5 Years	6 Years	7 Years	8 Years	9 Years	10 Years	11 Years	12 Years	15 Years	20 Years	25 Years	30 Years	35 Years	40 Years
1	0.823	0.857	0.881	0.900	0.914	0.925	0.934	0.941	0.958	0.973	0.982	0.988	0.991	0.994
2	0.635	0.706	0.756	0.793	0.822	0.845	0.864	0.879	0.913	0.945	0.963	0.975	0.982	0.987
3	0.436	0.545	0.622	0.680	0.724	0.760	0.789	0.813	0.865	0.915	0.943	0.961	0.972	0.980
4	0.225	0.374	0.480	0.560	0.621	0.670	0.710	0.743	0.814	0.883	0.922	0.946	0.962	0.973
5	0.000	0.193	0.330	0.432	0.511	0.574	0.626	0.668	0.760	0.849	0.899	0.931	0.951	0.965
6		0.000	0.170	0.297	0.395	0.473	0.536	0.589	0.703	0.813	0.875	0.914	0.939	0.957
7			0.000	0.153	0.271	0.365	0.441	0.505	0.642	0.775	0.850	0.896	0.927	0.948
8				0.000	0.139	0.250	0.341	0.416	0.578	0.734	0.823	0.878	0.914	0.938
9					0.000	0.129	0.234	0.321	0.509	0.691	0.794	0.858	0.900	0.928
10						0.000	0.120	0.220	0.436	0.645	0.764	0.837	0.885	0.918
11							0.000	0.113	0.359	0.597	0.731	0.815	0.869	0.906
12								0.000	0.277	0.545	0.697	0.791	0.852	0.894
15									0.000	0.371	0.580	0.710	0.796	0.854
20										0.000	0.333	0.540	0.676	0.768
25											0.000	0.310	0.514	0.652
30												0.000	0.295	0.496
35													0.000	0.285
40														0.000

For Mortgages with an Interest Rate of 6.25% and an Original Term of:

Age of Loan in Years	5 Years	6 Years	7 Years	8 Years	9 Years	10 Years	11 Years	12 Years	15 Years	20 Years	25 Years	30 Years	35 Years	40 Years
1	0.824	0.858	0.882	0.901	0.915	0.926	0.935	0.942	0.958	0.974	0.983	0.988	0.992	0.994
2	0.637	0.707	0.757	0.795	0.824	0.847	0.865	0.881	0.914	0.946	0.965	0.976	0.983	0.988
3	0.438	0.547	0.624	0.682	0.727	0.762	0.791	0.815	0.867	0.917	0.945	0.963	0.974	0.981
4	0.226	0.376	0.482	0.562	0.624	0.673	0.713	0.746	0.817	0.886	0.925	0.948	0.964	0.974
5	0.000	0.194	0.331	0.434	0.514	0.577	0.629	0.671	0.764	0.852	0.903	0.933	0.953	0.967
6		0.000	0.171	0.299	0.397	0.476	0.540	0.592	0.707	0.817	0.879	0.917	0.942	0.959
7			0.000	0.154	0.273	0.368	0.445	0.508	0.646	0.779	0.854	0.900	0.930	0.951
8				0.000	0.141	0.253	0.344	0.419	0.582	0.739	0.828	0.882	0.918	0.942
9					0.000	0.130	0.236	0.324	0.514	0.696	0.799	0.863	0.904	0.932
10						0.000	0.122	0.223	0.441	0.651	0.769	0.842	0.890	0.922
11							0.000	0.115	0.363	0.603	0.737	0.821	0.875	0.911
12								0.000	0.281	0.551	0.703	0.797	0.858	0.900
15									0.000	0.376	0.588	0.718	0.803	0.861
20										0.000	0.339	0.548	0.685	0.777
25											0.000	0.317	0.523	0.662
30												0.000	0.302	0.506
35													0.000	0.292
40														0.000

Remaining Principal Balance Factors

For Mortgages with an Interest Rate of 6.50% and an Original Term of:

Age of Loan in Years	5 Years	6 Years	7 Years	8 Years	9 Years	10 Years	11 Years	12 Years	15 Years	20 Years	25 Years	30 Years	35 Years	40 Years
1	0.825	0.859	0.883	0.901	0.915	0.927	0.936	0.943	0.959	0.975	0.983	0.989	0.992	0.995
2	0.638	0.709	0.759	0.796	0.825	0.848	0.867	0.882	0.916	0.948	0.966	0.977	0.984	0.989
3	0.439	0.548	0.626	0.684	0.729	0.765	0.794	0.818	0.869	0.919	0.947	0.964	0.975	0.983
4	0.227	0.377	0.484	0.564	0.626	0.675	0.715	0.748	0.820	0.889	0.927	0.951	0.966	0.976
5	0.000	0.195	0.333	0.437	0.517	0.580	0.632	0.675	0.767	0.856	0.906	0.936	0.956	0.969
6		0.000	0.172	0.301	0.400	0.479	0.543	0.596	0.711	0.821	0.883	0.921	0.945	0.962
7			0.000	0.155	0.275	0.370	0.448	0.512	0.651	0.784	0.858	0.904	0.934	0.954
8				0.000	0.142	0.255	0.347	0.422	0.587	0.744	0.832	0.887	0.922	0.945
9					0.000	0.132	0.238	0.327	0.518	0.702	0.805	0.868	0.909	0.936
10						0.000	0.123	0.225	0.445	0.657	0.775	0.848	0.895	0.926
11							0.000	0.116	0.367	0.608	0.744	0.826	0.880	0.916
12								0.000	0.284	0.557	0.710	0.804	0.864	0.905
15									0.000	0.381	0.595	0.726	0.810	0.867
20										0.000	0.345	0.557	0.694	0.785
25											0.000	0.323	0.532	0.672
30												0.000	0.309	0.516
35													0.000	0.299
40														0.000

For Mortgages with an Interest Rate of 6.75% and an Original Term of:

Age of Loan in Years	5 Years	6 Years	7 Years	8 Years	9 Years	10 Years	11 Years	12 Years	15 Years	20 Years	25 Years	30 Years	35 Years	40 Years
1	0.826	0.860	0.884	0.902	0.916	0.927	0.937	0.944	0.960	0.976	0.984	0.989	0.993	0.995
2	0.640	0.710	0.761	0.798	0.827	0.850	0.869	0.884	0.917	0.949	0.967	0.978	0.985	0.990
3	0.441	0.550	0.628	0.686	0.731	0.767	0.796	0.820	0.872	0.921	0.949	0.966	0.977	0.984
4	0.228	0.379	0.487	0.567	0.629	0.678	0.718	0.751	0.823	0.891	0.929	0.953	0.968	0.978
5	0.000	0.196	0.335	0.439	0.520	0.583	0.635	0.678	0.771	0.859	0.909	0.939	0.958	0.971
6		0.000	0.173	0.303	0.402	0.482	0.546	0.600	0.715	0.825	0.886	0.924	0.948	0.964
7			0.000	0.156	0.277	0.373	0.451	0.516	0.655	0.788	0.863	0.908	0.937	0.956
8				0.000	0.143	0.257	0.350	0.426	0.591	0.749	0.837	0.891	0.925	0.948
9					0.000	0.133	0.241	0.330	0.523	0.707	0.810	0.873	0.913	0.940
10						0.000	0.124	0.227	0.450	0.662	0.781	0.853	0.899	0.930
11							0.000	0.117	0.371	0.614	0.750	0.832	0.885	0.920
12								0.000	0.288	0.563	0.716	0.810	0.870	0.910
15									0.000	0.386	0.602	0.733	0.817	0.873
20										0.000	0.351	0.565	0.702	0.794
25											0.000	0.330	0.541	0.682
30												0.000	0.316	0.525
35													0.000	0.307
40														0.000

Remaining Principal Balance Factors

For Mortgages with an Interest Rate of 7.00% and an Original Term of:

Age of Loan in Years	5 Years	6 Years	7 Years	8 Years	9 Years	10 Years	11 Years	12 Years	15 Years	20 Years	25 Years	30 Years	35 Years	40 Years
1	0.827	0.861	0.885	0.903	0.917	0.928	0.937	0.945	0.961	0.976	0.985	0.990	0.993	0.995
2	0.641	0.712	0.762	0.800	0.829	0.852	0.870	0.886	0.919	0.951	0.968	0.979	0.986	0.990
3	0.442	0.552	0.630	0.689	0.734	0.769	0.798	0.822	0.874	0.923	0.951	0.967	0.978	0.985
4	0.229	0.381	0.489	0.569	0.632	0.681	0.721	0.754	0.826	0.894	0.932	0.955	0.969	0.979
5	0.000	0.197	0.337	0.442	0.522	0.586	0.638	0.681	0.774	0.863	0.912	0.941	0.960	0.973
6		0.000	0.174	0.305	0.405	0.485	0.550	0.603	0.719	0.829	0.890	0.927	0.950	0.966
7			0.000	0.158	0.279	0.376	0.455	0.519	0.659	0.793	0.867	0.911	0.940	0.959
8				0.000	0.145	0.259	0.352	0.429	0.596	0.754	0.842	0.895	0.929	0.951
9					0.000	0.134	0.243	0.333	0.527	0.712	0.815	0.877	0.917	0.943
10						0.000	0.126	0.230	0.454	0.668	0.786	0.858	0.904	0.934
11							0.000	0.119	0.375	0.620	0.756	0.838	0.890	0.925
12								0.000	0.291	0.569	0.723	0.816	0.875	0.914
15									0.000	0.392	0.609	0.740	0.824	0.879
20										0.000	0.357	0.573	0.711	0.802
25											0.000	0.336	0.550	0.691
30												0.000	0.323	0.535
35													0.000	0.314
40														0.000

For Mortgages with an Interest Rate of 7.25% and an Original Term of:

Age of Loan in Years	5 Years	6 Years	7 Years	8 Years	9 Years	10 Years	11 Years	12 Years	15 Years	20 Years	25 Years	30 Years	35 Years	40 Years
1	0.828	0.862	0.886	0.904	0.918	0.929	0.938	0.946	0.962	0.977	0.985	0.990	0.994	0.996
2	0.643	0.714	0.764	0.801	0.830	0.853	0.872	0.887	0.921	0.952	0.969	0.980	0.987	0.991
3	0.444	0.554	0.632	0.691	0.736	0.772	0.801	0.825	0.876	0.925	0.952	0.969	0.979	0.986
4	0.230	0.383	0.491	0.572	0.634	0.684	0.724	0.757	0.829	0.897	0.934	0.957	0.971	0.980
5	0.000	0.198	0.339	0.444	0.525	0.589	0.642	0.685	0.778	0.866	0.915	0.944	0.962	0.974
6		0.000	0.176	0.307	0.408	0.488	0.553	0.607	0.723	0.833	0.893	0.930	0.953	0.968
7			0.000	0.159	0.281	0.379	0.458	0.523	0.663	0.797	0.871	0.915	0.943	0.961
8				0.000	0.146	0.262	0.355	0.433	0.600	0.759	0.846	0.899	0.932	0.954
9					0.000	0.136	0.245	0.336	0.532	0.718	0.820	0.882	0.921	0.946
10						0.000	0.127	0.232	0.458	0.673	0.792	0.863	0.908	0.938
11							0.000	0.120	0.379	0.626	0.761	0.843	0.895	0.929
12								0.000	0.295	0.574	0.729	0.822	0.880	0.919
15									0.000	0.397	0.616	0.747	0.831	0.885
20										0.000	0.363	0.581	0.719	0.809
25											0.000	0.342	0.559	0.701
30												0.000	0.330	0.545
35													0.000	0.321
40														0.000

Remaining Principal Balance Factors

For Mortgages with an Interest Rate of 7.50% and an Original Term of:

Age of Loan in Years	5 Years	6 Years	7 Years	8 Years	9 Years	10 Years	11 Years	12 Years	15 Years	20 Years	25 Years	30 Years	35 Years	40 Years
1	0.829	0.863	0.887	0.905	0.919	0.930	0.939	0.947	0.962	0.978	0.986	0.991	0.994	0.996
2	0.644	0.715	0.765	0.803	0.832	0.855	0.874	0.889	0.922	0.953	0.971	0.981	0.987	0.991
3	0.445	0.556	0.634	0.693	0.738	0.774	0.803	0.827	0.878	0.927	0.954	0.970	0.980	0.987
4	0.231	0.384	0.493	0.574	0.637	0.687	0.727	0.760	0.832	0.899	0.936	0.959	0.973	0.982
5	0.000	0.199	0.341	0.446	0.528	0.592	0.645	0.688	0.781	0.869	0.917	0.946	0.964	0.976
6		0.000	0.177	0.309	0.410	0.491	0.556	0.610	0.726	0.836	0.897	0.933	0.955	0.970
7			0.000	0.160	0.284	0.382	0.461	0.527	0.668	0.801	0.875	0.918	0.946	0.964
8				0.000	0.147	0.264	0.358	0.436	0.604	0.763	0.851	0.903	0.935	0.957
9					0.000	0.137	0.248	0.339	0.536	0.723	0.825	0.886	0.924	0.949
10						0.000	0.128	0.234	0.463	0.679	0.797	0.868	0.912	0.941
11							0.000	0.122	0.383	0.631	0.767	0.848	0.899	0.932
12								0.000	0.298	0.580	0.735	0.827	0.886	0.923
15									0.000	0.402	0.623	0.754	0.837	0.890
20										0.000	0.369	0.589	0.727	0.817
25											0.000	0.349	0.568	0.710
30												0.000	0.336	0.554
35													0.000	0.328
40														0.000

For Mortgages with an Interest Rate of 7.75% and an Original Term of:

Age of Loan in Years	5 Years	6 Years	7 Years	8 Years	9 Years	10 Years	11 Years	12 Years	15 Years	20 Years	25 Years	30 Years	35 Years	40 Years
1	0.830	0.864	0.888	0.906	0.920	0.931	0.940	0.947	0.963	0.978	0.986	0.991	0.994	0.996
2	0.646	0.717	0.767	0.805	0.834	0.857	0.875	0.891	0.924	0.955	0.972	0.982	0.988	0.992
3	0.447	0.558	0.636	0.695	0.740	0.776	0.805	0.829	0.881	0.929	0.956	0.971	0.981	0.988
4	0.232	0.386	0.495	0.577	0.639	0.689	0.730	0.763	0.834	0.902	0.939	0.960	0.974	0.983
5	0.000	0.200	0.343	0.449	0.531	0.595	0.648	0.691	0.784	0.872	0.920	0.948	0.966	0.978
6		0.000	0.178	0.311	0.413	0.494	0.560	0.614	0.730	0.840	0.900	0.936	0.958	0.972
7			0.000	0.161	0.286	0.384	0.464	0.530	0.672	0.806	0.878	0.922	0.949	0.966
8				0.000	0.148	0.266	0.361	0.440	0.609	0.768	0.855	0.907	0.939	0.959
9					0.000	0.138	0.250	0.342	0.541	0.728	0.830	0.890	0.928	0.952
10						0.000	0.130	0.237	0.467	0.684	0.802	0.873	0.916	0.944
11							0.000	0.123	0.387	0.637	0.773	0.854	0.904	0.936
12								0.000	0.301	0.586	0.741	0.833	0.890	0.927
15									0.000	0.407	0.629	0.761	0.843	0.896
20										0.000	0.375	0.597	0.735	0.842
25											0.000	0.355	0.577	0.719
30												0.000	0.343	0.564
35													0.000	0.336
40														0.000

Remaining Principal Balance Factors

For Mortgages with an Interest Rate of 8.00% and an Original Term of:

Age of Loan in Years	5 Years	6 Years	7 Years	8 Years	9 Years	10 Years	11 Years	12 Years	15 Years	20 Years	25 Years	30 Years	35 Years	40 Years
1	0.831	0.865	0.889	0.907	0.921	0.932	0.941	0.948	0.964	0.979	0.987	0.992	0.995	0.996
2	0.647	0.718	0.769	0.806	0.835	0.858	0.877	0.892	0.925	0.956	0.973	0.983	0.989	0.993
3	0.448	0.560	0.638	0.697	0.743	0.778	0.808	0.831	0.883	0.931	0.957	0.973	0.982	0.988
4	0.233	0.388	0.497	0.579	0.642	0.692	0.732	0.766	0.837	0.904	0.941	0.962	0.975	0.984
5	0.000	0.202	0.345	0.451	0.533	0.598	0.651	0.694	0.788	0.875	0.923	0.951	0.968	0.979
6		0.000	0.179	0.313	0.415	0.497	0.563	0.617	0.734	0.844	0.903	0.938	0.960	0.974
7			0.000	0.163	0.288	0.387	0.468	0.534	0.676	0.810	0.882	0.925	0.951	0.968
8				0.000	0.150	0.268	0.364	0.443	0.613	0.773	0.859	0.910	0.942	0.962
9					0.000	0.139	0.252	0.345	0.545	0.733	0.834	0.894	0.931	0.955
10						0.000	0.131	0.239	0.471	0.689	0.808	0.877	0.920	0.948
11							0.000	0.124	0.391	0.642	0.779	0.859	0.908	0.940
12								0.000	0.305	0.592	0.747	0.839	0.895	0.931
15									0.000	0.413	0.636	0.768	0.849	0.901
20										0.000	0.381	0.605	0.743	0.831
25											0.000	0.362	0.585	0.728
30												0.000	0.350	0.573
35													0.000	0.343
40														0.000

For Mortgages with an Interest Rate of 8.25% and an Original Term of:

Age of Loan in Years	5 Years	6 Years	7 Years	8 Years	9 Years	10 Years	11 Years	12 Years	15 Years	20 Years	25 Years	30 Years	35 Years	40 Years
1	0.831	0.866	0.890	0.908	0.922	0.933	0.942	0.949	0.965	0.979	0.987	0.992	0.995	0.997
2	0.648	0.720	0.770	0.808	0.837	0.860	0.878	0.894	0.927	0.957	0.974	0.983	0.989	0.993
3	0.450	0.561	0.640	0.699	0.745	0.781	0.810	0.834	0.885	0.933	0.959	0.974	0.983	0.989
4	0.234	0.389	0.500	0.581	0.645	0.695	0.735	0.769	0.840	0.907	0.943	0.964	0.977	0.985
5	0.000	0.203	0.347	0.454	0.536	0.601	0.654	0.698	0.791	0.878	0.925	0.953	0.970	0.980
6		0.000	0.180	0.315	0.418	0.500	0.566	0.621	0.738	0.847	0.906	0.941	0.962	0.975
7			0.000	0.164	0.290	0.390	0.471	0.537	0.680	0.814	0.886	0.928	0.954	0.970
8				0.000	0.151	0.271	0.367	0.447	0.617	0.777	0.863	0.914	0.945	0.964
9					0.000	0.141	0.255	0.349	0.549	0.738	0.839	0.898	0.935	0.958
10						0.000	0.133	0.242	0.476	0.695	0.813	0.882	0.924	0.951
11							0.000	0.126	0.395	0.648	0.784	0.864	0.912	0.943
12								0.000	0.308	0.597	0.753	0.844	0.900	0.935
15									0.000	0.418	0.643	0.774	0.855	0.906
20										0.000	0.387	0.613	0.751	0.838
25											0.000	0.368	0.594	0.736
30												0.000	0.357	0.582
35													0.000	0.250
40														0.000

Remaining Principal Balance Factors

For Mortgages with an Interest Rate of 8.50% and an Original Term of:

Age of Loan in Years	5 Years	6 Years	7 Years	8 Years	9 Years	10 Years	11 Years	12 Years	15 Years	20 Years	25 Years	30 Years	35 Years	40 Years
1	0.832	0.867	0.891	0.909	0.923	0.934	0.943	0.950	0.966	0.980	0.988	0.992	0.995	0.997
2	0.650	0.721	0.772	0.810	0.839	0.861	0.880	0.895	0.928	0.958	0.975	0.984	0.990	0.994
3	0.451	0.563	0.642	0.701	0.747	0.783	0.812	0.836	0.887	0.935	0.960	0.975	0.984	0.990
4	0.235	0.391	0.502	0.584	0.647	0.697	0.738	0.771	0.843	0.909	0.945	0.966	0.978	0.986
5	0.000	0.204	0.348	0.456	0.539	0.604	0.657	0.701	0.794	0.881	0.928	0.955	0.971	0.982
6		0.000	0.182	0.317	0.421	0.503	0.570	0.624	0.742	0.851	0.909	0.943	0.964	0.977
7			0.000	0.165	0.292	0.393	0.474	0.541	0.684	0.818	0.889	0.931	0.956	0.972
8				0.000	0.152	0.273	0.370	0.450	0.622	0.782	0.867	0.917	0.947	0.966
9					0.000	0.142	0.257	0.352	0.554	0.743	0.844	0.902	0.938	0.960
10						0.000	0.134	0.244	0.480	0.700	0.818	0.886	0.928	0.953
11							0.000	0.127	0.400	0.654	0.790	0.868	0.916	0.946
12								0.000	0.312	0.603	0.759	0.849	0.904	0.938
15									0.000	0.423	0.649	0.781	0.861	0.910
20										0.000	0.392	0.620	0.758	0.845
25											0.000	0.375	0.602	0.744
30												0.000	0.364	0.591
35													0.000	0.357
40														0.000

For Mortgages with an Interest Rate of 8.75% and an Original Term of:

Age of Loan in Years	5 Years	6 Years	7 Years	8 Years	9 Years	10 Years	11 Years	12 Years	15 Years	20 Years	25 Years	30 Years	35 Years	40 Years
1	0.833	0.867	0.892	0.910	0.924	0.935	0.943	0.951	0.966	0.981	0.988	0.993	0.995	0.997
2	0.651	0.723	0.773	0.811	0.840	0.863	0.882	0.897	0.929	0.960	0.976	0.985	0.991	0.994
3	0.453	0.565	0.645	0.704	0.749	0.785	0.814	0.838	0.889	0.937	0.962	0.976	0.985	0.991
4	0.236	0.393	0.504	0.586	0.650	0.700	0.741	0.774	0.845	0.912	0.947	0.967	0.979	0.987
5	0.000	0.205	0.350	0.458	0.541	0.607	0.660	0.704	0.797	0.884	0.930	0.957	0.973	0.983
6		0.000	0.183	0.319	0.423	0.506	0.573	0.628	0.745	0.854	0.912	0.946	0.966	0.978
7			0.000	0.166	0.294	0.396	0.477	0.545	0.688	0.822	0.893	0.934	0.958	0.973
8				0.000	0.154	0.275	0.373	0.454	0.626	0.786	0.871	0.920	0.950	0.968
9					0.000	0.144	0.259	0.355	0.558	0.747	0.848	0.906	0.941	0.962
10						0.000	0.135	0.247	0.484	0.705	0.823	0.890	0.931	0.956
11							0.000	0.129	0.404	0.659	0.795	0.873	0.920	0.949
12								0.000	0.315	0.609	0.765	0.854	0.908	0.942
15									0.000	0.428	0.656	0.787	0.866	0.915
20										0.000	0.398	0.628	0.766	0.851
25											0.000	0.381	0.611	0.753
30												0.000	0.371	0.600
35													0.000	0.364
40														0.000

Remaining Principal Balance Factors

For Mortgages with an Interest Rate of 9.00% and an Original Term of:

Age of Loan in Years	5 Years	6 Years	7 Years	8 Years	9 Years	10 Years	11 Years	12 Years	15 Years	20 Years	25 Years	30 Years	35 Years	40 Years
1	0.834	0.868	0.893	0.911	0.924	0.935	0.944	0.951	0.967	0.981	0.989	0.993	0.996	0.997
2	0.653	0.724	0.775	0.813	0.842	0.865	0.883	0.898	0.931	0.961	0.977	0.986	0.991	0.994
3	0.454	0.567	0.647	0.706	0.751	0.787	0.816	0.840	0.891	0.938	0.963	0.978	0.986	0.991
4	0.237	0.395	0.506	0.589	0.652	0.703	0.743	0.777	0.848	0.914	0.949	0.969	0.980	0.988
5	0.000	0.206	0.352	0.461	0.544	0.610	0.664	0.707	0.801	0.887	0.933	0.959	0.974	0.984
6		0.000	0.184	0.321	0.426	0.509	0.576	0.631	0.749	0.858	0.915	0.948	0.968	0.980
7			0.000	0.168	0.296	0.398	0.481	0.548	0.692	0.826	0.896	0.936	0.960	0.975
8				0.000	0.155	0.277	0.376	0.457	0.630	0.791	0.875	0.924	0.952	0.970
9					0.000	0.145	0.262	0.358	0.563	0.752	0.852	0.910	0.944	0.965
10						0.000	0.137	0.249	0.489	0.710	0.827	0.894	0.934	0.959
11							0.000	0.130	0.408	0.664	0.800	0.878	0.924	0.952
12								0.000	0.319	0.614	0.770	0.859	0.912	0.945
15									0.000	0.433	0.662	0.793	0.871	0.919
20										0.000	0.404	0.635	0.773	0.857
25											0.000	0.388	0.619	0.761
30												0.000	0.378	0.609
35													0.000	0.372
40														0.000

For Mortgages with an Interest Rate of 9.25% and an Original Term of:

Age of Loan in Years	5 Years	6 Years	7 Years	8 Years	9 Years	10 Years	11 Years	12 Years	15 Years	20 Years	25 Years	30 Years	35 Years	40 Years
1	0.835	0.869	0.893	0.911	0.925	0.936	0.945	0.952	0.968	0.982	0.989	0.994	0.996	0.998
2	0.654	0.726	0.777	0.814	0.843	0.866	0.885	0.900	0.932	0.962	0.978	0.986	0.992	0.995
3	0.456	0.569	0.649	0.708	0.753	0.790	0.819	0.842	0.893	0.940	0.965	0.979	0.987	0.992
4	0.238	0.396	0.508	0.591	0.655	0.705	0.746	0.780	0.851	0.916	0.951	0.970	0.982	0.989
5	0.000	0.207	0.354	0.463	0.547	0.613	0.667	0.710	0.804	0.890	0.935	0.961	0.976	0.985
6		0.000	0.185	0.323	0.428	0.512	0.579	0.635	0.753	0.861	0.918	0.950	0.969	0.981
7			0.000	0.169	0.299	0.401	0.484	0.552	0.696	0.830	0.899	0.939	0.962	0.977
8				0.000	0.156	0.280	0.379	0.461	0.635	0.795	0.879	0.927	0.955	0.972
9					0.000	0.146	0.264	0.361	0.567	0.757	0.857	0.913	0.947	0.967
10						0.000	0.138	0.252	0.493	0.715	0.832	0.898	0.937	0.961
11							0.000	0.132	0.412	0.670	0.805	0.882	0.927	0.955
12								0.000	0.322	0.620	0.776	0.864	0.916	0.948
15									0.000	0.439	0.669	0.799	0.876	0.923
20										0.000	0.410	0.643	0.780	0.863
25											0.000	0.394	0.627	0.768
30												0.000	0.384	0.618
35													0.000	0.379
40														0.000

Remaining Principal Balance Factors

For Mortgages with an Interest Rate of 9.50% and an Original Term of:

Age of Loan in Years	5 Years	6 Years	7 Years	8 Years	9 Years	10 Years	11 Years	12 Years	15 Years	20 Years	25 Years	30 Years	35 Years	40 Years
1	0.836	0.870	0.894	0.912	0.926	0.937	0.946	0.953	0.968	0.982	0.990	0.994	0.996	0.998
2	0.656	0.727	0.778	0.816	0.845	0.868	0.886	0.901	0.934	0.963	0.978	0.987	0.992	0.995
3	0.457	0.570	0.651	0.710	0.756	0.792	0.821	0.845	0.895	0.942	0.966	0.980	0.988	0.992
4	0.240	0.398	0.510	0.594	0.658	0.708	0.749	0.782	0.853	0.918	0.952	0.971	0.983	0.989
5	0.000	0.208	0.356	0.465	0.550	0.616	0.670	0.714	0.807	0.893	0.937	0.962	0.977	0.986
6		0.000	0.186	0.325	0.431	0.515	0.583	0.638	0.756	0.864	0.921	0.953	0.971	0.982
7			0.000	0.170	0.301	0.404	0.487	0.555	0.700	0.833	0.903	0.942	0.964	0.978
8				0.000	0.157	0.282	0.382	0.464	0.639	0.799	0.883	0.930	0.957	0.974
9					0.000	0.148	0.267	0.364	0.571	0.762	0.861	0.917	0.949	0.969
10						0.000	0.140	0.254	0.497	0.720	0.837	0.902	0.940	0.963
11							0.000	0.133	0.416	0.675	0.810	0.886	0.931	0.957
12								0.000	0.326	0.625	0.781	0.869	0.920	0.951
15									0.000	0.444	0.675	0.805	0.881	0.927
20										0.000	0.416	0.650	0.787	0.869
25											0.000	0.400	0.635	0.776
30												0.000	0.391	0.626
35													0.000	0.386
40														0.000

For Mortgages with an Interest Rate of 9.75% and an Original Term of:

Age of Loan in Years	5 Years	6 Years	7 Years	8 Years	9 Years	10 Years	11 Years	12 Years	15 Years	20 Years	25 Years	30 Years	35 Years	40 Years
1	0.837	0.871	0.895	0.913	0.927	0.938	0.947	0.954	0.969	0.983	0.990	0.994	0.996	0.998
2	0.657	0.729	0.780	0.818	0.846	0.869	0.888	0.903	0.935	0.964	0.979	0.988	0.993	0.995
3	0.459	0.572	0.653	0.712	0.758	0.794	0.823	0.847	0.897	0.943	0.967	0.981	0.988	0.993
4	0.241	0.400	0.512	0.596	0.660	0.711	0.751	0.785	0.856	0.921	0.954	0.973	0.984	0.990
5	0.000	0.210	0.358	0.468	0.552	0.619	0.673	0.717	0.810	0.895	0.940	0.964	0.978	0.987
6		0.000	0.188	0.327	0.434	0.518	0.586	0.642	0.760	0.868	0.923	0.955	0.973	0.983
7			0.000	0.171	0.303	0.407	0.490	0.559	0.704	0.837	0.906	0.944	0.966	0.980
8				0.000	0.159	0.284	0.385	0.468	0.643	0.803	0.886	0.933	0.959	0.975
9					0.000	0.149	0.269	0.367	0.576	0.766	0.865	0.920	0.952	0.971
10						0.000	0.141	0.257	0.501	0.725	0.841	0.906	0.943	0.966
11							0.000	0.134	0.420	0.680	0.815	0.890	0.934	0.960
12								0.000	0.330	0.631	0.786	0.873	0.924	0.954
15									0.000	0.449	0.681	0.811	0.886	0.931
20										0.000	0.422	0.657	0.793	0.875
25											0.000	0.407	0.643	0.783
30												0.000	0.398	0.634
35													0.000	0.393
40														0.000

Remaining Principal Balance Factors

For Mortgages with an Interest Rate of 10.00% and an Original Term of:

Age of Loan in Years	5 Years	6 Years	7 Years	8 Years	9 Years	10 Years	11 Years	12 Years	15 Years	20 Years	25 Years	30 Years	35 Years	40 Years
1	0.838	0.872	0.896	0.914	0.928	0.939	0.947	0.955	0.970	0.983	0.991	0.994	0.997	0.998
2	0.658	0.730	0.781	0.819	0.848	0.871	0.889	0.904	0.936	0.965	0.980	0.988	0.993	0.996
3	0.460	0.574	0.655	0.714	0.760	0.796	0.825	0.849	0.899	0.945	0.969	0.982	0.989	0.993
4	0.242	0.401	0.514	0.598	0.663	0.713	0.754	0.788	0.858	0.923	0.956	0.974	0.985	0.991
5	0.000	0.211	0.360	0.470	0.555	0.622	0.676	0.720	0.813	0.898	0.942	0.966	0.980	0.988
6		0.000	0.189	0.329	0.436	0.521	0.589	0.645	0.763	0.871	0.926	0.957	0.974	0.984
7			0.000	0.173	0.305	0.410	0.494	0.562	0.708	0.841	0.909	0.946	0.968	0.981
8				0.000	0.160	0.286	0.388	0.471	0.647	0.807	0.890	0.935	0.961	0.977
9					0.000	0.150	0.271	0.370	0.580	0.771	0.869	0.923	0.954	0.972
10						0.000	0.142	0.259	0.506	0.730	0.846	0.909	0.946	0.968
11							0.000	0.136	0.424	0.685	0.820	0.894	0.937	0.962
12								0.000	0.333	0.636	0.792	0.878	0.927	0.956
15									0.000	0.454	0.688	0.817	0.891	0.934
20										0.000	0.428	0.664	0.800	0.880
25											0.000	0.413	0.651	0.790
30												0.000	0.405	0.643
35													0.000	0.400
40														0.000

For Mortgages with an Interest Rate of 10.25% and an Original Term of:

Age of Loan in Years	5 Years	6 Years	7 Years	8 Years	9 Years	10 Years	11 Years	12 Years	15 Years	20 Years	25 Years	30 Years	35 Years	40 Years
1	0.839	0.873	0.897	0.915	0.929	0.939	0.948	0.955	0.970	0.984	0.991	0.995	0.997	0.998
2	0.660	0.732	0.783	0.821	0.850	0.872	0.891	0.906	0.937	0.966	0.981	0.989	0.993	0.996
3	0.462	0.576	0.657	0.716	0.762	0.798	0.827	0.851	0.901	0.947	0.970	0.982	0.990	0.994
4	0.243	0.403	0.517	0.601	0.665	0.716	0.757	0.790	0.861	0.925	0.957	0.975	0.985	0.991
5	0.000	0.212	0.362	0.473	0.558	0.625	0.679	0.723	0.816	0.901	0.944	0.967	0.981	0.989
6		0.000	0.190	0.331	0.439	0.524	0.592	0.648	0.767	0.874	0.929	0.959	0.976	0.986
7			0.000	0.174	0.307	0.412	0.497	0.566	0.712	0.844	0.912	0.949	0.970	0.982
8				0.000	0.161	0.289	0.391	0.475	0.651	0.812	0.893	0.938	0.964	0.978
9					0.000	0.152	0.274	0.373	0.584	0.775	0.873	0.926	0.956	0.974
10						0.000	0.144	0.261	0.510	0.735	0.850	0.913	0.949	0.970
11							0.000	0.137	0.428	0.691	0.825	0.898	0.940	0.964
12								0.000	0.337	0.641	0.797	0.882	0.931	0.959
15									0.000	0.459	0.694	0.822	0.895	0.938
20										0.000	0.433	0.671	0.806	0.885
25											0.000	0.419	0.658	0.797
30												0.000	0.411	0.651
35													0.000	0.407
40														0.000

Remaining Principal Balance Factors

For Mortgages with an Interest Rate of 10.50% and an Original Term of:

Age of Loan in Years	5 Years	6 Years	7 Years	8 Years	9 Years	10 Years	11 Years	12 Years	15 Years	20 Years	25 Years	30 Years	35 Years	40 Years
1	0.839	0.874	0.898	0.916	0.929	0.940	0.949	0.956	0.971	0.984	0.991	0.995	0.997	0.998
2	0.661	0.733	0.784	0.822	0.851	0.874	0.892	0.907	0.939	0.967	0.982	0.989	0.994	0.996
3	0.463	0.578	0.659	0.718	0.764	0.800	0.829	0.853	0.903	0.948	0.971	0.983	0.990	0.994
4	0.244	0.405	0.519	0.603	0.668	0.719	0.759	0.793	0.863	0.927	0.959	0.976	0.986	0.992
5	0.000	0.213	0.364	0.475	0.561	0.628	0.682	0.726	0.819	0.903	0.946	0.969	0.982	0.989
6		0.000	0.191	0.333	0.442	0.527	0.596	0.652	0.770	0.877	0.931	0.960	0.977	0.986
7			0.000	0.175	0.309	0.415	0.500	0.570	0.716	0.848	0.915	0.951	0.971	0.983
8				0.000	0.163	0.291	0.394	0.478	0.656	0.816	0.897	0.941	0.965	0.980
9					0.000	0.153	0.276	0.377	0.589	0.780	0.876	0.929	0.959	0.976
10						0.000	0.145	0.264	0.514	0.740	0.854	0.916	0.951	0.971
11							0.000	0.139	0.432	0.696	0.829	0.902	0.943	0.967
12								0.000	0.340	0.647	0.802	0.886	0.934	0.961
15									0.000	0.464	0.700	0.828	0.900	0.941
20										0.000	0.439	0.678	0.812	0.890
25											0.000	0.426	0.666	0.804
30												0.000	0.418	0.659
35													0.000	0.413
40														0.000

For Mortgages with an Interest Rate of 10.75% and an Original Term of:

Age of Loan in Years	5 Years	6 Years	7 Years	8 Years	9 Years	10 Years	11 Years	12 Years	15 Years	20 Years	25 Years	30 Years	35 Years	40 Years
1	0.840	0.875	0.899	0.917	0.930	0.941	0.950	0.957	0.972	0.985	0.992	0.995	0.997	0.998
2	0.663	0.735	0.786	0.824	0.853	0.875	0.894	0.909	0.940	0.968	0.982	0.990	0.994	0.997
3	0.465	0.580	0.661	0.720	0.766	0.802	0.831	0.855	0.905	0.950	0.972	0.984	0.991	0.995
4	0.245	0.407	0.521	0.605	0.670	0.721	0.762	0.795	0.866	0.929	0.960	0.978	0.987	0.993
5	0.000	0.214	0.365	0.477	0.563	0.631	0.685	0.729	0.822	0.906	0.948	0.970	0.983	0.990
6		0.000	0.193	0.335	0.444	0.530	0.599	0.655	0.774	0.880	0.933	0.962	0.978	0.987
7			0.000	0.176	0.312	0.418	0.503	0.573	0.720	0.851	0.918	0.953	0.973	0.984
8				0.000	0.164	0.293	0.397	0.482	0.660	0.820	0.900	0.943	0.967	0.981
9					0.000	0.154	0.279	0.380	0.593	0.784	0.880	0.932	0.961	0.977
10						0.000	0.147	0.266	0.519	0.745	0.858	0.919	0.954	0.973
11							0.000	0.140	0.436	0.701	0.834	0.906	0.946	0.969
12								0.000	0.344	0.652	0.807	0.890	0.937	0.963
15									0.000	0.470	0.706	0.833	0.904	0.944
20										0.000	0.445	0.685	0.819	0.895
25											0.000	0.432	0.673	0.810
30												0.000	0.424	0.666
35													0.000	0.420
40														0.000

Remaining Principal Balance Factors

For Mortgages with an Interest Rate of 11.00% and an Original Term of:

Age of Loan in Years	5 Years	6 Years	7 Years	8 Years	9 Years	10 Years	11 Years	12 Years	15 Years	20 Years	25 Years	30 Years	35 Years	40 Years
1	0.841	0.875	0.900	0.917	0.931	0.942	0.950	0.957	0.972	0.985	0.992	0.995	0.997	0.999
2	0.664	0.736	0.788	0.825	0.854	0.877	0.895	0.910	0.941	0.969	0.983	0.990	0.995	0.997
3	0.466	0.581	0.662	0.722	0.768	0.805	0.833	0.857	0.907	0.951	0.973	0.985	0.991	0.995
4	0.246	0.408	0.523	0.608	0.673	0.724	0.765	0.798	0.868	0.931	0.962	0.979	0.988	0.993
5	0.000	0.215	0.367	0.480	0.566	0.634	0.688	0.732	0.825	0.908	0.950	0.972	0.984	0.991
6		0.000	0.194	0.337	0.447	0.533	0.602	0.659	0.777	0.883	0.936	0.964	0.979	0.988
7			0.000	0.178	0.314	0.421	0.507	0.577	0.724	0.855	0.920	0.955	0.974	0.985
8				0.000	0.165	0.296	0.400	0.485	0.664	0.823	0.903	0.945	0.969	0.982
9					0.000	0.156	0.281	0.383	0.597	0.788	0.884	0.935	0.963	0.979
10						0.000	0.148	0.269	0.523	0.749	0.862	0.923	0.956	0.975
11							0.000	0.142	0.440	0.706	0.838	0.909	0.948	0.970
12								0.000	0.347	0.657	0.812	0.894	0.940	0.965
15									0.000	0.475	0.712	0.838	0.908	0.947
20										0.000	0.451	0.691	0.824	0.899
25											0.000	0.438	0.680	0.817
30												0.000	0.431	0.674
35													0.000	0.427
40														0.000

For Mortgages with an Interest Rate of 11.25% and an Original Term of:

Age of Loan in Years	5 Years	6 Years	7 Years	8 Years	9 Years	10 Years	11 Years	12 Years	15 Years	20 Years	25 Years	30 Years	35 Years	40 Years
1	0.842	0.876	0.900	0.918	0.932	0.943	0.951	0.958	0.973	0.986	0.992	0.996	0.998	0.999
2	0.666	0.738	0.789	0.827	0.856	0.878	0.897	0.911	0.942	0.970	0.984	0.991	0.995	0.997
3	0.468	0.583	0.664	0.725	0.770	0.807	0.836	0.859	0.909	0.952	0.974	0.986	0.992	0.995
4	0.247	0.410	0.525	0.610	0.675	0.726	0.767	0.801	0.871	0.933	0.963	0.980	0.989	0.994
5	0.000	0.217	0.369	0.482	0.569	0.636	0.691	0.735	0.828	0.911	0.951	0.973	0.985	0.991
6		0.000	0.195	0.339	0.449	0.536	0.605	0.662	0.780	0.886	0.938	0.966	0.981	0.989
7			0.000	0.179	0.316	0.424	0.510	0.580	0.727	0.858	0.923	0.957	0.976	0.986
8				0.000	0.167	0.298	0.403	0.488	0.668	0.827	0.906	0.948	0.971	0.983
9					0.000	0.157	0.283	0.386	0.601	0.793	0.887	0.937	0.965	0.980
10						0.000	0.150	0.271	0.527	0.754	0.866	0.926	0.958	0.976
11							0.000	0.143	0.444	0.711	0.843	0.913	0.951	0.972
12								0.000	0.351	0.662	0.816	0.898	0.943	0.967
15									0.000	0.480	0.717	0.843	0.912	0.950
20										0.000	0.456	0.698	0.830	0.904
25											0.000	0.444	0.687	0.823
30												0.000	0.437	0.681
35													0.000	0.434
40														0.000

Remaining Principal Balance Factors

For Mortgages with an Interest Rate of 11.50% and an Original Term of:

Age of Loan in Years	5 Years	6 Years	7 Years	8 Years	9 Years	10 Years	11 Years	12 Years	15 Years	20 Years	25 Years	30 Years	35 Years	40 Years
1	0.843	0.877	0.901	0.919	0.933	0.943	0.952	0.959	0.973	0.986	0.993	0.996	0.998	0.999
2	0.667	0.739	0.791	0.828	0.857	0.880	0.898	0.913	0.944	0.971	0.984	0.991	0.995	0.997
3	0.470	0.585	0.666	0.727	0.773	0.809	0.838	0.861	0.910	0.954	0.975	0.986	0.992	0.996
4	0.248	0.412	0.527	0.612	0.678	0.729	0.770	0.803	0.873	0.935	0.965	0.981	0.989	0.994
5	0.000	0.218	0.371	0.485	0.571	0.639	0.694	0.738	0.831	0.913	0.953	0.974	0.986	0.992
6		0.000	0.196	0.341	0.452	0.539	0.609	0.665	0.784	0.889	0.940	0.967	0.982	0.990
7			0.000	0.180	0.318	0.426	0.513	0.584	0.731	0.861	0.925	0.959	0.977	0.987
8				0.000	0.168	0.300	0.406	0.492	0.672	0.831	0.909	0.950	0.972	0.984
9					0.000	0.159	0.286	0.389	0.606	0.797	0.891	0.940	0.967	0.981
10						0.000	0.151	0.274	0.531	0.759	0.870	0.929	0.960	0.978
11							0.000	0.145	0.448	0.716	0.847	0.916	0.953	0.974
12								0.000	0.354	0.667	0.821	0.902	0.945	0.969
15									0.000	0.485	0.723	0.848	0.915	0.953
20										0.000	0.462	0.704	0.836	0.908
25											0.000	0.450	0.694	0.829
30												0.000	0.444	0.689
35													0.000	0.440
40														0.000

For Mortgages with an Interest Rate of 11.75% and an Original Term of:

Age of Loan in Years	5 Years	6 Years	7 Years	8 Years	9 Years	10 Years	11 Years	12 Years	15 Years	20 Years	25 Years	30 Years	35 Years	40 Years
1	0.844	0.878	0.902	0.920	0.933	0.944	0.953	0.960	0.974	0.987	0.993	0.996	0.998	0.999
2	0.668	0.741	0.792	0.830	0.859	0.881	0.899	0.914	0.945	0.972	0.985	0.992	0.996	0.998
3	0.471	0.587	0.668	0.729	0.775	0.811	0.840	0.863	0.912	0.955	0.976	0.987	0.993	0.996
4	0.249	0.414	0.529	0.615	0.680	0.731	0.772	0.806	0.875	0.936	0.966	0.982	0.990	0.994
5	0.000	0.219	0.373	0.487	0.574	0.642	0.697	0.741	0.834	0.915	0.955	0.975	0.987	0.993
6		0.000	0.197	0.343	0.455	0.542	0.612	0.669	0.787	0.891	0.942	0.969	0.983	0.990
7			0.000	0.182	0.320	0.429	0.516	0.587	0.735	0.865	0.928	0.961	0.978	0.988
8				0.000	0.170	0.302	0.409	0.495	0.676	0.835	0.912	0.952	0.974	0.985
9					0.000	0.160	0.288	0.392	0.610	0.801	0.894	0.942	0.968	0.982
10						0.000	0.152	0.276	0.535	0.763	0.874	0.931	0.962	0.979
11							0.000	0.146	0.452	0.720	0.851	0.919	0.956	0.975
12								0.000	0.358	0.672	0.826	0.905	0.948	0.971
15									0.000	0.490	0.729	0.852	0.919	0.955
20										0.000	0.468	0.711	0.841	0.912
25											0.000	0.456	0.701	0.835
30												0.000	0.450	0.696
35													0.000	0.447
40														0.000

Remaining Principal Balance Factors

For Mortgages with an Interest Rate of 12.00% and an Original Term of:

Age of Loan in Years	5 Years	6 Years	7 Years	8 Years	9 Years	10 Years	11 Years	12 Years	15 Years	20 Years	25 Years	30 Years	35 Years	40 Years
1	0.845	0.879	0.903	0.921	0.934	0.945	0.953	0.960	0.975	0.987	0.993	0.996	0.998	0.999
2	0.670	0.742	0.794	0.831	0.860	0.883	0.901	0.915	0.946	0.973	0.986	0.992	0.996	0.998
3	0.473	0.589	0.670	0.731	0.777	0.813	0.842	0.865	0.914	0.956	0.977	0.988	0.993	0.996
4	0.250	0.415	0.531	0.617	0.683	0.734	0.775	0.808	0.877	0.938	0.967	0.982	0.990	0.995
5	0.000	0.220	0.375	0.489	0.577	0.645	0.700	0.744	0.837	0.917	0.957	0.977	0.987	0.993
6		0.000	0.199	0.345	0.457	0.545	0.615	0.672	0.790	0.894	0.944	0.970	0.984	0.991
7			0.000	0.183	0.323	0.432	0.519	0.590	0.738	0.868	0.930	0.963	0.980	0.989
8				0.000	0.171	0.305	0.412	0.499	0.680	0.838	0.915	0.954	0.975	0.986
9					0.000	0.161	0.291	0.395	0.614	0.805	0.897	0.945	0.970	0.984
10						0.000	0.154	0.279	0.540	0.767	0.878	0.934	0.964	0.980
11							0.000	0.148	0.456	0.725	0.855	0.922	0.958	0.977
12								0.000	0.361	0.677	0.830	0.909	0.950	0.973
15									0.000	0.495	0.734	0.857	0.922	0.958
20										0.000	0.473	0.717	0.846	0.916
25											0.000	0.462	0.708	0.840
30												0.000	0.457	0.703
35													0.000	0.453
40														0.000

For Mortgages with an Interest Rate of 12.25% and an Original Term of:

Age of Loan in Years	5 Years	6 Years	7 Years	8 Years	9 Years	10 Years	11 Years	12 Years	15 Years	20 Years	25 Years	30 Years	35 Years	40 Years
1	0.846	0.880	0.904	0.922	0.935	0.946	0.954	0.961	0.975	0.988	0.994	0.997	0.998	0.999
2	0.671	0.744	0.795	0.833	0.862	0.884	0.902	0.917	0.947	0.974	0.986	0.993	0.996	0.998
3	0.474	0.590	0.672	0.733	0.779	0.815	0.844	0.867	0.915	0.958	0.978	0.988	0.994	0.997
4	0.251	0.417	0.534	0.620	0.685	0.736	0.777	0.811	0.880	0.940	0.969	0.983	0.991	0.995
5	0.000	0.221	0.377	0.492	0.579	0.648	0.703	0.747	0.839	0.920	0.958	0.978	0.988	0.994
6		0.000	0.200	0.347	0.460	0.548	0.618	0.675	0.794	0.897	0.946	0.971	0.985	0.992
7			0.000	0.184	0.325	0.435	0.523	0.594	0.742	0.871	0.933	0.964	0.981	0.990
8				0.000	0.172	0.307	0.415	0.502	0.684	0.842	0.918	0.956	0.976	0.987
9					0.000	0.163	0.293	0.399	0.618	0.809	0.901	0.947	0.972	0.985
10						0.000	0.155	0.282	0.544	0.772	0.881	0.937	0.966	0.982
11							0.000	0.149	0.460	0.730	0.859	0.925	0.960	0.978
12								0.000	0.365	0.682	0.835	0.912	0.953	0.974
15									0.000	0.500	0.740	0.862	0.926	0.960
20										0.000	0.479	0.723	0.851	0.920
25											0.000	0.468	0.714	0.846
30												0.000	0.463	0.710
35													0.000	0.460
40														0.000

Remaining Principal Balance Factors

For Mortgages with an Interest Rate of 12.50% and an Original Term of:

Age of Loan in Years	5 Years	6 Years	7 Years	8 Years	9 Years	10 Years	11 Years	12 Years	15 Years	20 Years	25 Years	30 Years	35 Years	40 Years
1	0.846	0.881	0.905	0.922	0.936	0.946	0.955	0.962	0.976	0.988	0.994	0.997	0.998	0.999
2	0.673	0.745	0.797	0.834	0.863	0.886	0.904	0.918	0.948	0.974	0.987	0.993	0.996	0.998
3	0.476	0.592	0.674	0.735	0.781	0.817	0.846	0.869	0.917	0.959	0.979	0.989	0.994	0.997
4	0.253	0.419	0.536	0.622	0.688	0.739	0.780	0.813	0.882	0.942	0.970	0.984	0.992	0.996
5	0.000	0.222	0.379	0.494	0.582	0.651	0.705	0.750	0.842	0.922	0.960	0.979	0.989	0.994
6		0.000	0.201	0.349	0.462	0.551	0.621	0.678	0.797	0.899	0.948	0.973	0.986	0.992
7			0.000	0.186	0.327	0.438	0.526	0.597	0.746	0.874	0.935	0.966	0.982	0.990
8				0.000	0.174	0.309	0.418	0.506	0.688	0.845	0.920	0.958	0.978	0.988
9					0.000	0.164	0.295	0.402	0.622	0.813	0.904	0.949	0.973	0.986
10						0.000	0.157	0.284	0.548	0.776	0.885	0.939	0.968	0.983
11							0.000	0.151	0.464	0.735	0.863	0.928	0.962	0.980
12								0.000	0.368	0.687	0.839	0.915	0.955	0.976
15									0.000	0.505	0.745	0.866	0.929	0.962
20										0.000	0.485	0.729	0.856	0.923
25											0.000	0.474	0.721	0.851
30												0.000	0.469	0.717
35													0.000	0.466
40														0.000

For Mortgages with an Interest Rate of 12.75% and an Original Term of:

Age of Loan in Years	5 Years	6 Years	7 Years	8 Years	9 Years	10 Years	11 Years	12 Years	15 Years	20 Years	25 Years	30 Years	35 Years	40 Years
1	0.847	0.881	0.905	0.923	0.937	0.947	0.955	0.962	0.976	0.988	0.994	0.997	0.998	0.999
2	0.647	0.747	0.798	0.836	0.865	0.887	0.905	0.919	0.949	0.975	0.987	0.993	0.997	0.998
3	0.477	0.594	0.676	0.737	0.783	0.819	0.847	0.871	0.919	0.960	0.980	0.989	0.994	0.997
4	0.254	0.421	0.538	0.624	0.690	0.741	0.782	0.815	0.884	0.943	0.971	0.985	0.992	0.996
5	0.000	0.224	0.381	0.496	0.585	0.653	0.708	0.753	0.845	0.924	0.961	0.980	0.989	0.994
6		0.000	0.202	0.351	0.465	0.554	0.624	0.682	0.800	0.902	0.950	0.974	0.986	0.993
7			0.000	0.187	0.329	0.440	0.529	0.601	0.749	0.877	0.937	0.967	0.983	0.991
8				0.000	0.175	0.312	0.421	0.509	0.692	0.849	0.923	0.960	0.979	0.989
9					0.000	0.166	0.298	0.405	0.626	0.817	0.907	0.951	0.975	0.987
10						0.000	0.158	0.287	0.552	0.780	0.888	0.942	0.969	0.984
11							0.000	0.152	0.468	0.739	0.867	0.931	0.964	0.981
12								0.000	0.372	0.692	0.843	0.918	0.957	0.977
15									0.000	0.510	0.750	0.870	0.932	0.964
20										0.000	0.490	0.735	0.861	0.927
25											0.000	0.480	0.727	0.856
30												0.000	0.475	0.723
35													0.000	0.473
40														0.000

Remaining Principal Balance Factors

For Mortgages with an Interest Rate of 13.00% and an Original Term of:

Age of Loan in Years	5 Years	6 Years	7 Years	8 Years	9 Years	10 Years	11 Years	12 Years	15 Years	20 Years	25 Years	30 Years	35 Years	40 Years
1	0.848	0.882	0.906	0.924	0.937	0.948	0.956	0.963	0.977	0.989	0.994	0.997	0.998	0.999
2	0.675	0.748	0.800	0.837	0.866	0.888	0.906	0.921	0.950	0.976	0.988	0.994	0.997	0.998
3	0.479	0.596	0.678	0.739	0.785	0.821	0.849	0.873	0.920	0.961	0.981	0.990	0.995	0.997
4	0.255	0.422	0.540	0.626	0.692	0.744	0.785	0.818	0.886	0.945	0.972	0.986	0.993	0.996
5	0.000	0.225	0.383	0.499	0.587	0.656	0.711	0.756	0.847	0.926	0.963	0.981	0.990	0.995
6		0.000	0.204	0.354	0.468	0.557	0.627	0.685	0.803	0.905	0.952	0.975	0.987	0.993
7			0.000	0.188	0.331	0.443	0.532	0.604	0.753	0.880	0.940	0.969	0.984	0.992
8				0.000	0.176	0.314	0.424	0.512	0.695	0.852	0.926	0.962	0.980	0.990
9					0.000	0.167	0.300	0.408	0.630	0.821	0.910	0.954	0.976	0.987
10						0.000	0.160	0.289	0.556	0.785	0.891	0.944	0.971	0.985
11							0.000	0.154	0.472	0.744	0.871	0.934	0.966	0.982
12								0.000	0.376	0.697	0.847	0.922	0.959	0.979
15									0.000	0.515	0.755	0.874	0.935	0.966
20										0.000	0.496	0.741	0.866	0.930
25											0.000	0.486	0.733	0.861
30												0.000	0.481	0.730
35													0.000	0.479
40														0.000

For Mortgages with an Interest Rate of 13.25% and an Original Term of:

Age of Loan in Years	5 Years	6 Years	7 Years	8 Years	9 Years	10 Years	11 Years	12 Years	15 Years	20 Years	25 Years	30 Years	35 Years	40 Years
1	0.849	0.883	0.907	0.925	0.938	0.949	0.957	0.964	0.977	0.989	0.995	0.997	0.999	0.999
2	0.677	0.750	0.801	0.839	0.867	0.890	0.908	0.922	0.952	0.977	0.988	0.994	0.997	0.998
3	0.480	0.598	0.680	0.741	0.787	0.823	0.851	0.874	0.992	0.963	0.981	0.991	0.995	0.997
4	0.256	0.424	0.542	0.629	0.695	0.746	0.787	0.820	0.888	0.946	0.973	0.986	0.993	0.996
5	0.000	0.226	0.385	0.501	0.590	0.659	0.714	0.758	0.850	0.928	0.964	0.982	0.991	0.995
6		0.000	0.205	0.356	0.470	0.559	0.631	0.688	0.806	0.907	0.954	0.976	0.988	0.994
7			0.000	0.189	0.334	0.446	0.535	0.608	0.756	0.883	0.942	0.970	0.985	0.992
8				0.000	0.178	0.316	0.427	0.516	0.699	0.856	0.928	0.963	0.981	0.990
9					0.000	0.169	0.303	0.411	0.634	0.824	0.912	0.956	0.977	0.988
10						0.000	0.161	0.292	0.560	0.789	0.895	0.946	0.973	0.986
11							0.000	0.155	0.476	0.748	0.874	0.936	0.967	0.983
12								0.000	0.379	0.702	0.851	0.924	0.961	0.980
15									0.000	0.520	0.760	0.878	0.938	0.968
20										0.000	0.501	0.747	0.870	0.933
25											0.000	0.492	0.740	0.866
30												0.000	0.487	0.736
35													0.000	0.485
40														0.000

Remaining Principal Balance Factors

For Mortgages with an Interest Rate of 13.50% and an Original Term of:

Age of Loan in Years	5 Years	6 Years	7 Years	8 Years	9 Years	10 Years	11 Years	12 Years	15 Years	20 Years	25 Years	30 Years	35 Years	40 Years
1	0.850	0.884	0.908	0.925	0.939	0.949	0.957	0.964	0.978	0.989	0.995	0.997	0.999	0.999
2	0.678	0.751	0.802	0.840	0.869	0.891	0.909	0.923	0.953	0.977	0.989	0.994	0.997	0.999
3	0.482	0.599	0.682	0.743	0.789	0.825	0.853	0.876	0.924	0.964	0.982	0.991	0.995	0.998
4	0.257	0.426	0.544	0.631	0.697	0.749	0.790	0.823	0.890	0.948	0.974	0.987	0.993	0.997
5	0.000	0.227	0.386	0.504	0.592	0.662	0.717	0.761	0.853	0.930	0.965	0.983	0.991	0.996
6		0.000	0.206	0.358	0.473	0.562	0.634	0.691	0.809	0.909	0.955	0.978	0.989	0.994
7			0.000	0.191	0.336	0.449	0.538	0.611	0.760	0.886	0.944	0.972	0.986	0.993
8				0.000	0.179	0.319	0.430	0.519	0.703	0.859	0.930	0.965	0.982	0.991
9					0.000	0.170	0.305	0.414	0.638	0.828	0.915	0.957	0.978	0.989
10						0.000	0.163	0.294	0.564	0.793	0.898	0.949	0.974	0.987
11							0.000	0.157	0.480	0.753	0.878	0.939	0.969	0.984
12								0.000	0.383	0.707	0.855	0.927	0.963	0.981
15									0.000	0.525	0.765	0.882	0.940	0.970
20										0.000	0.507	0.752	0.874	0.936
25											0.000	0.498	0.746	0.871
30												0.000	0.493	0.742
35													0.000	0.491
40														0.000

For Mortgages with an Interest Rate of 13.75% and an Original Term of:

Age of Loan in Years	5 Years	6 Years	7 Years	8 Years	9 Years	10 Years	11 Years	12 Years	15 Years	20 Years	25 Years	30 Years	35 Years	40 Years
1	0.851	0.885	0.909	0.926	0.940	0.950	0.958	0.965	0.978	0.990	0.995	0.998	0.999	0.999
2	0.679	0.753	0.804	0.842	0.870	0.892	0.910	0.924	0.954	0.978	0.989	0.995	0.997	0.999
3	0.483	0.601	0.684	0.745	0.791	0.827	0.855	0.878	0.925	0.965	0.983	0.991	0.996	0.998
4	0.258	0.427	0.546	0.633	0.700	0.751	0.792	0.825	0.893	0.949	0.975	0.988	0.994	0.997
5	0.000	0.228	0.388	0.506	0.595	0.665	0.720	0.764	0.855	0.932	0.967	0.983	0.992	0.996
6		0.000	0.207	0.360	0.475	0.565	0.637	0.694	0.812	0.912	0.957	0.979	0.989	0.995
7			0.000	0.192	0.338	0.452	0.542	0.614	0.763	0.889	0.946	0.973	0.986	0.993
8				0.000	0.181	0.321	0.433	0.523	0.707	0.862	0.933	0.967	0.983	0.992
9					0.000	0.171	0.308	0.417	0.642	0.832	0.918	0.959	0.980	0.990
10						0.000	0.164	0.297	0.568	0.797	0.901	0.951	0.975	0.988
11							0.000	0.159	0.483	0.757	0.881	0.941	0.971	0.985
12								0.000	0.386	0.711	0.859	0.930	0.965	0.982
15									0.000	0.530	0.770	0.886	0.943	0.971
20										0.000	0.512	0.758	0.879	0.939
25											0.000	0.504	0.751	0.875
30												0.000	0.499	0.748
35													0.000	0.497
40														0.000

Remaining Principal Balance Factors

For Mortgages with an Interest Rate of 14.00% and an Original Term of:

Age of Loan in Years	5 Years	6 Years	7 Years	8 Years	9 Years	10 Years	11 Years	12 Years	15 Years	20 Years	25 Years	30 Years	35 Years	40 Years
1	0.851	0.886	0.909	0.927	0.940	0.951	0.959	0.965	0.979	0.990	0.995	0.998	0.999	0.999
2	0.681	0.754	0.805	0.843	0.872	0.894	0.911	0.926	0.955	0.979	0.990	0.995	0.998	0.999
3	0.485	0.603	0.686	0.747	0.793	0.829	0.857	0.880	0.927	0.966	0.984	0.992	0.996	0.998
4	0.259	0.429	0.548	0.636	0.702	0.754	0.794	0.827	0.895	0.951	0.976	0.988	0.994	0.997
5	0.000	0.229	0.390	0.508	0.598	0.667	0.722	0.767	0.858	0.934	0.968	0.984	0.992	0.996
6		0.000	0.209	0.362	0.478	0.568	0.640	0.697	0.815	0.914	0.959	0.980	0.990	0.995
7			0.000	0.193	0.340	0.454	0.545	0.618	0.767	0.891	0.948	0.974	0.987	0.994
8				0.000	0.182	0.323	0.436	0.526	0.711	0.865	0.935	0.968	0.984	0.992
9					0.000	0.173	0.310	0.420	0.646	0.835	0.921	0.961	0.981	0.990
10						0.000	0.166	0.299	0.572	0.801	0.904	0.953	0.977	0.988
11							0.000	0.160	0.487	0.761	0.885	0.943	0.972	0.986
12								0.000	0.390	0.716	0.863	0.933	0.967	0.983
15									0.000	0.534	0.775	0.890	0.945	0.973
20										0.000	0.517	0.763	0.883	0.942
25											0.000	0.509	0.757	0.879
30												0.000	0.505	0.754
35													0.000	0.503
40														0.000

For Mortgages with an Interest Rate of 14.25% and an Original Term of:

Age of Loan in Years	5 Years	6 Years	7 Years	8 Years	9 Years	10 Years	11 Years	12 Years	15 Years	20 Years	25 Years	30 Years	35 Years	40 Years
1	0.852	0.886	0.910	0.928	0.941	0.951	0.959	0.966	0.979	0.990	0.995	0.998	0.999	0.999
2	0.682	0.755	0.807	0.844	0.873	0.895	0.913	0.927	0.956	0.980	0.990	0.995	0.998	0.999
3	0.486	0.605	0.688	0.749	0.795	0.830	0.859	0.882	0.928	0.967	0.984	0.992	0.996	0.998
4	0.260	0.431	0.550	0.638	0.704	0.756	0.797	0.830	0.897	0.952	0.977	0.989	0.995	0.997
5	0.000	0.231	0.392	0.511	0.600	0.670	0.725	0.770	0.860	0.936	0.969	0.985	0.993	0.996
6		0.000	0.210	0.364	0.480	0.571	0.643	0.701	0.818	0.916	0.960	0.981	0.991	0.995
7			0.000	0.195	0.342	0.457	0.548	0.621	0.770	0.894	0.949	0.975	0.988	0.994
8				0.000	0.183	0.326	0.439	0.529	0.714	0.868	0.937	0.970	0.985	0.993
9					0.000	0.174	0.313	0.424	0.650	0.839	0.923	0.963	0.982	0.991
10						0.000	0.167	0.302	0.576	0.805	0.907	0.955	0.978	0.989
11							0.000	0.162	0.491	0.766	0.888	0.946	0.973	0.987
12								0.000	0.393	0.720	0.867	0.935	0.968	0.984
15									0.000	0.539	0.780	0.893	0.948	0.974
20										0.000	0.523	0.768	0.887	0.944
25											0.000	0.515	0.763	0.884
30												0.000	0.511	0.760
35													0.000	0.509
40														0.000

Remaining Principal Balance Factors

For Mortgages with an Interest Rate of 14.50% and an Original Term of:

Age of Loan in Years	5 Years	6 Years	7 Years	8 Years	9 Years	10 Years	11 Years	12 Years	15 Years	20 Years	25 Years	30 Years	35 Years	40 Years
1	0.853	0.887	0.911	0.928	0.942	0.952	0.960	0.967	0.980	0.991	0.996	0.998	0.999	1.000
2	0.684	0.757	0.808	0.846	0.874	0.896	0.914	0.928	0.957	0.980	0.991	0.996	0.998	0.999
3	0.488	0.606	0.690	0.750	0.797	0.832	0.861	0.883	0.930	0.968	0.985	0.993	0.996	0.998
4	0.261	0.433	0.552	0.640	0.707	0.758	0.799	0.832	0.899	0.954	0.978	0.990	0.995	0.998
5	0.000	0.232	0.394	0.513	0.603	0.673	0.728	0.772	0.863	0.937	0.970	0.986	0.993	0.997
6		0.000	0.211	0.366	0.483	0.574	0.646	0.704	0.821	0.918	0.962	0.982	0.991	0.996
7			0.000	0.196	0.345	0.460	0.551	0.624	0.773	0.897	0.951	0.977	0.989	0.995
8				0.000	0.185	0.328	0.441	0.533	0.718	0.871	0.939	0.971	0.986	0.993
9					0.000	0.176	0.315	0.427	0.654	0.842	0.926	0.964	0.983	0.992
10						0.000	0.169	0.304	0.580	0.809	0.910	0.957	0.979	0.990
11							0.000	0.163	0.495	0.770	0.891	0.948	0.975	0.988
12								0.000	0.397	0.725	0.870	0.938	0.970	0.985
15									0.000	0.544	0.785	0.897	0.950	0.976
20										0.000	0.528	0.774	0.891	0.947
25											0.000	0.520	0.768	0.888
30												0.000	0.517	0.766
35													0.000	0.515
40														0.000

For Mortgages with an Interest Rate of 14.75% and an Original Term of:

Age of Loan in Years	5 Years	6 Years	7 Years	8 Years	9 Years	10 Years	11 Years	12 Years	15 Years	20 Years	25 Years	30 Years	35 Years	40 Years
1	0.854	0.888	0.912	0.929	0.942	0.953	0.961	0.967	0.980	0.991	0.996	0.998	0.999	1.000
2	0.685	0.758	0.810	0.847	0.876	0.898	0.915	0.929	0.957	0.981	0.991	0.996	0.998	0.999
3	0.489	0.608	0.691	0.752	0.798	0.834	0.862	0.885	0.931	0.969	0.985	0.993	0.997	0.998
4	0.262	0.434	0.555	0.643	0.709	0.761	0.801	0.834	0.901	0.955	0.979	0.990	0.995	0.998
5	0.000	0.233	0.396	0.515	0.606	0.675	0.731	0.775	0.865	0.939	0.972	0.987	0.994	0.997
6		0.000	0.213	0.368	0.486	0.577	0.649	0.707	0.824	0.921	0.963	0.982	0.992	0.996
7			0.000	0.197	0.347	0.463	0.554	0.628	0.777	0.899	0.953	0.978	0.989	0.995
8				0.000	0.186	0.330	0.444	0.536	0.722	0.874	0.941	0.972	0.987	0.994
9					0.000	0.177	0.317	0.430	0.658	0.846	0.928	0.966	0.984	0.992
10						0.000	0.170	0.307	0.584	0.812	0.912	0.959	0.980	0.991
11							0.000	0.165	0.499	0.774	0.894	0.950	0.976	0.989
12								0.000	0.400	0.729	0.874	0.940	0.971	0.986
15									0.000	0.549	0.789	0.900	0.952	0.977
20										0.000	0.533	0.779	0.894	0.949
25											0.000	0.526	0.774	0.892
30												0.000	0.523	0.771
35													0.000	0.521
40														0.000

Remaining Principal Balance Factors

For Mortgages with an Interest Rate of 15.00% and an Original Term of:

Age of Loan in Years	5 Years	6 Years	7 Years	8 Years	9 Years	10 Years	11 Years	12 Years	15 Years	20 Years	25 Years	30 Years	35 Years	40 Years
1	0.855	0.889	0.913	0.930	0.943	0.953	0.961	0.968	0.981	0.991	0.996	0.998	0.999	1.000
2	0.686	0.760	0.811	0.849	0.877	0.899	0.916	0.930	0.958	0.981	0.991	0.996	0.998	0.999
3	0.491	0.610	0.693	0.754	0.800	0.836	0.864	0.887	0.933	0.970	0.986	0.993	0.997	0.999
4	0.264	0.436	0.557	0.645	0.711	0.763	0.804	0.836	0.902	0.956	0.980	0.991	0.996	0.998
5	0.000	0.234	0.398	0.518	0.608	0.678	0.733	0.778	0.868	0.941	0.973	0.987	0.994	0.997
6		0.000	0.214	0.370	0.488	0.580	0.652	0.710	0.827	0.923	0.964	0.983	0.992	0.996
7			0.000	0.199	0.349	0.465	0.557	0.631	0.780	0.902	0.955	0.979	0.990	0.995
8				0.000	0.188	0.333	0.447	0.539	0.725	0.877	0.943	0.973	0.987	0.994
9					0.000	0.179	0.320	0.433	0.662	0.849	0.930	0.967	0.985	0.993
10						0.000	0.172	0.310	0.588	0.816	0.915	0.960	0.981	0.991
11							0.000	0.166	0.503	0.778	0.898	0.952	0.977	0.989
12								0.000	0.404	0.734	0.877	0.942	0.973	0.987
15									0.000	0.554	0.794	0.903	0.954	0.978
20										0.000	0.538	0.784	0.898	0.952
25											0.000	0.532	0.779	0.895
30												0.000	0.528	0.777
35													0.000	0.527
40														0.000

For Mortgages with an Interest Rate of 15.25% and an Original Term of:

Age of Loan in Years	5 Years	6 Years	7 Years	8 Years	9 Years	10 Years	11 Years	12 Years	15 Years	20 Years	25 Years	30 Years	35 Years	40 Years
1	0.856	0.890	0.913	0.931	0.944	0.954	0.962	0.968	0.981	0.992	0.996	0.998	0.999	1.000
2	0.688	0.761	0.813	0.850	0.878	0.900	0.918	0.931	0.959	0.982	0.992	0.996	0.998	0.999
3	0.492	0.612	0.695	0.756	0.802	0.838	0.866	0.889	0.934	0.971	0.987	0.994	0.997	0.999
4	0.265	0.438	0.559	0.647	0.714	0.765	0.806	0.839	0.904	0.958	0.981	0.991	0.996	0.998
5	0.000	0.235	0.400	0.520	0.611	0.681	0.736	0.780	0.870	0.943	0.974	0.988	0.994	0.997
6		0.000	0.215	0.372	0.491	0.583	0.655	0.713	0.830	0.925	0.966	0.984	0.993	0.997
7			0.000	0.200	0.351	0.468	0.560	0.634	0.783	0.904	0.956	0.980	0.991	0.996
8				0.000	0.189	0.335	0.450	0.543	0.729	0.880	0.945	0.975	0.988	0.994
9					0.000	0.180	0.322	0.436	0.666	0.852	0.933	0.969	0.985	0.993
10						0.000	0.173	0.312	0.592	0.820	0.918	0.962	0.982	0.992
11							0.000	0.168	0.507	0.782	0.901	0.954	0.979	0.990
12								0.000	0.407	0.738	0.880	0.945	0.974	0.988
15									0.000	0.558	0.798	0.907	0.956	0.980
20										0.000	0.544	0.789	0.901	0.954
25											0.000	0.537	0.784	0.899
30												0.000	0.534	0.782
35													0.000	0.532
40														0.000

Remaining Principal Balance Factors

For Mortgages with an Interest Rate of 15.50% and an Original Term of:

Age of Loan in Years	5 Years	6 Years	7 Years	8 Years	9 Years	10 Years	11 Years	12 Years	15 Years	20 Years	25 Years	30 Years	35 Years	40 Years
1	0.856	0.890	0.914	0.931	0.944	0.955	0.963	0.969	0.982	0.992	0.996	0.998	0.999	1.000
2	0.689	0.763	0.814	0.851	0.880	0.902	0.919	0.933	0.960	0.983	0.992	0.996	0.998	0.999
3	0.494	0.613	0.697	0.758	0.804	0.840	0.868	0.890	0.935	0.972	0.987	0.994	0.997	0.999
4	0.266	0.440	0.561	0.649	0.716	0.768	0.808	0.841	0.906	0.959	0.981	0.992	0.996	0.998
5	0.000	0.237	0.402	0.522	0.613	0.684	0.739	0.783	0.872	0.944	0.975	0.988	0.995	0.998
6		0.000	0.216	0.374	0.493	0.585	0.658	0.716	0.833	0.927	0.967	0.985	0.993	0.997
7			0.000	0.202	0.353	0.471	0.563	0.637	0.786	0.907	0.958	0.981	0.991	0.996
8				0.000	0.190	0.337	0.453	0.546	0.732	0.883	0.947	0.976	0.989	0.995
9					0.000	0.182	0.325	0.439	0.670	0.856	0.935	0.970	0.986	0.994
10						0.000	0.175	0.315	0.596	0.823	0.920	0.964	0.983	0.992
11							0.000	0.169	0.511	0.786	0.903	0.956	0.980	0.991
12								0.000	0.411	0.742	0.884	0.947	0.975	0.989
15									0.000	0.563	0.803	0.910	0.958	0.981
20										0.000	0.549	0.793	0.905	0.956
25											0.000	0.542	0.789	0.903
30												0.000	0.539	0.787
35													0.000	0.538
40														0.000

For Mortgages with an Interest Rate of 15.75% and an Original Term of:

Age of Loan in Years	5 Years	6 Years	7 Years	8 Years	9 Years	10 Years	11 Years	12 Years	15 Years	20 Years	25 Years	30 Years	35 Years	40 Years
1	0.857	0.891	0.915	0.932	0.945	0.955	0.963	0.969	0.982	0.992	0.997	0.998	0.999	1.000
2	0.690	0.764	0.815	0.853	0.881	0.903	0.920	0.934	0.961	0.983	0.992	0.997	0.998	0.999
3	0.495	0.615	0.699	0.760	0.806	0.842	0.870	0.892	0.937	0.973	0.988	0.994	0.997	0.999
4	0.267	0.441	0.563	0.652	0.718	0.770	0.811	0.843	0.908	0.960	0.982	0.992	0.996	0.998
5	0.000	0.238	0.404	0.525	0.616	0.686	0.742	0.786	0.875	0.946	0.976	0.989	0.995	0.998
6		0.000	0.218	0.376	0.496	0.588	0.661	0.719	0.835	0.929	0.968	0.986	0.993	0.997
7			0.000	0.203	0.356	0.474	0.567	0.641	0.790	0.909	0.959	0.982	0.992	0.996
8				0.000	0.192	0.340	0.456	0.549	0.736	0.886	0.949	0.977	0.990	0.995
9					0.000	0.183	0.327	0.442	0.673	0.859	0.937	0.971	0.987	0.994
10						0.000	0.176	0.317	0.600	0.827	0.923	0.965	0.984	0.993
11							0.000	0.171	0.514	0.790	0.906	0.958	0.981	0.991
12								0.000	0.414	0.747	0.887	0.949	0.977	0.989
15									0.000	0.568	0.807	0.913	0.960	0.982
20										0.000	0.554	0.798	0.908	0.958
25											0.000	0.548	0.794	0.906
30												0.000	0.545	0.792
35													0.000	0.544
40														0.000

Remaining Principal Balance Factors

For Mortgages with an Interest Rate of 16.00% and an Original Term of:

Age of Loan in Years	5 Years	6 Years	7 Years	8 Years	9 Years	10 Years	11 Years	12 Years	15 Years	20 Years	25 Years	30 Years	35 Years	40 Years
1	0.858	0.892	0.916	0.933	0.946	0.956	0.964	0.970	0.983	0.993	0.997	0.999	0.999	1.000
2	0.692	0.765	0.817	0.854	0.882	0.904	0.921	0.935	0.962	0.984	0.993	0.997	0.999	0.999
3	0.497	0.617	0.701	0.762	0.808	0.843	0.871	0.893	0.938	0.973	0.988	0.995	0.998	0.999
4	0.268	0.443	0.565	0.654	0.721	0.772	0.813	0.845	0.910	0.961	0.983	0.992	0.997	0.998
5	0.000	0.239	0.406	0.527	0.618	0.689	0.744	0.788	0.877	0.947	0.977	0.990	0.995	0.998
6		0.000	0.219	0.378	0.498	0.591	0.664	0.722	0.838	0.931	0.969	0.986	0.994	0.997
7			0.000	0.204	0.358	0.476	0.570	0.644	0.793	0.911	0.961	0.983	0.992	0.996
8				0.000	0.193	0.342	0.459	0.553	0.739	0.889	0.951	0.978	0.990	0.996
9					0.000	0.185	0.330	0.445	0.677	0.862	0.939	0.973	0.988	0.994
10						0.000	0.178	0.320	0.604	0.831	0.925	0.967	0.985	0.993
11							0.000	0.173	0.518	0.794	0.909	0.959	0.982	0.992
12								0.000	0.418	0.751	0.890	0.951	0.978	0.990
15									0.000	0.572	0.811	0.916	0.962	0.983
20										0.000	0.559	0.803	0.911	0.960
25											0.000	0.553	0.799	0.909
30												0.000	0.550	0.797
35													0.000	0.549
40														0.000

For Mortgages with an Interest Rate of 16.25% and an Original Term of:

Age of Loan in Years	5 Years	6 Years	7 Years	8 Years	9 Years	10 Years	11 Years	12 Years	15 Years	20 Years	25 Years	30 Years	35 Years	40 Years
1	0.859	0.893	0.916	0.934	0.947	0.956	0.964	0.970	0.983	0.993	0.997	0.999	0.999	1.000
2	0.693	0.767	0.818	0.856	0.884	0.905	0.922	0.936	0.963	0.984	0.993	0.997	0.999	0.999
3	0.498	0.619	0.703	0.764	0.810	0.845	0.873	0.895	0.939	0.974	0.989	0.995	0.998	0.999
4	0.269	0.445	0.567	0.656	0.723	0.775	0.815	0.847	0.912	0.963	0.984	0.993	0.997	0.999
5	0.000	0.240	0.408	0.529	0.621	0.691	0.747	0.791	0.879	0.949	0.978	0.990	0.996	0.998
6		0.000	0.220	0.381	0.501	0.594	0.667	0.725	0.841	0.933	0.971	0.987	0.994	0.997
7			0.000	0.206	0.360	0.479	0.573	0.647	0.796	0.914	0.962	0.983	0.993	0.997
8				0.000	0.195	0.344	0.462	0.556	0.743	0.891	0.953	0.979	0.991	0.996
9					0.000	0.186	0.332	0.448	0.681	0.865	0.941	0.974	0.988	0.995
10						0.000	0.179	0.322	0.608	0.834	0.928	0.968	0.986	0.994
11							0.000	0.174	0.522	0.798	0.912	0.961	0.983	0.992
12								0.000	0.421	0.755	0.893	0.953	0.979	0.991
15									0.000	0.577	0.815	0.918	0.964	0.984
20										0.000	0.564	0.807	0.914	0.962
25											0.000	0.558	0.804	0.913
30												0.000	0.556	0.802
35													0.000	0.555
40														0.000

Remaining Principal Balance Factors

For Mortgages with an Interest Rate of 16.50% and an Original Term of:

Age of Loan in Years	5 Years	6 Years	7 Years	8 Years	9 Years	10 Years	11 Years	12 Years	15 Years	20 Years	25 Years	30 Years	35 Years	40 Years
1	0.860	0.894	0.917	0.934	0.947	0.957	0.965	0.971	0.983	0.993	0.997	0.999	0.999	1.000
2	0.694	0.768	0.820	0.857	0.885	0.907	0.923	0.937	0.964	0.985	0.993	0.997	0.999	0.999
3	0.500	0.620	0.705	0.766	0.812	0.847	0.875	0.897	0.941	0.975	0.989	0.995	0.998	0.999
4	0.270	0.446	0.569	0.658	0.725	0.777	0.817	0.849	0.913	0.964	0.984	0.993	0.997	0.999
5	0.000	0.241	0.409	0.532	0.623	0.694	0.749	0.793	0.881	0.950	0.979	0.991	0.996	0.998
6		0.000	0.221	0.383	0.504	0.597	0.670	0.728	0.843	0.934	0.972	0.988	0.995	0.998
7			0.000	0.207	0.362	0.482	0.576	0.650	0.799	0.916	0.964	0.984	0.993	0.997
8				0.000	0.196	0.347	0.465	0.559	0.746	0.894	0.954	0.980	0.991	0.996
9					0.000	0.188	0.335	0.452	0.684	0.868	0.943	0.975	0.989	0.995
10						0.000	0.181	0.325	0.612	0.837	0.930	0.969	0.987	0.994
11							0.000	0.176	0.526	0.801	0.914	0.963	0.984	0.993
12								0.000	0.425	0.759	0.896	0.955	0.980	0.991
15									0.000	0.581	0.819	0.921	0.965	0.985
20										0.000	0.569	0.812	0.917	0.964
25											0.000	0.563	0.808	0.916
30												0.000	0.561	0.807
35													0.000	0.560
40														0.000

For Mortgages with an Interest Rate of 16.75% and an Original Term of:

Age of Loan in Years	5 Years	6 Years	7 Years	8 Years	9 Years	10 Years	11 Years	12 Years	15 Years	20 Years	25 Years	30 Years	35 Years	40 Years
1	0.860	0.894	0.918	0.935	0.948	0.958	0.965	0.972	0.984	0.993	0.997	0.999	0.999	1.000
2	0.696	0.770	0.821	0.858	0.886	0.908	0.925	0.938	0.965	0.985	0.994	0.997	0.999	0.999
3	0.501	0.622	0.706	0.768	0.813	0.849	0.876	0.898	0.942	0.976	0.990	0.996	0.998	0.999
4	0.271	0.448	0.571	0.660	0.727	0.779	0.819	0.851	0.915	0.965	0.985	0.994	0.997	0.999
5	0.000	0.243	0.411	0.534	0.626	0.697	0.752	0.796	0.883	0.952	0.979	0.991	0.996	0.998
6		0.000	0.223	0.385	0.506	0.600	0.673	0.731	0.846	0.936	0.973	0.988	0.995	0.998
7			0.000	0.208	0.365	0.485	0.579	0.653	0.802	0.918	0.965	0.985	0.993	0.997
8				0.000	0.197	0.349	0.468	0.562	0.750	0.896	0.956	0.981	0.992	0.996
9					0.000	0.189	0.337	0.455	0.688	0.871	0.945	0.976	0.990	0.996
10						0.000	0.183	0.327	0.615	0.841	0.932	0.971	0.987	0.994
11							0.000	0.177	0.530	0.805	0.917	0.964	0.984	0.993
12								0.000	0.428	0.763	0.899	0.956	0.981	0.992
15									0.000	0.586	0.823	0.924	0.967	0.986
20										0.000	0.574	0.816	0.920	0.965
25											0.000	0.569	0.813	0.919
30												0.000	0.566	0.812
35													0.000	0.565
40														0.000

Remaining Principal Balance Factors

For Mortgages with an Interest Rate of 17.00% and an Original Term of:

Age of Loan in Years	5 Years	6 Years	7 Years	8 Years	9 Years	10 Years	11 Years	12 Years	15 Years	20 Years	25 Years	30 Years	35 Years	40 Years
1	0.861	0.895	0.919	0.936	0.948	0.958	0.966	0.972	0.984	0.993	0.997	0.999	0.999	1.000
2	0.697	0.771	0.822	0.860	0.887	0.909	0.926	0.939	0.965	0.986	0.994	0.997	0.999	1.000
3	0.503	0.624	0.708	0.769	0.815	0.850	0.878	0.900	0.943	0.977	0.990	0.996	0.998	0.999
4	0.272	0.450	0.573	0.663	0.730	0.781	0.822	0.853	0.917	0.966	0.986	0.994	0.997	0.999
5	0.000	0.244	0.413	0.536	0.629	0.699	0.755	0.799	0.886	0.953	0.980	0.992	0.996	0.998
6		0.000	0.224	0.387	0.509	0.602	0.676	0.734	0.849	0.938	0.974	0.989	0.995	0.998
7			0.000	0.210	0.367	0.487	0.582	0.657	0.805	0.920	0.966	0.986	0.994	0.997
8				0.000	0.199	0.352	0.471	0.566	0.753	0.899	0.957	0.982	0.992	0.997
9					0.000	0.191	0.340	0.458	0.692	0.874	0.947	0.977	0.990	0.996
10						0.000	0.184	0.330	0.619	0.844	0.934	0.972	0.988	0.995
11							0.000	0.179	0.533	0.809	0.919	0.966	0.985	0.994
12								0.000	0.432	0.767	0.902	0.958	0.982	0.992
15									0.000	0.590	0.827	0.926	0.968	0.986
20										0.000	0.579	0.820	0.923	0.967
25											0.000	0.574	0.817	0.922
30												0.000	0.572	0.816
35													0.000	0.571
40														0.000

For Mortgages with an Interest Rate of 17.25% and an Original Term of:

Age of Loan in Years	5 Years	6 Years	7 Years	8 Years	9 Years	10 Years	11 Years	12 Years	15 Years	20 Years	25 Years	30 Years	35 Years	40 Years
1	0.862	0.896	0.919	0.936	0.949	0.959	0.967	0.973	0.985	0.994	0.997	0.999	1.000	1.000
2	0.698	0.772	0.824	0.861	0.889	0.910	0.927	0.940	0.966	0.986	0.994	0.998	0.999	1.000
3	0.504	0.626	0.710	0.771	0.817	0.852	0.880	0.901	0.944	0.977	0.991	0.996	0.998	0.999
4	0.274	0.452	0.575	0.665	0.732	0.783	0.824	0.855	0.918	0.967	0.986	0.994	0.998	0.999
5	0.000	0.245	0.415	0.539	0.631	0.702	0.757	0.801	0.888	0.954	0.981	0.992	0.997	0.999
6		0.000	0.225	0.389	0.511	0.605	0.678	0.736	0.851	0.940	0.975	0.989	0.996	0.998
7			0.000	0.211	0.369	0.490	0.585	0.660	0.808	0.922	0.968	0.986	0.994	0.998
8				0.000	0.200	0.354	0.474	0.569	0.756	0.901	0.959	0.983	0.993	0.997
9					0.000	0.192	0.342	0.461	0.695	0.877	0.949	0.978	0.991	0.996
10						0.000	0.186	0.333	0.623	0.847	0.936	0.973	0.989	0.995
11							0.000	0.181	0.537	0.812	0.922	0.967	0.986	0.994
12								0.000	0.435	0.771	0.905	0.960	0.983	0.993
15									0.000	0.595	0.831	0.929	0.970	0.987
20										0.000	0.583	0.824	0.926	0.968
25											0.000	0.579	0.822	0.924
30												0.000	0.577	0.820
35													0.000	0.576
40														0.000

Remaining Principal Balance Factors

For Mortgages with an Interest Rate of 17.50% and an Original Term of:

Age of Loan in Years	5 Years	6 Years	7 Years	8 Years	9 Years	10 Years	11 Years	12 Years	15 Years	20 Years	25 Years	30 Years	35 Years	40 Years
1	0.863	0.897	0.920	0.937	0.950	0.959	0.967	0.973	0.985	0.994	0.998	0.999	1.000	1.000
2	0.700	0.774	0.825	0.862	0.890	0.911	0.928	0.941	0.967	0.987	0.995	0.998	0.999	1.000
3	0.506	0.627	0.712	0.773	0.819	0.854	0.881	0.903	0.945	0.978	0.991	0.996	0.998	0.999
4	0.275	0.453	0.577	0.667	0.734	0.786	0.826	0.858	0.920	0.968	0.987	0.995	0.998	0.999
5	0.000	0.246	0.417	0.541	0.634	0.704	0.760	0.804	0.890	0.956	0.982	0.992	0.997	0.999
6		0.000	0.227	0.391	0.514	0.608	0.681	0.739	0.854	0.941	0.976	0.990	0.996	0.998
7			0.000	0.212	0.371	0.493	0.588	0.663	0.811	0.924	0.969	0.987	0.995	0.998
8				0.000	0.202	0.356	0.477	0.572	0.760	0.904	0.960	0.983	0.993	0.997
9					0.000	0.194	0.344	0.464	0.699	0.879	0.950	0.979	0.991	0.996
10						0.000	0.187	0.335	0.627	0.850	0.938	0.974	0.989	0.996
11							0.000	0.182	0.541	0.816	0.924	0.968	0.987	0.994
12								0.000	0.439	0.775	0.907	0.961	0.984	0.993
15									0.000	0.599	0.835	0.931	0.971	0.988
20										0.000	0.588	0.829	0.928	0.970
25											0.000	0.584	0.826	0.927
30												0.000	0.582	0.825
35													0.000	0.581
40														0.000

For Mortgages with an Interest Rate of 17.75% and an Original Term of:

Age of Loan in Years	5 Years	6 Years	7 Years	8 Years	9 Years	10 Years	11 Years	12 Years	15 Years	20 Years	25 Years	30 Years	35 Years	40 Years
1	0.864	0.897	0.921	0.938	0.950	0.960	0.968	0.974	0.985	0.994	0.998	0.999	1.000	1.000
2	0.701	0.775	0.826	0.863	0.891	0.912	0.929	0.942	0.968	0.987	0.995	0.998	0.999	1.000
3	0.507	0.629	0.714	0.775	0.821	0.856	0.883	0.904	0.947	0.979	0.991	0.996	0.999	0.999
4	0.276	0.455	0.579	0.669	0.736	0.788	0.828	0.860	0.922	0.969	0.987	0.995	0.998	0.999
5	0.000	0.248	0.419	0.543	0.636	0.707	0.762	0.806	0.892	0.957	0.983	0.993	0.997	0.999
6		0.000	0.228	0.393	0.516	0.611	0.684	0.742	0.856	0.943	0.977	0.990	0.996	0.998
7			0.000	0.214	0.373	0.496	0.591	0.666	0.814	0.926	0.970	0.988	0.995	0.998
8				0.000	0.203	0.359	0.480	0.575	0.763	0.906	0.962	0.984	0.993	0.997
9					0.000	0.195	0.347	0.467	0.703	0.882	0.952	0.980	0.992	0.997
10						0.000	0.189	0.338	0.630	0.853	0.940	0.975	0.990	0.996
11							0.000	0.184	0.545	0.819	0.926	0.970	0.988	0.995
12								0.000	0.442	0.779	0.910	0.963	0.985	0.994
15									0.000	0.603	0.839	0.934	0.973	0.989
20										0.000	0.593	0.833	0.931	0.971
25											0.000	0.589	0.830	0.930
30												0.000	0.587	0.829
35													0.000	0.586
40														0.000

Mortgage or Deed of Trust: What System Each State Uses

State	Security Instrument	State	Security Instrument
Alabama	Mortgage	Maine	Mortgage
Alaska	Deed of Trust	Maryland	Deed of Trust
Arizona	Deed of Trust	Massachusetts	Mortgage
Arkansas	Mortgage	Michigan	Mortgage
California	Deed of Trust	Minnesota	Mortgage
Colorado	Deed of Trust	Mississippi	Deed of Trust
Connecticut	Open-End Mortgage	Missouri	Deed of Trust
		Montana	Deed of Trust
Delaware	Mortgage	Nebraska	Deed of Trust
District of Columbia	Deed of Trust	Nevada	Deed of Trust
Florida	Mortgage	New Hampshire	Mortgage
Georgia	Security Deed	New Jersey	Mortgage
Hawaii	Mortgage	New Mexico	Mortgage
Idaho	Deed of Trust	New York	Mortgage
Illinois	Mortgage	North Carolina	Deed of Trust
Indiana	Mortgage	North Dakota	Mortgage
Iowa	Mortgage	Ohio	Open-End Mortgage
Kansas	Mortgage		
Kentucky	Mortgage	Oklahoma	Mortgage
Louisiana	Mortgage	Oregon	Deed of Trust

State	Security Instrument	State	Security Instrument
Pennsylvania	Mortgage	Vermont	Mortgage
Rhode Island	Mortgage	Virginia	Deed of Trust
South Carolina	Mortgage	Washington	Deed of Trust
South Dakota	Mortgage	West Virginia	Deed of Trust
Tennessee	Deed of Trust	Wisconsin	Mortgage
Texas	Deed of Trust	Wyoming	Mortgage
Utah	Deed of Trust		

APPENDIX

L

Internet Resources

Web Site Name	Internet Address
Calculation Tools/Downloads	
CNet	shareware.cnet.com
Download.Com	www.download.com
FinanCenter	www.financenter.com
Microsoft	www.microsoft.com
ZD Net	www.zdnet.com/downloads
Government/Association/Corporate Sites	
Fannie Mae - Corporate Site	www.fanniemae.com
Fannie Mae - HomePath	www.homepath.com/
Fannie Mae Foundation	www.fanniemaefoundation.org/
Freddie Mac - Corporate Site	www.freddiemac.com/
Freddie Mac - HomeSteps	www.homesteps.com/
Mortgage Bankers Association of America	www.mbaa.org
U.S. Dept. of Housing and Urban Development	www.hud.gov
Veterans Affairs (VA)	www.va.gov
Credit Report Sites	
Fair, Isaac and Company, Inc.	www.myfico.com
Equifax	www.equifax.com
Experian	www.experian.com/consumer/
Trans Union LLC	www.transunion.com
Industry Newspapers	
U S Mortgage News	www.nfns.com
National Mortgage News	www.nationalmortgagenews.com

Resources at This Site						Comments
Current Interest Rates	Lenders in Your Area	Mortgage Calculation Tools	Consumer Advice and Information	Mortgage Industry News	On-Line Application	
		X				
		X				
		X				Very complete set of tools
		X				
		X				
			X	X		
	X	X	X			Consumer information.
			X			Community outreach organization that promotes home ownership, aimed at first-time borrowers, immigrants, minorities. Foreign language guides—Spanish, Chinese, Russian, Polish, Portuguese, Haitian-Creole, Korean and Vietnamese.
X		X	X	X		Best information on "Credit Scoring" and how your credit history will affect your application.
			X			Find a low-cost home.
		X	X	X		
		X	X	X		Information on FHA loans.
			X			Information on V.A. loans.
		X	X			Best information on "Credit Scoring"
						(800) 685-1111
						(800) 311-4769
						(800) 888-4213
X		X	X	X		Rates from hundreds of lenders by state
				X		

Web Site Name	Internet Address

Multi-Lender Sites *There are thousands of lenders on the web. These are representative of the thousands, but a listing here does not constitute a recommendation.

Web Site Name	Internet Address
Approved Buyers Network	www.approvedbuyer.com
GetSmart.com	www.getsmart.com
Mortgage LoanPage	www.loanpage.com
Myers LoanApp	www.loan.app.com

Single-Lender Sites *There are thousands of lenders on the web. These are representative of the thousands, but a listing here does not constitute a recommendation.

Web Site Name	Internet Address
Barrons Mortgage Group, Ltd.	www.barronsmtg.com
Countrywide Home Loans	www.countrywide.com
E-Loan	www.eloan.com
IndyMac Bank	www.indymacmortgage.com
Intuit's "QuickenMortgage"	mortgage.quicken.com
LowRatesUSA.com	www.lowratesusa.com
Veterans Choice Mortgage	www.veteranschoicemortgage.com

On-Line Information Services

Web Site Name	Internet Address
HSH Associates	www.hsh.com/
Mortgage Mag	www.mortgagemag.com/
Mortgage Market Information Services	www.interest.com/
CNNMoney	money.cnn.com

State Housing Finance Agencies/Associations

Web Site Name	Internet Address
Alabama HFA	www.ahfa.com/
Alaska HFC	www.ahfc.state.ak.us/
Arizona DoC	www.state.az.us/commerce
Arkansas DFA	www.state.ar.us/adfa/
California HFA	www.chfa.ca.gov/
Colorado HFA	www.colohfa.org/
Connecticut HFA	www.chfa.org
Delaware SHA	www2.state.de.us/dsha/
District of Columbia HFA	www.dchfa.org

Resources at This Site						Comments
Current Interest Rates	Lenders in Your Area	Mortgage Calculation Tools	Consumer Advice and Information	Mortgage Industry News	On-Line Application	
X	X	X	X			Large network of lenders and agents
X	X	X	X		X	
	X		X			
X		X	X	X	X	Long list of mortgage calculation tools
X		X	X		X	Nation's largest mortgage lender.
X		X	X			
X		X	X		X	Nice site
X		X	X		X	
X		X	X		X	
						VA loan specialty site
X	X	X	X	X		
	X					Large list of mortgage lenders on the internet.
X	X	X	X	X		
X		X				
			X			
			X			
			X			
			X			
			X			
			X			
			X			
			X			
			X			

Web Site Name	Internet Address
Florida HFC	www.floridahousing.org/
Georgia DCA/HFA	www.dca.state.ga.us/
Hawaii, HCDC of	www.hcdch.state.hi.us/
Idaho HFA	www.ihfa.org/
Illinois HDA	www.ihda.org/
Indiana HFA	www.indianahousing.org/
Iowa FA	www.ifahome.com/
Kansas DoC&H	kansascommerce.com/
Kentucky HC	www.kyhousing.org/
Louisiana HFA	www.lhfa.state.la.us/
Maine SHA	www.mainehousing.org/
Maryland DHCD	www.dhcd.state.md.us/
MassHousing	www.mhfa.com/
Michigan SHDA	www.mshda.org/
Minnesota HFA	www.mhfa.state.mn.us/
Mississippi HC	www.mshomecorp.com/
Missouri HDC	www.mhdc.com/
Montana BoH/HD	www.com.state.mt.us/
Nebraska IFA	www.nifa.org/
Nevada HD	nvhousing.state.nv.us/
New Hampshire HFA	www.nhhfa.org/
New Jersey HMFA	www.state.nj.us/dca/hmfa/
New Mexico MFA	www.nmmfa.org/
New York DHCR	www.dhcr.state.ny.us/
New York HDC	www.nychdc.com/
New York HFA/SONYMA	www.nyhomes.org/
North Carolina HFA	www.nchfa.state.nc.us/
North Dakota HFA	www.ndhfa.state.nd.us/
Ohio HFA	www.odod.state.oh.us/ohfa
Oklahoma HFA	www.ohfa.org/
Oregon HCSD	www.hcs.state.or.us/
Pennsylvania HFA	www.phfa.org/
Puerto Rico HFC	www.gdb-pur.com/
Rhode Island HMFC	www.rihousing.com/

Resources at This Site						Comments
Current Interest Rates	Lenders in Your Area	Mortgage Calculation Tools	Consumer Advice and Information	Mortgage Industry News	On-Line Application	
			X			
			X			
			X			
			X			
			X			
			X			
			X			
			X			
			X			
			X			
			X			
			X			
			X			
			X			
			X			
			X			
			X			
			X			
			X			
			X			
			X			
			X			
			X			
			X			
			X			
			X			
			X			
			X			
			X			
			X			
			X			
			X			
			X			
			X			
			X			
			X			

Web Site Name	Internet Address
South Carolina SHFDA	www.sha.state.sc.us/
South Dakota HDA	www.sdhda.org/
Tennessee HDA	www.state.tn.us/thda
Texas DHCA	www.tdhca.state.tx.us/
Utah HC	www.utahhousingcorp.org/
Vermont HFA	www.vhfa.org/
Virgin Islands HFA	
Virginia HDA	www.vhda.com/
Washington State HFC	www.wshfc.org/
West Virginia HDF	www.wvhdf.com/
Wisconsin HEDA	www.wheda.com/
Wyoming CDA	www.wyomingcda.com/
National Council of State Housing Agencies	www.ncsha.org
National Association of Local Housing Finance Agencies	www.nalhfa.org

Resources at This Site						Comments
Current Interest Rates	Lenders in Your Area	Mortgage Calculation Tools	Consumer Advice and Information	Mortgage Industry News	On-Line Application	
			X			
			X			
			X			
			X			
			X			
			X			
			X			
			X			
			X			
			X			
			X			
			X			
			X			
			X			

Glossary

abstract of title (abstract) History of a parcel of real estate, compiled from public records, listing transfers of ownership and claims against the property.

acceleration clause Provision in a mortgage document stating that if a payment is missed or any other provision violated the whole debt becomes immediately due and payable.

acknowledgment Formal declaration before a public official that one has signed a document.

acre Land measure equal to 43,560 square feet.

adjustable-rate mortgage (ARM) Loan whose interest rate is changed periodically to keep pace with current levels.

adjusted basis Original cost of property plus any later improvements and minus a figure for depreciation claimed.

adjusted sales price Sales price minus commissions, legal fees, and other costs of selling.

agent Person authorized to act on behalf of another in dealings with third parties.

agreement of sale (purchase agreement, sales agreement, contract to purchase) Written contract detailing terms under which buyer agrees to buy and seller agrees to sell.

alienation clause (due-on-sale, nonassumption) Provision in a mortgage document stating that the loan must be paid in full if ownership is transferred, sometimes contingent upon other occurrences.

amortization Gradual payment of a debt through regular installments that cover both interest and principal.

appraisal Estimate of value of real estate, presumably by an expert.

appreciation Increase in value or worth of property.

"as is" Present condition of property being transferred, with no guaranty or warranty provided by the seller.

assessed valuation Value placed on property as a basis for levying property taxes; not identical with appraised or market value.

assignment Transfer of a contract from one party to another.

assumable mortgage Loan that may be passed to the next owner of the property.

assumption Takeover of a loan by any qualified buyer (available for FHA and VA loans).

automatic renewal clause Provision that allows a listing contract to be renewed indefinitely unless canceled by the property owner.

balloon loan Mortgage in which the remaining balance becomes fully due and payable at a predetermined time.

balloon payment Final payment on a balloon loan.

bill of sale Written document transferring personal property.

binder Preliminary agreement of sale, usually accompanied by earnest money (term also used with property insurance).

bond Written promise to repay a loan, often with an accompanying mortgage that pledges real estate as security; roughly the same as promissory note.

broker Person licensed by the state to represent another for a fee in real estate transactions.

building code Regulations of local government stipulating requirements and standards for building and construction.

buydown The payment of additional points to a mortgage lender in return for a lower interest rate on the loan.

buyer's broker Agent who takes the buyer as client, is obligated to put the buyer's interests above all others, and owes specific fiduciary duties to the buyer.

buyers' market Situation in which supply of homes for sale exceeds demand.

cap Limit (typically about 2 percent) by which an adjustable-mortgage rate might be increased or decreased at any one time.

capital gain Taxable profit on the sale of an appreciated asset.

caveat emptor Let the buyer beware.

ceiling Limit beyond which an adjustable mortgage rate may never be raised; also known as lifetime cap.

certificate of occupancy Document issued by local governmental agency stating that property meets standards for occupancy.

chattel Personal property.

client The broker's principal, to whom fiduciary duties are owed.

closing (settlement, escrow, passing papers) Conclusion of a real estate sale, at which time title is transferred and necessary funds change hands.

closing costs One-time charges paid by buyer and seller on the day property changes hands.

closing statement Statement prepared for buyer and seller listing debits and credits, completed by the person in charge of the closing.

cloud (on title) Outstanding claim or encumbrance that challenges the owner's clear title.

commission Fee paid (usually by a seller) for a broker's services in securing a buyer for property; commonly a percentage of sales price.

commitment (letter) Written promise to grant a mortgage loan.

common elements Parts of a condominium Planned Unit Development (PUD) in which each owner holds an interest (swimming pool, etc.).

comparable Recently sold similar property, used to estimate market value.

comparative market analysis Method of valuing homes using study of comparables, property that failed to sell, and other property currently on the market.

conditional commitment Lender's promise to make a loan subject to the fulfillment of specified conditions.

conditional offer Purchase offer in which the buyer proposes to purchase only after certain occurrences (sale of another home, securing of financing, etc.).

condominium Type of ownership involving individual ownership of dwelling units and common ownership of shared areas.

consideration   Anything of value given to induce another to enter into a contract.

contingency   Condition (inserted into the contract) which must be satisfied before the buyer purchases a house.

contract   Legally enforceable agreement to do (or not to do) a particular thing.

contract for deed (land contract)   Method of selling by which the buyer receives possession but the seller retains title.

conventional mortgage   Loan arranged between lender and borrower with no governmental guarantee or insurance.

cost basis   Accounting figure that includes original cost of property plus certain expenses to purchase, money spent on permanent improvements and other costs, minus any depreciation claimed on tax returns over the years.

curtesy   In some states, rights a widower obtains to a portion of his deceased wife's real property.

customer   Typically, the buyer, as opposed to the principal (seller).

days on market (DOM)   Number of days between the time a house is put on the market and the date of a firm sale contract.

deed   Formal written document transferring title to real estate; a new deed is used for each transfer.

deed of trust   Document by which title to property is held by a neutral third party until a debt is paid; used instead of a mortgage in some states.

deed restriction (restrictive covenant)   Provision placed in a deed to control use and occupancy of the property by future owners.

default   Failure to make mortgage payment or other violation of terms stated in the note.

deferred maintenance   Needed repairs that have been put off.

deficiency judgment   Personal claim against the debtor, when foreclosed property does not yield enough at sale to pay off loans against it.

delivery   Legal transfer of a deed to the new property owner, the moment at which transfer of title occurs.

depreciation   Decrease in value of property because of deterioration or obsolescence; sometimes, an artificial bookkeeping concept valuable as a tax shelter.

direct endorsement   Complete processing of an FHA mortgage application by an authorized local lender; the authority granted to a lender by the FHA to process and approve mortgage loans without prior approval from the FHA.

documentary tax stamp   Charge levied by state or local governments when real estate is transferred or mortgaged.

dower   In some states, the rights of a widow to a portion of her deceased husband's property.

down payment   Cash to be paid by the buyer at closing.

earnest money   Buyer's "good faith" deposit accompanying purchase offer.

easement   Permanent right to use another's property (telephone lines, common driveway, footpath, etc.).

encroachment   Unauthorized intrusion of a building or improvement onto another's land.

encumbrance   Claim against another's real estate (unpaid tax, mortgage, easement, etc.).

equity   Money realized when property is sold and all the claims against it are paid; commonly, sales price minus present mortgage and closing costs.

escrow   Funds given to a third party to be held pending some occurrence; may refer to earnest money, funds collected by a lender for the payment of taxes and insurance charges, funds withheld at closing to insure uncompleted repairs, or in some states the entire process of closing.

exclusive agency   Listing agreement under which only the listing office can sell the property and keep the commission, except if the owner sells the house, in which case no commission is paid.

exclusive right-to-sell Listing agreement under which the owner promises to pay a commission if the property is sold during the listing period by anyone, even the owner.

fair market value See *market value.*

FHA Federal Housing Administration (HUD), which insures mortgages to protect the lending institution in case of default.

FHA mortgage Loan made by a local lending institution and insured by the FHA, with the borrower paying the premium.

fee simple (absolute) Highest possible degree of ownership of land.

fiduciary Person in a position of trust or responsibility with specific duties to act in the best interest of the client.

first mortgage Mortgage holding priority over the claims of subsequent lenders against the same property.

fixture Personal property that has become part of the real estate.

foreclosure Legal procedure for enforcing payment of a debt by seizing and selling the mortgaged property.

front foot Measurement of land along a street or waterfront—each front foot is one foot wide and extends to the depth of the lot.

grantee Buyer, who receives a deed.

grantor Seller, who gives a deed.

guaranteed sale Promise by the listing broker that if the property cannot be sold by a specific date, the broker will buy it, usually at a sharply discounted price.

hazard insurance Insurance on a property against fire and similar risks.

homeowner's policy Policy which puts many kinds of insurance together into one package.

improvements Permanent additions that increase the value of a home.

index Benchmark measure of current interest levels, used to calculate periodic changes in rates charged on adjustable rate mortgages.

joint tenancy Ownership by two or more persons, each with an undivided ownership—if one dies, the property goes automatically to the survivor.

junior mortgage Mortgage subordinate to another.

land contract Type of layaway installment plan for buying a house; sought by a buyer who does not have enough down payment to qualify for a bank loan or to persuade the seller to turn over title.

lien Claim against property for the payment of a debt: mechanic's lien, mortgage, unpaid taxes, judgments.

lis pendens Notice that litigation is pending on property.

listing agreement (listing) Written employment agreement between a property owner and a real estate broker, authorizing the broker to find a buyer.

listing presentation Proposal submitted orally or in writing by a real estate agent who seeks to put a prospective seller's property on the market.

loan servicing Handling paperwork of collecting loan payments, checking property tax and insurance coverage, handling delinquencies.

lock-in Guarantee that the borrower will receive the rate in effect at the time of loan application.

maintenance fees Payments made by the unit owner of a condominium to the homeowners association for expenses incurred in upkeep of the common areas.

margin Percentage (typically about 2.5 percent) added to the index to calculate mortgage rate adjustment.

marketable title Title free of liens, clouds, and defects; a title that will be freely accepted by a buyer.

market value Most likely price a given property will bring if widely exposed on the market, assuming fully informed buyer and seller.

mechanic's lien Claim placed against property by unpaid workers or suppliers.

meeting of the minds Agreement by buyer and seller on the provisions of a contract.

mortgage Lien or claim against real property given as security for a loan; the homeowner "gives" the mortgage; the lender "takes" it.

mortgagee Lender.

mortgagor Borrower.

multiple listing service (MLS) Arrangement by which brokers work together on the sale of each other's listed homes, with shared commissions.

negative amortization Arrangement under which the shortfall in a mortgage payment is added to the amount borrowed; gradual raising of a debt.

net listing Arrangement under which the seller receives a specific sum from the sales price and the agent keeps the rest as sales commission (open to abuses, illegal in most states).

note See *bond*.

PITI Abbreviation for principal, interest, taxes, and insurance, often lumped together in a monthly mortgage payment.

plat Map or chart of a lot, subdivision, or community, showing boundary lines, buildings, and easements.

PMI Private mortgage insurance; insurance issued by a private company, which insures the lender against loss in the event that the borrower defaults on the mortgage.

point (discount point) One percent of a new mortgage being placed, paid in a one-time lump sum to the lender.

portfolio loans Loans made by a bank that keeps its mortgages as assets in its own portfolio; also called nonconforming loans.

prepayment Payment of a mortgage loan before its due date.

prepayment penalty Charge levied by the lender for paying off a mortgage before its maturity date.

principal Party (typically the seller) who hires and pays an agent; also, the outstanding balance of the mortgage; part of the loan proceeds.

procuring cause Actions by a broker that bring about the desired results.

prorations Expenses such as taxes that are divided to the date of settlement between buyer and seller at closing.

purchase-money mortgage Mortgage for the purchase of real property, commonly a mortgage "taken back" by the seller.

quitclaim deed Deed that completely transfers whatever ownership the grantor may have had, but makes no claim of ownership in the first place.

real property Land and the improvements on it.

REALTOR® Registered name for a member of the National Association of REALTORS®.

redlining Practice of refusing to provide loans or insurance in a certain neighborhood.

RESPA Real Estate Settlement Procedures Act, requiring advance disclosure to the borrower of information pertinent to the loan.

restrictive covenant See *deed restriction*.

reverse mortgage Arrangement under which an elderly homeowner, who does not need to meet income or credit requirements, can draw against the equity in the home with no immediate repayment.

salesperson Holder of an entry-level license who is allowed to assist a broker legally responsible for the sale-person's activities; synonymous in some areas with agent.

seller's broker Agent who takes the seller as a client, is legally obligated to a set of fiduciary duties, and is required to put the seller's interests above all others.

sellers' market Situation in which demand for homes exceeds the supply offered for sale.

settlement   See *closing*.

specific performance   Lawsuit requesting that a contract be exactly carried out, usually asking that the seller be ordered to convey the property as previously agreed.

subagency   Legal process by which the seller who lists property for sale with a broker takes on the broker's associates and cooperating firms in a multiple listing system as agents.

survey   Map made by a licensed surveyor who measures the land and charts its boundaries, improvements, and relationship to the property surrounding it.

time is of the essence   Legal phrase in a contract, requiring punctual performance of all obligations.

title   Rights of ownership, control, and possession of property.

title insurance   Policy protecting the insured against loss or damage due to defects in the title; the owner's policy protects the buyer, the mortgagee's policy protects the lender; paid with a one-time premium.

title search   Check of the public records, usually at the local courthouse, to make sure that no adverse claims affect the value of the title.

VA   Department of Veterans Affairs (formerly Veterans Administration), which guarantees a veteran's mortgage so that a lender is willing to make the loan with little or no down payment.

vendee   Buyer.

vendor   Seller.

warranty deed   Most valuable type of deed, in which the grantor makes formal assurance of title.

zoning   Laws of local government establishing building codes and regulations on usage of property.

Index

The Mortgage Kit

For special discounts on 20 or more copies of this edition of *The Mortgage Kit*, please call Dearborn Trade Special Sales at 800-621-9621, extension 4307.